THE MONTREAL STORY TELLERS

Memoirs, Photographs, Critical E

EDITED BY J.R. (TIM) STRUTHERS

Véhicule Press

MONTRÉAL

for my editors and mentors:

VIRGINIA J. ROCK, my first teacher in graduate school, and a model to me of excellence and human commitment in education;

CARL F. KLINCK, from whom I received my initial instruction in Canadian literature, a strong sense of the importance of literary history, and an understanding of the high standards of professional scholarship;

NORM IBSEN, who, in his capacity as Book Review Editor of *The London Free Press*, encouraged a great many of my earliest writings on Canadian literature, particularly on the short story;

JACK DAVID and ROBERT LECKER, who commissioned my first two works on Hugh Hood, and guided me into a career as bibliographer, interviewer, literary critic, editor, and publisher;

STAN DRAGLAND, under whose direction and care my Ph.D. dissertation was written, who sensitized my approach to writing, and who reinforced my judgement that significant contributions to literary history are here and now in the making;

WIN SCHELL, publisher of Ergo Productions, whose courage, individuality, and wit have helped to shape my attitudes and actions, and who believes with me that Southwestern Ontario is the Quality-Control Centre of Canada;

JAMES GELINAS, joint-labourer with me on this and other projects, humorist, and connoisseur of style;

and most importantly my wife, MARIANNE MICROS, who has enlarged and vitalized my world, has given me some comprehension of the nature of the creative artist, and daily strengthens my vision, my resolve.

Published with the assistance of the Canada Council.

CONTENTS

Hugh Hood
TRUSTING THE TALE

Being a Compendious Account of the Montreal Story Teller Fiction Performance Group: Who they Were and Where they Came From and What they Thought they were Up To, and Why: Together with a Summary of their Successes and their Failures, Loves, Losses, Convictions and Perplexities, in the Hope of Straightening Things Out.

Now that the frivolous excesses of The Modern are shrouded like the thought of Marx and Freud in the fogs of the past, and we can begin to see around certain mighty shadows to the slopes and peaks of what has lasted and is lasting, we can propose a Chuzzlewichian undertaking of this nature without fear of its being wholly misunderstood. Let it be observed, then, that the coming-on of the 1970s was an Age of Poets. There were almost too many poets; they seemed to lurk in every corner, poets in churches and coffee-houses. Poets on the airwaves and at the barricades, on board ship, at the controls in the cockpit, and before the cameras. Poets coming and going in little automobiles and climbing up and down oscillating ladders, much like anxious chimpanzees in vaudeville, on the whole conveying the same peppy impression of a great deal of harmless activity being carried on to no very discernible purpose. We had all had our collective asses bored off by poets at poetry readings, and were reluctant to attend any more of them, having rooted suspicions that poetry readings were a Bad Thing, a Noxious Undertaking, Sir, intimations, finally, that they might best be quelled, restrained, sat upon, if possible even suppressed altogether.

It was in some such frame of mind as this that John Metcalf telephoned to me in the dying days of 1970, during "that flat prolonged week that follows Christmas," to see if perhaps he and I and some other like-minded persons could work a shakedown on the poets, and divert the attention of their stupefied audiences to the more wholesome, godly, clearly more decent action of listening to stories being read or told to them, action to which the human mind naturally accommodates itself, as over against the artificial, hothouse-scented, and effete flutterings of Poesy.

Metcalf and I had passed large part of our time in the teaching of literature, and it struck us that compelling children and adolescents to kowtow to the work of the poets was a false and trivial program fostered by cultural mandarins who never bothered to observe that the children and teenagers who were dragooned into this exposure to literature, Literature, My Good Man, with a Capital Letter and with All Due Respect, actually hated poetry, didn't like to sit captive in some smelly auditorium while sonorous nonsense rolled past them, like booming bowling balls (a touch of alliteration, there) in some cavernous alley. Poetry readings weren't like TV. They did you good and you couldn't change channels. The voice went on and on until the principal finally got up and said that the afternoon was over. We figured that there ought to be a way to organise rival readings by persons whose writings had Narrative Content, Humour, the Joys of the Familiar, Story.

I had met John Metcalf a year or two earlier, through Earle Toppings who had been an editor at Ryerson Press when I published my first two books there. Earle worked with John over a couple of anthologies in which selections from my work appeared. The three of us finally got together for a meeting one afternoon in Montreal which developed into a round-the-clock party with a notably high level of liquor consumption and a number of comic incidents that I hope to write up for money one day, and so will not reveal here. I had furnished John with some short notes to my anthology pieces and had read his stories in *Tamarack*, and in the selection included in Clarke, Irwin's *New Canadian Writing* series. When we met, we became close friends and will doubtless continue on that footing.

We met again in Fredericton in the fall of 1970 at a conference of Canadian fiction writers and critics which included Rudy Wiebe, Dave Godfrey, David Helwig, Harry Bruce, Dennis Duffy, Kent Thompson, Bill New, Alec Lucas, and a host of others, a week-long affair to which I brought my wife and children, for a family holiday. My wife says that the first sentence John Metcalf ever spoke to her, in the coffee-shop of the Lord Beaverbrook Hotel at noon one day, was, "I've just been reading a magazine advertisement which said, 'How do you know where you'll be, when your laxative starts to work?'" This precise tone of close and disenchanted observation shot through with nervous hilarity has characterised Metcalf's work, and endeared him to an ever-increasing circle of close readers with deepening intensity of response, over the subsequent decade. It is the Metcalf *tone* that most fixes itself upon us.

He thought we could muscle in on the poets and snake some of the money away from them. Why not get together a bunch of the guys who were writing stories around Montreal, make up a program, and get some reading dates in the schools? If there is one thing Montreal possesses, it is schools and school commissions. Setting up school commissions in their several fields of jurisdiction seems to have been the national sport of Quebeckers in the last century, as building railroads to nowhere was that of Ontarians. Talking to me on the phone on December 28th, 1970 — give or take a day — John said — and I can still hear that unplaceable languorous drawl in the receiver — "Now look here, Hugh, I mean there must be some way to fiddle these poetry sods out of their ill-gotten perks, mustn't there?" I couldn't have agreed more. I told him that I could easily get hold of three or four other story writers who felt the same way, to arrange a meeting. As things worked out, I believe that I was the only one of the group of five who had known all the others before we formed our subversive small clan.

I had seen Clark Blaise's stories in another volume of the Clarke, Irwin *New Canadian Writing* series, and I knew he was living and teaching in Montreal. Ray Smith and I had met at a party given by renowned CBC Radio Arts biggie Robert Weaver, in a Dorchester Street hotel in Montreal around the time of Expo. Weaver used to take these vast sweeps across the country making contacts with writers whose work he promoted to good effect in the pages of *Tamarack*, or on one of the various radio programs he was responsible for, sometimes in one or another of the Toronto newspaper columns he and his friends wrote. I'd attended two or three of Weaver's parties (an earlier one fairly accurately sketched in my novel *White Figure, White Ground*) before this, but the 1967 gathering was the first one from which I came away with a new friend. I mentioned casually to Ray Smith that I played touch football every Saturday in Kent Park, and that we were always looking for new players who would come out regularly. Sometime later he phoned me to ask the exact location of the game; then he appeared the following Saturday and played in the group for several seasons afterwards. I collected more intense perceptions of Ray Smith's character and ideas as an artist through touch football than through any conversations we ever had about writing.

Raymond Fraser had been running a small literary magazine called *Intercourse*, which he'd been able to carry through a dozen numbers almost unaided. I believe the magazine had been conceived in collaboration with a couple of other people, because Ray once told me that the name of the mag wasn't his idea, and that he'd have changed it except that it had acquired a certain audience-recognition-factor almost at once. The material in *Intercourse* couldn't have been more innocent and decent in character under any name; perhaps the title was something of a misrepresentation. But by the time he'd produced a dozen issues, Ray was getting requests for back files from libraries all over North America, which gave the publication considerable momentum. He never put forward any imperialistic claims for *Intercourse*, at no time suggesting, for instance, that the magazine might be considered the organ of a movement. He had good ones and bum ones in the run of back issues, mostly good ones, good writers who were glad to have a poem or a story in his magazine. It was when I read a statement somewhere by Alden Nowlan to the effect that Ray Fraser was writing "the best short stories in Canada" that I decided to try *Intercourse* with a story of my own called "Worst Thing Ever" which was about a geriatric nurse who marries one of her patients in the hope of prolonging his life and practising her healing art to its fullest reach. The story appears in *The Fruit Man, The Meat Man & The Manager*, but was published first in Ray's magazine.

I'd never met Ray at this time, nor his girlfriend Sharon Johnston who was herself, coincidentally, a geriatric nurse. When "Worst Thing Ever" arrived on Ray's desk he was sure that I must have known something about him and Sharon, because of the nature and the development of the story; this might have induced him to accept it for publication. He telephoned me shortly afterwards, and like Ray Smith he wanted to play touch football. The three of us had some pretty close contact long before the birth of the Montreal Story Teller Group.

10

Fraser had written a good deal of poetry, which might have aroused suspicions in the breast of muse-hating Metcalf or myself, but these poems were redeemed by a very strong sense of anecdote, and by their generous and touching humanity. And Ray was a copious author of short stories, and has since published two novels and a story collection. He used to amaze — and even annoy — John Metcalf, the most Flaubertian of laborious composers, by turning up at our readings with a sheaf of manuscript clutched in one hand and a mickey of rum in the other. When it was his turn to go on, he would page through his papers, mumbling incoherently. "Just wrote these last night and this morning," he would say, brandishing three or four longish stories. Metcalf would turn his face to the wall, then covertly examine his own contribution to the reading: it would be short, in perfectly formed minute handwriting in black ink, the final copy of something that had been drafted one word at a time over many weeks, about which he retained serious artistic reservations.

Ray Fraser would wamble onto the platform and read one of his pieces, which would excite shouts of approval and a lot of laughter, especially from the young men in the audience, and then John would follow him and draw the same delighted laughter and admiration with some meticulously crafted literary structure which was flawless at all points. My two sons, who witnessed group readings a couple of times, retain to this day charmed memories of a story Ray Fraser read one night in a collegiate auditorium about some wizened Atlantic character who got pissed on Screech and inflamed by some powerful aphrodisiac, went home, climbed the stairs to his grim apartment, and there, in an indecisive priapic grapple with his ancient wife, bit off one of her tits, admittedly not much of a mouthful. This narrative fragment, offensive to many in the audience, unthinkable as recitation before listeners of feminist conviction, pleased and persuaded Dwight and John Hood as no story of mine has ever done. They revere Metcalf too; his are the only books which my son Dwight will read at a single sitting, with focussed attention and a fixed grin.

There were differences among us of character, artistic postulate, age. Though we are often identified as a group of story writers, it seems just worth mentioning that we've produced something like fifteen novels: eight of mine, two by Fraser and John Metcalf, one each by Clark and Ray Smith. We had an extremely wide range of material to draw upon,

11

stories set in England and the southern U.S.A., and Cape Breton and New Brunswick, in Toronto and New York and New England, and in wholly imaginary places. Most importantly, we had all written about Montreal in extraordinarily different ways. *A North American Education*, *Going Down Slow*, *Around the Mountain*, many of Fraser's fantastic tales from *Intercourse*, and some masked, opaque, complex structures in various parts of Ray Smith's works provided a teeming body of material which we believed suitable for performance before high school and college audiences.

We would guarantee that at least three of us would appear in any given program. The readings would last about two hours, with a longish intermission; we would answer questions at the end of the second hour. We would do our best to ensure that the material read would seem interesting and in some way related to the lives of our hearers. If we were performing away from Montreal, as we did now and then, we might offer selections less local in focus. I might read something from *You Cant Get There From Here*. Ray Smith might try over one of his more Borgesian pieces. Fraser might produce almost anything from one day to the next; you never really knew.

All these matters were decided among us at a first meeting in my home, one Sunday afternoon in January of 1971. We all envisaged making vast sums of money from the readings, once we got established as a going entity with a reputation for putting on a good show. My wife executed a poster for us, which was reproduced very handsomely on expensive poster stock supplied by my friend Hank Dowden, foreman in a lithography shop in Montreal West, with whom I'd played hockey for many years. I used to have several hundred of these posters around the house, gathering dust and taking up filing space. I wonder where they are now.

I've been introduced now and then in the years since as the man who originated the idea of public readings of fiction in this country. That isn't true. The original idea was John Metcalf's, and all five of us appeared at the first reading, at Rosemere High School, just off the island of Montreal to the north, on a fearsomely cold afternoon in February, 1971. I do believe that we were the first persons to produce a performance of just this kind in Canada, perhaps anywhere.

We did not think of ourselves as in any sense a *literary* movement. If we had any principles in common as a group (except a dedication to large

12

fees) they were more educational than literary in nature. Four of us had done a considerable amount of teaching, in high school or CEGEP or college or university. Clark Blaise was giving highly effective writing courses at Concordia. Ray Smith taught at one of the more remotely concealed campuses of Dawson College. John Metcalf had been a high school teacher *de carrière*, as *Going Down Slow* suggests. My own acquaintance with university instruction is very long. Ray Fraser, however, would never admit to having taught anybody anything.

As I ponder these matters at a decade's remove, I'm inclined to revise my earlier belief that our relations were purely those of friendship, rather than theoretical and technical in nature. I see that I wrote at least two stories that were meant as admiring imitations of the style and conceptions of other writers in the group. "The Dog Explosion" is dedicated to Raymond Fraser and Sharon Johnston, and is meant to be an outrageous and extravagant narrative, fabulous, something like the pieces that Ray delivered at our readings and often printed in his magazine. My imitation isn't very close, I'm ready enough to admit, but the intention was there, the unforced admiration, and the wish to write with Ray Fraser's insouciance and refusal to be bound by the canons of credibility, his freedom.

Clark Blaise was at that time writing a gripping series of parables, half story/half essay, which treated modern urban life in a horrified and nearly desperate tone, pieces like "Eyes," "The Voice of the Elephant," and "Is Oakland Drowning?", some of which haven't found their way into his collections. These studies, nightmarish in imagery, troubled and deeply pessimistic in voice, seemed to me to exhibit an imagination of disaster possessed in those distant days by no other writer in the country. I wanted to try my hand at the minatory, hortatory, distinctly scriptural pessimism which these stories expressed so powerfully; they had the accents of Jeremiah, my favourite Old Testament prophet, a brave and persistent person. My story "Dark Glasses," praised in another context by Dave Godfrey, is an essay in the manner of Clark Blaise which nobody has spotted as such. Perhaps it is an unsuccessful pastiche, though the story may have points to be made in its favour on other grounds.

Clark once or twice permitted a minor influence of mine on his own writing. After recounting the terrible events of a certain midwinter evening, when his new Volvo died on him in the middle of nowhere, and he had to find a towtruck in the existential void, proposing these desperate real-life circumstances as the basis of a fiction, he asked me what the title should be. Without hesitation I produced the phrase "He raises me up," which became the title of the finished narrative. I'd been thinking of the Resurrection of Christ, and its movement in the hearts of mankind. Clark used the phrase in a somewhat different sense, just as he and I might select the same prospect of Montreal — driving up *Pie IX* on the way to Saint-Vincent de Paul — and give it diametrically opposed readings.

Clark also once remarked, in a puzzled plaintive small voice, as we were driving to a reading in his car, "Hard to be more Canadian than Hugh Hood."

Relations with John Metcalf were easier to establish on the level of friendship than on that of artistic practice. John and I have similar preoccupations with the discipline of the artist, with getting the work lined-out right, with a high degree of polish and finish, but we have come to very distinct conclusions about the simple "how" of the thing. A clear simple example: I usually take a very long time to think out the implications of a story idea in my head, sometimes several years, before committing anything to paper. When I finally write my first draft it will require very little revision, most of the actual composing of the piece having been done mentally. Ray Smith once looked through a first draft of mine and was astonished to see how close it was to the final published version; a final draft for me is largely a matter of polishing and fine tuning.

John will take just as long over a story, but much more of his work seems to be done with a provisional draft actually in existence on his desk in manuscript form. He might take several weeks to do a first draft of a length which I could manage in three or four days, thinking about each word, almost from word to word, as he proceeds. There are merits to either system of composition, of course, and what suits me would not feel right to John at all. I remember reading somewhere that Hemingway would not compose at a typewriter, preferring to write his ideas down slowly in longhand, at a pace that suited him. At the same time, he found it easy to compose in a café, among a crowd of people eating and drinking, something that would be impossible for me. I very much enjoy the composition of the story in my head, which is never a systematic process. I don't think about the beginning, then about the middle, or anything as simple as that. It's largely a matter of revolving the situation of the narrative, and its geography, in my visual imagination, finding a good title — always an immense help — then perhaps finding an appropriate final line. Endings are of capital importance.

John and I have dedicated books to one another, and the story I finished last week, called "Every Piece Different," is dedicated to John Metcalf; it's a *cri du coeur* about how it feels to practise an art in Canada at the present time, a subject we've often talked about. "Every Piece Different" doesn't read like John's fiction about artists and writers, *General Ludd*, for example, or the brilliant novella "Private Parts." An accurate description of the differences in the art we actually manage to achieve on the page, when our premises, ethically speaking, are almost identical, would present a testing problem for a contemporary critic, somebody with the tools to get the job done, not necessarily a *Derridiste* or *Barthesien*, but a well-trained one.

John and Clark collaborated through the later 1970s on the annual Oberon Press anthology, *Best Canadian Stories*, and might be supposed to hold parallel convictions about what is good and bad in the fiction of the decade. Their collaboration began at the time when our group was beginning to break up, for various reasons which were never the result of personal differences. I have never been a member of a group of more agreeable people, and I can remember no serious personal differences of any kind. Alterations in personal circumstances, more than anything else, led to the breakup: departures from the city, new artistic perspectives and undertakings, doubts about writing stories designed to be read aloud, matters of that kind, some of lasting importance in the lives of the people concerned, some of technical interest to the conception of the nature of prose fiction, some transitory and temporary, brought the organisation to its predictable end.

We had a pretty good run from the time of our first appearance at Rosemere High School in February, 1971, until our final engagement, absolutely the last to be given anywhere on any stage, which to the best of my memory took place in the spring of 1976 at Concordia University in Montreal at a conference for secondary school teachers of literature, five years together in the course of which we must have given more than fifty readings of different kinds, in universities, colleges, CEGEPs, in high schools, to various societies and professional groups, sometimes in bookstores, once even in a primary school, where I tried the experiment

15

of actually *telling* a story, one I've never written down, to an audience
of seventh- and eighth-graders. The story went down extremely well as
a kind of impromptu recitation. The children thought it was very
funny, and it helped to put me in touch with the feeling of oral narration, where your material is organised in a completely different way
from that of formal literary practice. I enjoyed the experience of sitting
in front of sixty kids and telling them a funny story about trying to get
rid of a duck (never mind how) but it isn't really my medium. Of the
five of us, I think Ray Fraser is closest to the state of the natural informal raconteur, a narrative feeling best conveyed by the writing of Mark
Twain. The rest of us were pretty formal prose artists, requiring the
printed page and close solitary attention as conditions of effect. I began
to distrust the idea of reading my work aloud to audiences who might
be hearing a very carefully arranged text for the first time, without any
adequate preparation for its demands. I can't imagine trying to read my
later stories aloud, with any hope of bringing out their intentions.
When I found myself writing ''God Has Manifested Himself Unto Us
as Canadian Tire'' specifically for performance aloud, I felt like I was
turning into a standup comedian, somebody like the *diseuse* Lily Tomlin
— whose work I greatly admire. The first time I read ''Canadian Tire''
to a public audience, it worked out just as I'd expected. It got a lot of
laughs and made a big hit, but it felt to me, as I was acting it out, a kind
of performance that I'm not much suited to by nature. I don't want to
be a performer now. There was a time in my life when I very much
wanted to be a performer, a singer with a dance band or a movie actor,
but that was thirty-five years ago, and I didn't have the talent for either
medium. Whether Clark or John or Ray Smith or Ray Fraser ever had
similar ambitions and doubts, I can't say.

We all read rather effectively. Of the other four, the one whom I'd
least have expected to be a success on the platform was Clark Blaise, but
he was an amazingly persuasive reader. He insinuated his histrionics,
rather than allowing you to see that he was acting the story out. He
would stand there in dark, unobtrusive clothes, looking like what he is,
a grave, supernally intelligent, artist, and enthral the audience by some
recital of a series of terrific disasters, never raising his voice, but managing to chill everybody's imagination very sufficiently. Ray Smith
would read pieces of great length, many of them chapters from *Lord
Nelson Tavern*, which he was writing at this time. You'd think to

yourself, my God, they'll never sit still for all of that. But they would and did often sit through a solid forty minutes of Ray's elaborate, figured, labyrinthine investigation of the life of Nora Noon/Notty Midnight, because of the fascination of the intricate series of revelations released in such precise order, partly too because of Ray's impressive appearance on the platform; tall, very handsome, bearded, dressed in a thick woollen handmade poncho, sometimes with a guitar slung over one shoulder, he dominated these assemblies by his presence. Raymond Fraser commanded attention by opposite means; he would present himself as a scruffy type who had just risen from bed, thrown on his clothes, and snatched up a bundle of manuscript as he passed out the door of his apartment on the way to the reading; then he would read these hilarious and incredible tales of the lives of submerged and disaffected persons from strange places and marine deeps of society. He could make you feel desperately concerned about these people while at the same time laughing uncontrollably at the awful things that happened to them.

Metcalf was simply a superb reader. Still is. You can't really dig John's writing to the full unless you've heard him read some of it. He has the timing, the sense of nuance, of a Jack Benny. He had a boffo comedy turn, and I do not exaggerate. Now and then he and I would read together the scene from *Going Down Slow* where the phony folk singer, Blind Foxy John, who has lifted his act from old Alan Lomax records, appears in a Montreal club, causing great annoyance to the main character in the book, who breaks up the act and causes a hell of a disturbance. I used to read — and sing — Blind Foxy John's lines, and John would do all the other voices. The segment *played*, as performers say, like cream. That was immense fun to do, highly instructive as well. I've always wanted to be part of a music-hall act. If I ever get to work up an act and take it on the road, it will be with J. Metcalf, and I somehow suspect that the billing will be "Metcalf and Hood," purely for the sake of euphony.

We had some genuinely theatrical successes at our readings, some flops as well. The very first one we gave turned out to be a smashing success, for several intersecting reasons. It was organised by a friend of ours, Doug Rollins, a very close student of contemporary writing and a fine jazz musician, who happened to be head of the English department at Rosemere High. Doug spent a lot of time preparing his students for our appearance; they had all read something by each writer and were ready with acute questions. All five of us read something; there was a stream of comments and laughter. The school band was rehearsing some marches in a distant part of the building; you could hear the thrilling strains of football fight songs and military marches, as a background to the laughing and cheering in the auditorium. Somebody made a tape of the event and presented each of us with a copy; it had been made with a good deal of professionalism, the writers' voices being faded in and out against the background of crowd noise and music, creating a strong impression of spontaneity. Maybe that first appearance was our best. I can't remember that we ever surpassed it, though we certainly had our moments.

One spring afternoon a few months later we were reading in a second-floor classroom at Vanier College, on rue Sainte-Croix in Ville St.-Laurent. That particular two-block stretch of rue Sainte-Croix is minutely described in the story "The Village Inside" in *Around the Mountain*. The opening pages of the story provide a detailed picture of the buildings across the street from the college, then go on to work the look and feel of these buildings into the structure and meaning of what is being narrated. I'm fond of the story, which has had other admirers. Kent Thompson, for example, delivered a paper at the Ottawa University conference on Canadian short fiction, in 1975, which analyses this story in very close perspective. His analysis is printed in *Minus Canadian*, edited by Barry Cameron and Michael Dixon, who also offered papers at this conference. Kent's analysis of "The Village Inside" is searching and substantially correct, I think, but it is devoted to the central movement of the piece, rather than the opening pages, where I am trying to establish the notion of one historical moment existing in, and being delivered through, another. I used the old buildings across the street from the college to propose this notion.

While I was reading the story — which seemed a natural selection for our appearance there — about half the students in the room, maybe fifteen of them (it was a smallish crowd), got to their feet and moved quietly over towards the wide windowsills, where they sat or stood and gazed across at the very buildings I was describing in my story, whose appearance was greatly enhanced by the sunshine and mildness of the agreeable afternoon. There were whispers of "It's them," and "That's like us," and then a deep and attentive silence as I read through the rest

18

of the story. Out of the four or five years of my association with these men, that was the point at which the original idea behind the readings seemed to be working best for me. I got a sense of identification with the scene and with my hearers that must be very rare among contemporary writers and their audiences. There was something exceedingly moving in that quiet spontaneous drift towards the windows, to look at the reality of what my story was demonstrating, an "art in life in art in life" infinite-regress situation which I found very suggestive, like some of Magritte's work.

I mention highlights from my own readings; each of us would have many to recount, but those which one has experienced himself are probably the most accessible for re-telling. On another occasion we were reading at a small school away out in the east end of the city, not really a high school at all, but an annex of some overcrowded larger institution several blocks away. This was down near the docks area of Pier 51 and Pier 52, eastwards along the riverfront, where Domenico Lercaro steps ashore and starts walking inland as fast as he can, in my story "Socks." I prefaced my reading with the remark that the piers mentioned in the story were about a mile away from the school, "over there," giving a wave of the hand and a nod towards the Saint Lawrence, visible from the windows. I received the same delighted attention that I'd had in Ville St.-Laurent, the unmistakeable signs of the fundamental pleasure of recognition given by literary realism, not simply the naïve pleasure of identifying one's neighbourhood, district, or quarter, but the additional, much more complex pleasure of seeing one's place worked into the balance and design of the narration. In both these situations, it seemed to me that my listeners' response was much more subtle and mixed than I might have expected.

I think we were most successful in high schools and CEGEPs; certainly we gave most of our readings there. We appeared in inner-city high schools where the rich odour of cannabis floated along the halls and into the auditoriums, swirling intoxicatingly around the microphones, where you had to be careful not to read anything obviously literary. Clark Blaise's story "Eyes" used to fascinate audiences in such settings, especially the menacing closing lines concluding, "and your neighbors would turn upon you." These listeners obviously appreciated the sharp contrast between what Clark was describing, and his quiet, neat, self-contained personal appearance. It may have sur-

19

prised them that this unobtrusive gentleman knew so many of the same things they knew, better than they did themselves.

We circulated a letter asking for engagements in other parts of the country, receiving very few replies. We never read as a group in the West, or in Toronto. I do remember a single date at a high school in Ottawa, a distinct success. There were occasional university readings; we read as a group during the Learned Societies meetings at McGill one year, without making any great impact on the tired teachers of literature slouched in front of us, obviously longing to get back to the hospitality suites. "Don't come on too seriously to us," their limp forms seemed to suggest, "we're in the business too."

We got a fine reception at U.N.B., Fredericton campus, partly because several of us had been at the 1970 conference, partly because John Metcalf had been there as writer-in-residence for a time. I remember the Fredericton reading as one of our best; it isn't too surprising that Doug Rollins helped to organise it. He was now at work on his doctorate at U.N.B. I think our reading there was largely his production.

On that same trip we were driven in the dead of night down that shadowy long highway from Fredericton to Saint John, to read at the Saint John campus of U.N.B., an appearance organised and produced by Bill Prouty of the Saint John campus faculty. We'd wheedled a huge fee out of poor Professor Prouty's funding authority (but no huger than our talents would justify) and we found that we outnumbered our audience, which consisted of Prouty, a building-maintenance staff member who swept and garnished throughout our presentation, and two young women. We had them, five to four. And at that Bill Prouty handed over our cheque with barely a hint of dismay.

Since then I have read by myself to small audiences, never to one that small. Fourteen is the smallest number I've ever drawn. After a series of midwinter engagements where hardly anybody was able to get to the hall because of the cold or the storm, or because of simple lack of interest (much the most frequent motive, I suspect), I began to have qualms about readings. I once travelled almost seventeen hundred miles — eight hundred and fifty each way — to give a reading in late January in Edmundston, N.B., to an enthusiastic and responsive audience of twenty-eight people. There was an ice-storm in progress when I got in from Montreal, and as Edmundston is very hilly in places I had quite literally to crawl up the rink-like steps of the main building of *Collège Saint-Louis-Maillet* on my hands and knees. This seemed an appropriate posture.

All readings in front of a ''live'' audience by a writer like me, who depends so much on repeated scrutiny of his text by close readers, must seem a kind of begging for attention. I think that during the 1970s I gave well over a hundred readings, with the Montreal Story Tellers and without them. Looking back on the experience now, I should find it almost impossible to say whether or not I had attracted a significant number of new readers to my books by this means. I'm inclined to doubt it. Nothing is like reading a book but reading it. My work demands to be read silently and with close attention by mature men and women — there is nothing I could do to change this, even if I wished to — and a single reading won't do. I once read the story ''Breaking Off'' to a group of about thirty, including the very intelligent critic John Bentley Mays, at York University. They gave me a careful hearing, and the story held them to the end, but the question-and-answer session afterwards was largely a matter of providing the kit for assembling the story, so to speak, an explanation of points that no oral delivery could conceivably render. That was one of the last readings I gave, and I don't want to do any more, barring a very occasional informal private reading for some friend's class. Dickens, we know, felt differently, and his enthusiasm for public readings and performances seems actually to have helped to shorten his life. It wasn't the smallness of the audience at Edmundston or the dreadful January weather that disturbed me; it was the time it took to get there and back, and the physical fatigue that ensued.

I'd have gone on participating in group readings for an indefinite length of time, but the other guys had specific, practical motives for dropping out. Ray Fraser moved back to New Brunswick, taking up residence at Black River Bridge under the name of Captain Ray. Clark Blaise spent a sabbatical year in India with his wife, then accepted a position in Toronto. John Metcalf and his wife bought a farm near Delta, Ontario, and moved to the country to live. Only Ray Smith and I continue to live in Montreal, and both of us have been preoccupied with long forms of narration that may help to lessen our interest in readings. Ray has taken two or three tries at the novel in the last few years, in no case to his own satisfaction. The books have remained unpublished. *The Swing in the Garden* was the book I was writing when

Montreal Story Teller was peaking, and there was nothing in that novel I cared to try reading aloud to high school or college audiences; it would have been the wrong kind of material for spoken presentation, and neither *A New Athens* nor *Reservoir Ravine* furnishes anything that I'd risk at Cardinal Newman High in midtown Montreal. I did once read the "burning the money" sequence from *Reservoir Ravine* at a high school in Oromocto, N.B. The people who liked it best were all members of the teaching staff, and I'm not certain how much of it I got across to them.

It's an unstable art, the writing of fiction: there are so many stripes to it. You can be reaching one audience with powerful effectiveness, and missing every other potential hearer or reader. You may be reaching them all, but with qualified power. I'd like to hit every imaginable reader and/or hearer with maximum artistic force, to slay them from the stage with the flexibility and subtlety and histrionic charm of my appearance, to coax them on the printed page into fascinated reading after reading. To make them applaud and make them meditate and finally pray. But to do all that I'd have to be Inimitable. Wouldn't I?

1980

John Metcalf
TELLING TALES

Montreal Story Teller Fiction Performance Group — made up of myself, Clark Blaise, Ray Fraser, Hugh Hood, and Ray Smith, and formed to give public readings — was not a literary 'movement'. The word 'movement' implies common aims, excited talk, a manifesto scrawled on menus. Montreal Story Teller was united only in the base desire for emolument. At least, that's true of the beginning.

We did talk a lot among ourselves about the educational virtues of our activities, about snaring a new generation of readers, about charging the batteries of the teachers themselves. In the period of questions and answers which followed readings we did promote Canadian writers and writing with missionary zeal. But we all had more than a passing interest in used bills of small denomination.

Ray Smith, whose father was the manager of a bank, kept the accounts. These accounts were kept in a very *severe* book and were professionally incomprehensible. Ray worried about these accounts. The rest of us could not have cared less. Ray worried about reporting sums earned to the tax-gatherers. The rest of us felt he was being overly particular. Hugh's position was that such sums *were not taxable* — an example of the radical simplicity and profundity of much of Hugh's thought. In essence, his theory, with which I was and am in total agreement, was that *any* sum he was paid for reading, ten or ten thousand dollars, was an honorarium, a mere token, a formal gesture of gratitude, because his reading was beyond price. Honoraria could not rationally be considered as income. Therefore honoraria were not taxable. An argument which Hugh, to quote Hugh quoting W.C. Fields, often said would be found to hold water.

The most common questions we were asked were, "How much do

you earn?" and "Who do you write for?" This latter was not an untutored groping towards such a figment as V. Woolf's "Common Reader" but meant exactly what it said. It meant: "Which company pays you to write? *Reader's Digest? Maclean's?*" Such questions led to explanations of sales and royalties, returns and remainders. When the children grasped that we earned from stories less than they did from paper-routes or baby-sitting, they politely did their best to disguise their conviction that we were potty.

After twenty sessions or so of answering the same question, our advocacy of Truth, Beauty, The Joy of Art, etc. sounded a bit thin even to us.

But it was pleasing and sustaining simply to be together. Writing is a necessarily lonely occupation but writing in Canada approximates solitary confinement. I'm convinced that the lack of audience, the lack of response, accounts for the slow rate of composition of so many Canadian writers and their early silencing.

Together, sustained by each other, we could make light of the fact that no large bookstore in Montreal carried our books. We could make light of the fact that the paperback reissues of Clark's *A North American Education* and *Tribal Justice* were shelved in Classics Book Shop under 'Education' and 'Anthropology'. We could make light of the fact that no university in Montreal expressed the faintest interest in engaging us to read; that the *doyen* of Montreal literary journalists, John Richmond of *The Montreal Star*, refused to acknowledge our existence.

Well, he said, when Hugh once remonstrated, *you never invite me round to crack a bottle of sherry, do you, dear boy?*

Of course, this 'sustaining' was never articulated; it expressed itself in general hilarity. We never discussed literature or technique. We all had very high standards of craftsmanship and respected each other's craft but we did not offer criticism and wouldn't have accepted it. I think it was Thurber who said that in the literary world no one sits at anyone's feet unless they've been knocked there. Most of our journeys to and from readings were taken up with Hugh and Clark swapping baseball trivia or with Hugh's photographic horrible memory unwinding paragraphs from Chandler or Wodehouse; our task was to identify which books they came from. Ray and Ray often traded hints and wrinkles about home-brewing and bottling, sediment problems. Ray Smith, a superb cook, might reveal the latest round in his lengthy con-

24

troversy with a cooking expert on the CBC about the use of cheddar cheese in the manufacture of Welsh Rarebit. Ray claimed that with all *advertised* methods, cheddar went funny. Beer came into it somewhere. It usually did. Clark often detailed yet another financial reversal. On the day he told us his house had just burned down, we all, I think, accepted the news as somehow unexciting and *inevitable*. What I talked about, I can't remember. I really did try to place Hugh's quotations.

"Shall I give you a clue?"

"Yes."

"It's *before* 1935."

If one of us did comment on a compatriot's work, Ray Smith would attempt to guide us back to baseball or the great P.G. by saying, "I don't read books by Canadian writers." This plonking statement was not merely an attempt to end unwelcome topics; it was also true. Literary shop-talk of any kind seemed to cause him great distress. In this, he was much like Professor Alec Lucas of McGill who endeared himself to me one evening at a book-launching for a young poet. Free drink flowed. People were chatting of this and that. Waiters circulated with gratifying frequency. Then another professor called for silence and proposed that the young man read to us from his book. Professor Lucas said to me in a very loud and *petulant* voice,

"They always have to *spoil* these occasions."

I've said that we all had very high standards of craftsmanship. I should perhaps change that statement. We all liked Ray Fraser personally, of course, but perhaps only Hugh was a devotee of Ray's fiction.

Ray's stories were less stories than anecdotes or tales. They were typed on yellow newsprint and heavily influenced in style and subject matter by his former employment at the tabloid *Midnight*. Most of these yarns seemed to feature massive insobriety, murder, incest, mutilation, rape, anal crime, and genital abnormality.

Once when we were reading at the University of New Brunswick in Fredericton, Ray managed to clear a fair part of a large auditorium with a scabrous *conte* entitled "Spanish Jack" which detailed the aftermath of a Maritime Golden Ager's ingestion of cantharides. Or perhaps I've got it wrong. Perhaps it was the one about the underprivileged Maritimer in a knocking-shop who couldn't get it up. In memory, they tend to merge.

By the time he was but three sentences in, four nuns left in a marked manner.

The lay folk left later.

Ray published a selection of these yarns in a book called *The Black Horse Tavern*. My feathers were considerably ruffled when Dennis Duffy of all people reviewed the book and perversely declared it to be the best collection of stories since my own *The Lady Who Sold Furniture*.

Ray Smith was impressed by a certain *carefree* quality in Fraser sentences and after profound inebriated thought produced the following which he claimed was quintessential Fraser:

"She looked like an old bag of forty — which she was, by Christ!"

(The full effect requires that the sentence be read with a very long pause at the dash and with an emphasis on "was" and stronger emphasis and gravelly tone on the "by Christ!")

Ray had large numbers of these yellow stories which he stuffed into his army-surplus knapsack as he left the house. He read them unedited and sometimes with pages missing. Nothing fazed him. To sustain himself he always brought with him a mickey of brandy which was swigged in the wings. He always bought the cheapest brandy he could find. Amazing brandy. Brandy from countries one would not associate with the grape. Such as Patagonia. He often read last and was usually flushed.

I had urged Ray to clean these stories up because in some of the Catholic schools the bad language was not happily received. I did not want our agreement with the Catholic School Commission cancelled. We had a minor row on the subject; he promised that the next week his story would be as the driven snow.

The next week was a rushed affair. Hugh picked everyone up at 1 p.m. Ray was still in bed when we arrived. He threw on his clothes, grabbed up his knapsack. We rushed to the school. "No smut!" we reminded him before he went on stage. But in his haste he had grabbed up yet another impure tale.

He got himself launched into the matter and then found himself in a passage of abusive dialogue between two of his disgusting Maritime low-lifes. Backstage, we listened with great uneasiness as the dialogue wound up to one of the characters saying:

"By Christ! Someone ought to string the son of a whore up by his..."

26

At this point, Fraser, whose lips were already forming the word 'balls', remembered. He gazed out over the sea of Catholic girlhood, paralyzed.

The silence went on and on.

And on.

Suddenly, and triumphantly, he said, "*Thumbs!*"

I once heard Clark introduce one of his own readings by saying rather sadly that he was being paid more for reading aloud for one hour than he received in royalties in a year. It's sometimes impossible not to feel angry about this. We all of us would have preferred to sit at home and receive royalties. We would have preferred readers to listeners. Readers work harder and stand a chance of getting more. But as the principal of a school in which I once worked used to murmur when it was reported to him that children had again emptied their free milk into the grand piano, "We live in an imperfect world."

None of us was ever seduced, so far as I know, by the idea of performance. We all realized that writing and performing were entirely distinct activities and that, for us, writing was the sterner and more valuable task. My own work and Clark's lent itself most naturally to performance. Hugh's prose — certainly from his later novels but also in some of the stories — tends to be too complex to be grasped at a reading. The same is true of Clark's prose, of course, or mine, but our subtleties are of a different kind from Hugh's; we seem to be far more transparent. There are various reasons for this: much of Clark's work is in the first person and this creates an immediate intimacy; first-person writing seems to the unwary or unskilled listener less 'literary', the choice of a first-person narrator dictating a relatively simple syntax and vocabulary. In my own case, unskilled listeners probably fail to understand how complex and *literary* the simplicity is — particularly in dialogue. Behind the 'naturalness' of my dialogue, for which I've sometimes been commended, are echoes of such naturalistic writers as P.G., Firbank, Waugh, and Amis.

(The complexity of 'simplicity' is rarely grasped. A very crafty poet like John Newlove, for example, is generally seen as 'simple' which is both true and very much not true — a misunderstanding that won't be cured until we've managed to teach people to experience the 'how' of a work instead of grubbing about for an unfindable 'what'. An understanding which will occur, if the experience of my teaching career

27

is anything to go by, at about the same time that pigs take to the air.)

A possibly interesting sidelight — my years with Montreal Story Teller persuaded me that there is a strong, though not obvious, connection between a writer's conversational and literary style. An obvious example — a very small part of Hugh's literary complexity is the *formality* of his syntax, a formality which is mirrored in his speech. I suspect that a writer's literary range and style, the genres in which he is likely to succeed or fail, are intimately connected with the styles and patterns of his conversation.

Reading to a responsive audience is a pleasure for me. Reading to an *audience* isn't bad either; I recently supported Eastern Ontario Library Week by reading at the Brockville Public Library to an audience of the Chief Librarian, the Assistant Librarian, and my wife. And *she'd* heard it before.

There are particular reasons why my own work reads well — or *should* read well. I was at home very early in life with the idea of performance and with the handling of rhetoric because I listened every Sunday to two of my father's sermons. If he happened to be preaching elsewhere, I had the rare pleasure of hearing two of someone else's. And these were not your average Anglican chat but full-blown, non-conformist, three-quarters-of-an-hour jobs with plenty of side on the ball. I don't think I'm exaggerating or distorting when I say that even as a small child I developed a grasp of rhetorical structures.

When I was five or six, it was feared that my older brother's eyesight was failing. My mother, to spare his eyes, used to read his homework aloud to him. I can remember, vastly improbable as it sounds, being absolutely ravished by Shakespeare, literally felled by Malvolio. Another great source of pleasure at the time was *Toytown*, a serial for children on the BBC. I'm sure I drew no distinctions between Malvolio and Larry the Lamb. Which on reflection is probably a good thing.

It was only while writing this memoir that I realized how large a part radio and the spoken word played in forming the way I write and wish to write. When I was a child, the radio was switched on *to be listened to*. I cannot understand how it is possible to turn on radios for companionable noise and not hear what the horrid voices are talking about. If I catch even seconds of Don Harron's voice before the (usually ill-read) news, it causes me almost unbearable anguish. The effect upon me of Barbara Frum is even more marked. To this day, I hear *everything* and

28

increasingly envy those who don't.

I used to listen to many of the BBC programmes for children, the *William* stories, stories about Norman and Henry Bones-Boy Detectives, Dick Barton-Special Agent, and a host of others now largely forgotten. As I grew older, I listened to all the fine comedy programmes which culminated in the most entrancing radio programme ever produced, *The Goon Show*. The Goons created worlds in which I have never ceased to believe and in Major Bloodnok a character in that long tradition of military realists that you can stack up against Falstaff any day of the week.

I am always deeply affected by his shaken cry,

"No more curried eggs for me!"

Concurrent with the Goons, lesser but still adored performers lifted up my heart — Frankie Howerd and the simperingly lewd Benny Hill. Frankie Howerd's announcement to a female travel agent that he has come in to see her brochures, her *tours*, so appealed to me that I pinched it for *General Ludd*.

I was a devotee of splendidly coarse reviews in the theatre starring such stalwarts as 'Professor' Jimmy Edwards, Tony Hancock, and Harry Secombe, and of the great tradition of low farce.

On the BBC Third Programme in the fifties there were frequent plays, usually commissioned, by writers like N.F. Simpson, Giles Cooper, Harold Pinter, and Samuel Beckett. I can still remember coming home from school one evening and settling down to listen to a play by a playwright unknown to me then and being wrapped in increasing horror and delight. The actor was, I believe, Jack McGowran. The play was *All That Fall*.

And I'm afraid age hasn't cured me.

One of my treasured possessions is a record of the last music hall performance of the great Max Miller — "The Cheekie Chappie," as he was billed. I've listened to it countless times and never cease to marvel at the control he exercised over audiences. I sent a copy of it to John Mills knowing that it would tug at ancestral memory and he wrote back reminding me of a line Maxie had perpetrated during a live BBC broadcast — a jest about meeting a lady on a narrow mountain ledge and not knowing whether to block her passage or toss himself off.

But that gives nothing of the full wonders of the *voice*.

I listened to all this stuff intently and intensely, studied it almost, and

I realize now that it formed one important strand in my sense of accent and timing, of the voice as instrument. Reading and performance, then, is no trial for me. More important, it's no violation of my own work. When I'm writing, I'm always *listening* to what I'm doing. If it doesn't work aloud, I always change it because if it doesn't work aloud it doesn't work at all.

(One of the most perfect pieces of *voice* I've ever managed, a chunk I'm quite proud of, is the conversation between Jim Wells and Mr. Bhardwaj in Chapter Eleven of *General Ludd* — classy stuff, I thought, and memorable, though possibly caviar for the general as reviewers seem to have concentrated on the fancied sociological and political import of the tome.)

I have often changed what I had previously considered finished stories after a public reading. In fact, I use readings for just this purpose. I listen to myself, listen to the rhythms, and as I read make mental notes of where there's deadwood, awkwardnesses, where the timing is a beat or two off. I don't derive this information from the reaction of the audience — that would be perilous. The flow of adrenalin during a performance seems to stimulate an innate sense of what is correct.

It's impossible for me to tell the unvarnished truth about the members of Montreal Story Teller as readers, as performers, because the truth is doubtless enhanced by a heavy patina of love and affection. I think we were all damn good and good as a group.

Ray Smith tended to be rather nervous and rigid when he started and if he fluffed lines often apologized and started over. As he continued, he usually relaxed considerably, adding gesture and large movement. His rendition of "A Cynical Tale" from *Cape Breton is the Thought-Control Centre of Canada* was often very funny; there was the added pleasure of incongruity in watching arch suggestions of the feminine or homosexual conveyed by such a very huge man. Ray was a bit defeated at the beginning by the arcane nature of some of the stories in *Cape Breton*; they were not exactly what you might call a good read. This was not particularly surprising as the impulse behind them was almost 'anti-story'. Ray and I used to read together from the second section of his story "Peril" in an effort to jazz things up. Ray read all the narration and the part of Peril while I boomed the part of G.K. Chesterton.

(I do not mean to imply that Ray's work in *Cape Breton* was not good; I'm merely saying that I wouldn't have chosen it as a natural to

30

read to high school students. Or college students, come to that. "Peril" is a very funny story and moves in its final section into a delicate and affecting lyricism. It is also a very *odd* story. I also happen to think that it's among the best stories ever written in Canada.)

Later, when Ray was working on *Lord Nelson Tavern*, the nature of the material gave him greater scope and he was able to let himself go on monologues and more 'realistic' dialogue. These lively passages were usually in the voices of other people. It was always my impression listening to Ray that he had not worked through to an *authorial* voice with which he was entirely comfortable.

Clark Blaise's stories ran on wheels, as it were; Clark gave the impression that he was merely the almost invisible track on which they ran. The stories are so beautifully crafted and balanced in terms of their rhetoric that Clark seemed almost to disappear behind them. This was, of course, an illusion. Clark was never openly dramatic, never given to gesture, but he read fluently and *urgently* and with a fierce grip on the audience which tightened relentlessly. It was rather like watching an oddly silent pressure-cooker which you knew was capable of taking the roof off at any moment. This feeling of *contained* power, typical of Clark's performing style, was also somehow connected with Clark's temperament. I've never seen Clark not in control of himself but I'd pay large sums of money not to be there if or when.

Clark is an excellent mimic and it was amazing when, in those few stories which contain dialogue, voices other than the narrating voice flashed out. It was rather like lightning against a heavy sky, to hear Southern "cracker" voices or the precise imprecisions of East Indian English. At such times, Clark was riotously funny; I'm thinking fondly of his reading the Princess Hi-Yalla section in "A North American Education."

(I remember asking Clark once why he didn't use dialogue more often and I *think* he said that dialogue was too easy to write. This may be true. For him. Or it may not. I always got the impression that Clark quite literally *relaxed* when speaking in voices other than his 'own' and I sometimes felt that this relaxation frightened him.)

Ray Fraser's style and manner was confused and bumbling. One was always aware that Ray was *reading* something — not least because he often lost his place. If he provoked laughter, he would laugh himself and then find his place again, blushing, pushing his glasses higher with his thumb, a modest and nervous gesture. Ray sometimes gave the impression that he was as surprised as the audience at the way the events in the story were turning out — and this may well have been true.

Hugh Hood's reading style was again related to his matter. I've heard him read quite wildly on such stories as "Whos Paying for This Call" but that, like the story, was untypical. Hugh's normal reading style gave the impression, as do many of the stories, of being something like *heightened conversation*. There was an intimacy and familiarity about Hugh's reading — as though you too were very intelligent and he wished to share with you an interesting experience. This did not preclude emphasis and shading in delivery, of course, but the stance is rhetorically low-key. His style was so 'personal' and persuasive, so much someone 'talking', that I'm sure most listeners were unaware of the tropes being paraded in front of them.

Hugh did have one tremendous fault as a reader which worked against the willing suspension of disbelief. When I first heard him do it, I cringed. Later, I found it endearing. Now, my love for him is such that I would feel deprived if he read without indulging this mild eccentricity.

Hugh would stop in the middle of a paragraph, sometimes in the middle of a sentence, and start to chuckle at some rediscovered felicity. Sometimes he would shake his head as if amazed that he had got off such a perfect shot. He would say,

"You know, that's a *honey* of a sentence! I think I'll read that again."

And did.

Audiences didn't seem to find this particularly surprising but possibly because they thought we were all bloody weird anyway.

Of my own reading, I can't say much. Hugh's remarks on his own work while reading it suggest tremendous involvement in what he was doing, suggest almost an obliviousness of audience. When I read, I am fairly coldly concerned with manipulation of the audience. I am moving them to laughter or a moist eye but remain unmoved myself. From the intensity of their laughter or tension I do receive a current which enables me to pour it on the more — it's difficult to read powerfully to an audience of three — but I'm always fully aware that *I* am 'playing' *them*. It's an exhausting business because, although you're receiving current, you're giving out a hell of a lot more than you receive.

32

Unlike writing, the rewards are immediate, which explains why writers are attracted to the idea of reading their work. But the rewards are also ephemeral and, not being professional actors, we were all aware, I think, of some such image as seals being thrown gobbets of herring after launching themselves through hoops.

To have written something beautifully is its own reward but it also exists permanently on the page. I can scarcely comprehend the life of a professional actor. It must be rather like that of an addict needing daily, and larger, doses. I'm grateful to actors for all the pleasure they've given me and for what I've learned from them but I'm even more grateful I didn't become one. A writer, writing, is in some sort of relationship of equality with an ideal audience. I suspect that an actor's life is, paradoxically, more lonely than a writer's and that it is, essentially, masturbatory; I suspect that a good actor's relationship with an audience is tinged in some complicated way with contempt.

Most of the readings by Montreal Story Teller, apart from a relatively small number in universities, CEGEPs, and off-island Protestant schools, took place in schools under the jurisdiction of the Montreal Catholic School Commission. One of Hugh's former students at the University of Montreal happened to be the English Coordinator for the Commission and so was disposed to be helpful.

We were, of course, very interested in reading in the schools administered by the Protestant School Board of Greater Montreal but the Protestant Board had a very Protestant mistrust of the idea of parting with money — especially for the purpose of encouraging the profitless enjoyment of literature. I had worked for the Protestant School Board of Greater Montreal for some years and knew the personnel quite well. The Consultant in English with whom I had enjoyed a very friendly relationship, Charles Rittenhouse, had recently retired and had been replaced by a Welsh person. Hugh and I arranged to go to the Board offices on Fielding Avenue in Montreal to further press the case for Art, Beauty, and Truth, as telephonic communication had merely resulted in a lot of devious Welsh evasion. This visit ended in our both being banned for life from the Board offices and all schools and messuages under its jurisdiction.

Hugh is, by and large, a gentle, optimistic, cheerful character. He has many marked opinions which he is at all times more than willing to expound but always in a rational and compassionate spirit. I remember driving with him and my wife from Delta to Toronto. As we left the house in Delta my wife asked him why he didn't buckle his seat-belt. The answer, taking in a comprehensive survey through the ages of the doctrines of Free Will, Salvation, Law, and The Social Contract, lasted until we were approaching Oshawa. My wife often recalls this answer and now, when Hugh is visiting, visibly hesitates before asking him if he would like salt... pepper?

Hugh's cheerfulness and optimism must take its toll, however, because very infrequently he explodes into awe-inspiring rage. So it was that afternoon at the offices of the Protestant School Board of Greater Montreal.

Montreal at that time lived in fear of FLQ bombs and the Protestant Board had installed in the foyer of its headquarters an armed guard who refused to let us enter until we had identified ourselves and announced the nature of our business. His request was rather like poking a stick into an innocent-looking hole and being forced to run for one's life in front of an advancing wall of white-hot magma.

Hugh refused to identify himself. He refused to let *me* identify myself. He demanded to know the name of the guard. Of the receptionist. Of the switchboard girl. He wrote their names down in his note-book. By this time, covert phone-calls were being made. The Welsh person arrived. The mounting uproar roused ancient functionaries from their slumbers in the Boardroom. The Comptroller came and gawked. Down in their private elevator came Directors of Personnel and Consultants. Hugh, pinched of nostril and white with rage, was in full spate, reminding them, very reasonably in my opinion, that the schools they administered were paid for by *his* taxes; that all of them were *his* servants, not he theirs; that the building, perhaps more than any other, was a *public* building.

These politically unexceptionable remarks were followed by statements of a slightly more disputatious nature about the history and course of English-French relations, the part played by the Board in fostering and maintaining these social and political schisms, the accountability of the Board, the obvious political end to which their blind and high-handed attitudes would inevitably bring them. It was at about this point that the banning took place.

I must admit that there were some subsequent half-hearted gestures on their part towards reconciliation but these were curtly refused. It was a pity to have killed the Protestant Goose but we were in no mood then, or, come to that, now, to be fucked about by administrators or Welshmen.

Some of our readings stay more firmly in the mind than others. In one Catholic school we read in a sub-basement room which was festooned with lagged steam-pipes to a group of young slatterns — a Practical Class, I suspect, or a sorority rudely ripped from Domestic Science to form an audience. Their remarks about Clark's beard, Ray's size and probable endowment, and their projection of a contained but heightened sense of merriment filled me with foreboding. Was this, I asked myself, a natural audience for "Getting to Williamstown"? My fears were soon realized. As the outer limits of their attention span were reached, some three minutes into the reading, they deliberately began to fall off their chairs.

At another inner-city school — a nice euphemism, that — we were greeted by the principal, a large slab of a man whose ramrod bearing and aura suggested reflex violence, a sort of West Point General of a principal. His unsmiling face was marked from eye to chin by a purple scar. Those students we saw on our march to the auditorium seemed unnervingly quiet and self-effacing. The audience was unnaturally still and silent. The *feel* of the hall reminded me of those silent, panning shots in the pre-riot cafeteria in San Quentin. The teachers, all male, stood sentry in the aisles gazing at their charges. I would not go so far as to say that all the teachers were Christian Brothers but they were in the Christian Brothers class.

The reading was desperate from the start. We read our hearts out. We basely angled for laughs but got not a titter. It was like reading in a morgue. Even Ray Fraser's tale, yet another ill-judged offering, did not cause them to break ranks.

At the close of the ghastly proceedings, the principal expressed his thanks and invited the audience to express their appreciation. The applause sounded as if it were under water. The students were then marched out.

"Gentlemen," said the principal, "you will be so good as to follow me."

On the echoing march to the Office, I felt frankly nervous; I imagined Ray Fraser being held down by Christian Brothers and having his mouth washed out with soap and water. And for the rest of us, if we

35

were lucky, a general duffing up...

The Office was dominated by a massive steel safe. Chairs were brought in by a muscular man. Not a word had been spoken. The principal moved to the safe, turned wheels, heaved open the door. We stared. Inside were many bottles.

"Gentlemen," he said. "what is your pleasure?"

But not all our readings, of course, were so bizarre. The most successful ones were done for Doug Rollins at Rosemere High School and, later, at Dawson College. Doug Rollins, an old friend and superb teacher, provided audiences which had been prepared. They had read some of our work and had absorbed from Doug some ideas about the story form. They were also fired by his enthusiasm. The comparative sophistication of their questions after readings was remarkable.

It's difficult to know what sort of educational impact Montreal Story Teller made. At the time we were all aware, I think, of the missionary nature of the readings. To read Canadian matter and talk of Canadian concerns was then rather like carrying the Word to people who ate grubs and worshipped aeroplanes. One of our strengths was that we gave children the opportunity to hear and talk to living writers, creatures heretofore known only as names in italic on the contents page of an anthology or text. We appeared before them warts and all. And we talked, insistently, of being writers *in Canada*. I think this was valuable.

(I felt much the same way about the textbook I'd edited at about the same time — a book called *Sixteen by Twelve*. Writers were presented by means of photographs, brief biographies, and a chatty commentary to accompany the stories. It didn't really matter if the commentary were too difficult or even inaccurate and misleading; what mattered was the expression and impact of personality.)

The problem, though, was to wean the children from this immediately attractive stuff — from the holiday aspects of a reading, from the comedy of five grown men fooling about for their benefit — and to get them chomping on solid food, the words on the page. Personality only goes so far. We can't know how successful we were in this but we can make informed and gloomy guesses.

So far as *I* can see, still nothing much has changed. In spite of all the nationalist furore, the founding of the Writers' Union, and the proliferation of Canada Days in schools, Canadian writing is still foreign to

Canada. More to the point, perhaps, *writing* is foreign to Canada.

The educational world grinds on like the mills of God. For how many more decades, one wonders, will Canadian children have the moral and technical crudities of Hugh Garner imposed upon them? The first story I ever wrote is now beginning to be used in textbooks. It will still be 'in use' (and I'm afraid that's *exactly* what I mean) when I'm a toothless old fart mumbling into my nightly mug of warm milk. And young writers will be raging against the weathered monoliths that stand in their way.

I apologize in advance.

My book *Sixteen by Twelve* marches on — far too successfully. I'm afraid it will still be in use in twenty years. I put the thing together in 1969. When I did so, it was, I believe, the *only* vaguely contemporary gathering of stories for schools. A number of charmers have demanded to know how I, an ex-Brit and effete limejuicer, had the nerve to compile a book of Canadian stories for schools. My innate good manners have always prevented me from explaining in corrosive detail.

Towards the end, Montreal Story Teller was beginning to pall. The idea of being travelling clowns confident of being able to manipulate laughs held little appeal for any of us. We were writers. Serious people. We wanted to write serious stuff. I always had before me the vision of writing stuff of the same calibre as P.G.'s *The Mating Season*, a book to which I often turn for comfort.

(There's nothing better for a dark night of the soul than Bertie Wooster pretending to be Gussie Finknottle coaching Esmond Haddock in a souped-up version of the hunting song that Esmond is to sing at the King's Deverill Village Concert.)

We had read. We had preached and proselytized. But the literary landscape had not changed. We remained prophets without honour. The earth had not moved.

But if we were not especially effective in our Mission to the Heathen, we did have an educational impact on each other. I must qualify that immediately. I cannot speak for anyone else in Montreal Story Teller. I can say, however, that I was most definitely influenced by others in the group. What I learned is not easy to define. Listening to someone's story for the tenth (boring) time, the pieces in my own kaleidoscope would suddenly jink into a slightly different pattern.

Ray Smith's comments on and typical aggression towards the traditional story form raised red warning lights for me; he directed my attention towards dangers I'd never really seen. He forced me into more critical reading. I'd always felt that much 'experimental' writing was rather like farting Annie Laurie through a keyhole though not as demanding. The expertise was obvious, if it were well done, but the emotional power was lacking. Intimate acquaintance with Ray's story "Peril" skinned my eyeballs, as the necromancer in the first part of "Peril" says, quoting Gulley Jimson. Again.

Ray probably isn't aware of his influence on me — possibly because it's a largely cautionary one. Ray prevented me from perpetrating yet more gauche stories of sensitive youth. Ray has a thing about sensitive youth. Show Ray a sensitive youth in literature or life and he will don his leather coat and stride towards the Royal Pub on Guy Street, muttering.

(An example of the literary Ray at his most aggressive is the dour farce "Symbols in Agony" — a tale that dismembers Ray's vision of The Canadian Story. I remember his telling me once that his editor, Dennis Lee, had somehow managed to read the story without quite grasping that its intention was comic.)

Hugh's work reassured me of the *respectability* of writing openly about a moral world — and of writing openly. I don't mean by this anything so crude as that I saw Hugh merely as a moral influence. I mean something much more complicated.

My early writing had been constricted by rather strange notions of fictional chastity stemming from the doctrine 'Don't tell, show' carried to obsessively virginal lengths. Hugh offered me an example of how to relax my own style, of how to become less clenched. I didn't relax *in Hugh's manner* but that I managed to accept the possibility of relaxation is largely owing to his influence. His taste and erudition helped me get away from the conscious and precious effects of Imagism whose precepts informed, ineptly, my early prose efforts. The search for the old *mot* and my consciousness of the strictures of Hulme and Pound had induced literary constipation. I can't really remember now what is was I was attempting — probably something like the technique of a five-line H.D. lyric transferred to a 3000-word story but muddied by Hemingway mannerisms and totally contradicted by gobs of Dylan Thomas. Hugh's opinions and example were like a massive draught of laxative. Though it took a few years to work.

I had never really been *persuaded* by Modernism in prose and have never quite grasped what Post-Modernism *is*. It was Evelyn Waugh, I think, who said that James Joyce went mad to please the Americans; Hugh's comments on The Modern do not go quite this far but are similarly bracing.

Clark's work offered me constructional and rhetorical ideas. These influences haven't worked themselves out in open or obvious ways but stories of mine like "The Teeth of My Father," "The Eastmill Reception Centre," and "Private Parts: A Memoir" probably grew in their own dark from the seed of Clark's "Extractions and Contractions." I doubt that he'd acknowledge paternity.

It's probably also true to say, though, that Clark's stories fell into earth turned over by Ray Smith. And that the first-person voice that speaks in them owes much to Hugh. And much in them is also my own. And Waugh's. And Roger Longrigg's. And Richard Yates's. And also, perhaps, *Toytown*'s Larry the Lamb.

Influence does not work in obvious ways and it's probably impossible to trace unless one person has consciously copied another. But I think writers' minds tend to seize on technical and rhetorical goodies — which is to say the same as emotional possibilities — and carry them off to the dark cauldron where they cook with and are changed by the other ingredients of the ever-simmering stew.

At the beginning of this memoir I said that Montreal Story Teller was united only in its desire for honoraria. As a bond, that never loosened. But now, looking back, I think that we were held together by much more. We *grew* together. I don't think the group would have worked as it did unless we were getting from the association something more important than money. Four of us, at least, were writers obsessed by the idea of excellence, crazy about craft. The group gave us an association where craft was recognized and didn't have to be discussed; we were at home with each other, at home in the way that perhaps the disfigured are or the lame, that exiles are in a hostile land.

In my own case, at least, there was a sense in which membership in Montreal Story Teller was a way of helping to *define* myself; the company of other writers I respected helped to confirm that I was a writer indeed. We were all younger then, of course, and our hilarity and arrogance masked an uneasiness.

We're all probably too busy now, too differently obsessed to spend

39

time regularly in such readings. It's also probably true that we don't need each other in quite the way we did then. We all remain friends, of course, close friends, but we're living in different places, writing different things. Montreal Story Teller was an almost accidental coming together which worked and grew stronger because we were who we were at that particular point in our lives. For three of us, at least, Montreal Story Teller coincided, I think, with our apprenticeship.

Though we'd never have admitted it.

I had not thought much about the group in recent years before I started to write these recollections, but now I seem to see us as we were then and seem to hear those voices as we are driving down an endless road towards a reading somewhere — perhaps in the Maritimes.

We are all rather excited.

Ray Smith is being happily grumpy about the quality of food we can expect. Once when I was going out West I asked him if he had any restaurant recommendations.

"One cannot expect to eat well in Canada," he said, "*west of Guy Street.*"

What is he going on about now?

Lobsters. The wonder of lobsters from Cape Breton. The particular wonder of lobsters from his beloved Mabou. The impossibility of obtaining fresh lobster in New Brunswick. All lobsters are frozen and then exported to Toronto and then imported to Fredericton. Ray states this as fact.

Hugh offers statistics which prove that all foodstuffs in New Brunswick are 5¼% higher in price than in any other province. This leads on to arcane knowledge about distribution systems, capital, and monopoly. This, in turn, could well prompt Hugh to a discourse on the geography of distribution systems in the Canadian past, river systems, the Canadian Shield, glaciers...

But lobsters have prompted Ray Fraser to think of salmon which leads him into an amusing tale of poaching on the Miramichi, a tale that involves guides, American tourists, and dynamite.

Smoked salmon.

I offer an observation about the only pizza place in Fredericton when I lived there. It not only dotted turd-like mounds of hamburger on the pizzas but also proudly claimed: Made With Genuine Canadian Cheddar.

Clark is our resident French expert. So is Hugh but we're never sure if Hugh is making it up or not.

Ray Smith starts some French linguistic hare.

"What's the French for 'sanitary napkin', Clark?"

"*Le Tampax*," says Clark.

"*Cordon sanitaire*," says Hugh.

"Speaking of which," I say to Ray Smith, "remember that veal we had?"

"What veal?"

"In that restaurant in Old Montreal? Private house sort of place? Where the waiter said the can was upstairs and I went into a room where there was a woman watching television?"

"*I* wasn't with you. You must have been drunk."

"Sure you were!"

"No, I wasn't!"

"All right!" says Hugh. "Which one's this? 'As I sat in the bathtub, soaping a meditative foot and singing, if I remember correctly, "Pale Hands I Loved Beside the Shalimar"...'"

"But *why* can't I have one of your fruit pastilles, Hugh?"

"Buy your own fucking fruit pastilles."

Slowing through a small town, Hugh winds down the window to shout gratuitous advice to a hairy youth.

Clark wants to know if we're going to be paid that night or later. He starts to explain how he has to cover some cheques for school fees or mass dentistry or tax arrears and this leads to discussion with Hugh — high financial stuff concerning mortgage payments and the portability of university pensions — discussion which does not grip the rest of us as we're variously unemployed or on the pogey.

Ray and Ray are debating in which order when they arrive they're going to drink:

> Moosehead
> Schooner
> Tenpenny
> Oland's
> etc. etc.

Which prompts me to recall how after drinking Moosehead immoderately I was banned for life from the River Room of the Lord Beaverbrook Hotel in Fredericton for unplugging two amplified

Spanish singers from Saint John.

Hugh starts to invent unlikely and obscene names for Canadian wines.

The voices play on and on.

The headlights unroll the dark.

On either side of the road, trees.

We are driving towards an audience.

1981

Ray Smith
ONTOLOGICAL ARSEHOLES:
LIFE WITH MONTREAL STORY TELLER

I have never calculated the cost of my first published book, *Cape Breton is the Thought-Control Centre of Canada*, but my second, *Lord Nelson Tavern*, cost $50,000 (in 1970 dollars) and a marriage. The money breaks down about like this:

Wife	$25,000
Canada Council	10,000
Self	15,000

The Canada Council and Wifely contributions were in real cash money, coin of the realm; a small part of mine was also, but most is a calculation of lost salary and is therefore sort of imaginary, I suppose. Of course, *Lord Nelson* was not entirely responsible for the break-up. There were other, personal reasons, more my fault than hers; I am not just being polite. At the same time, the unpublished work of my apprenticeship along with two published books cost her more money and more happiness than I want to mention here. In return, she got the dedication for each book. Whether she considers that a good bargain or not, I don't know. Somehow, I doubt it.

Since *Lord Nelson Tavern* was published in 1974, I have written two novels. The first is about skiing and cost between sixty and seventy thousand 1977 dollars. The breakdown is:

Canada Council	$14,000
Jack McClelland	2,000
Self	50,000

About $10,000 of mine was savings; the rest was lost salary. When Jack McClelland reported on this book, he said it was "the worst manuscript I have seen from an established writer in all the years I've been in the business." John Metcalf, claiming Jack's taste was in his ass-

43

hole, demanded to read the book. His comment: "Jack was being polite; it is even worse." The reasons for this failure are complex. As the book will never be published, there is no point rehashing them here. Suffice it to say that I made certain monumental errors of judgement.

The most recent novel ran to over $80,000 in 1980 dollars of which $18,000 was from the Canada Council; none, and I'm sure this comes as no surprise, was from Jack McClelland. With, let's say for the sake of argument, about $10,000 for *Cape Breton* and other early work, the financial cost of my writing career has been over $200,000. The income to December 31st, 1982, is $38,009.59. The net on that is a loss to me, my ex-wife, Jack McClelland, and the Canada Council of $161,990.41. That's about $9,000 a year in the red every year for eighteen years.

Unadjusted for inflation.

I have tried in recent years to reduce the human cost by making sure my second wife has never supported me and therefore I can happily report that I write this on June 12th, 1983, our seventh wedding anniversary. The tensions of living with a writer as well as the lost salary over the years have, of course, affected her, but on the whole I think she looks upon my writing with a certain equanimity. At any rate, we're still married.

This tale of financial lunacy and disaster is commonplace among writers. So is the divorce.

A bit more on the most recent novel. It is a comic spy thriller which I think is a bloody marvel, a penetrating satire on the nature of Canadians and so on. The several friends who have read it seem to like it — one can never really trust them to tell the truth if they dislike a manuscript — but I can't find an editor who likes it. I think it will probably get published someday. And oddly enough, despite this tale of artistic, marital, and financial failure, I am still cheerful about the future. I recently did the first draft of a new short story, the first in fifteen years or so, and it is reasonably healthy. At least I can say that it has achieved a form, is not just words or sentences or scenes, but a made and grown thing. So that I can test my optimism, the title is, "In the night, Heinrich Himmler...''; perhaps it will turn up in one of the little magazines around 1986. I am not being ironic, for that is a reasonable wait for publication in a small magazine.

In any case, life has become too complicated—partly because of the racist, fascist regime of the P.Q.—for me to afford another novel, so although my career is not over, it is considerably reduced in scale from the glory years, the years of Montreal Story Teller.

You can see me in my pride in the photo Sam Tata did for our poster. I wasn't fat, by the way, but was standing with my pelvis stuck out. I could probably concoct some complex self-referral fiction about thinking of what I was thinking about when the photo was taken which was that I was wondering what I would think when I looked back at the photo ten years later, but I forget what I was thinking about. Probably hoping this was the last bloody shot and could we all get inside a nice warm bar and get outside a nice cool brew. And a few minutes later we did. As far as that goes, I don't often think back to those times, any more than any sensible person dwells on the past. Life goes on. But when I do remember, the memories are fine.

It is our first reading: Rosemere High School just north of Montreal and an audience of hundreds in the auditorium. A capable and interested staff has whipped the students into shape: many of them have actually read and studied stories we have written. We are among friends. What we don't realize is that this will be one of the very best audiences we will ever have.

Was I the first to read? I cannot remember, nor can I remember what I read. Probably a section of "Peril." I begin by lighting a cigarette to the vast approval of the students. I sip some water and begin. The audience is attentive and, despite a throat which keeps drying up, I read fairly well. Canadian culture has come to the school and Canadian culture is triumphant. Except that several minutes into the reading the school band strikes up from the rehearsal room behind the stage. While a teacher scurries off to shut them up, Canadian culture stands silent and amazed at the superb irony of the tune being played: "America the Beautiful."

Just in case one of the other Story Tellers has forgotten to mention it: John Metcalf started it all. Why, his argument ran, should the bloody poets be getting all the loot for reading their incomprehensible gibberish? Give them prose, give them characters, stories, give them life. But there was more to it than money. During the time the group was together, we must have spent at least ten minutes discussing whether or not we were actually bringing culture to the schools. The optimistic view was that students would benefit from seeing, in the flesh, people who had written stuff which was in their textbooks; or, conversely, from discovering that people in their textbooks were also in their phonebooks. The pessimistic view, usually from John, was that the students couldn't read the phonebook, never mind his books, and twenty-pound sledgehammers couldn't pound culture into those heads. I confess I was an optimist, and so remain.

We shared out the labours, such as they were. I did the accounts. (The book is open to accredited scholars upon appointment.) John and Hugh arranged the readings; or not, in the case of the notorious Protestant School Board of Greater Montreal. Hugh arranged (and paid) for both posters; his wife, Noreen, designed the first one. Hugh and Clark did the driving. Fraser brought the booze.

A little scene I did *before* reading John's.

The five of us are in Hugh's car driving to a reading. Probably along some ghastly six-laner like the Decarie Expressway. Known as "The Big Ditch," it has concrete walls fifty feet high. A dangerous and depressing place. Hugh gleefully extols freeways, concrete, and the Decarie.

"Yessir," he exults, "they ought to pave the island from end to end. Concrete is civilization."

He goes on in this vein. I never know if he is being serious or trying to get a rise out of someone. John plunges in. "You are being deliberately perverse, Hugh." John's ideal landscape is perhaps filled with the barren hills and green valleys of Yorkshire or Cumberland; he looks upon a life which includes the Decarie Expressway as something from Hieronymus Bosch, and his life here as a punishment for an adolescence spent in furtive wanking.

"Perverse?" Hugh cries. "Shit no. Do you realize that if the Romans..."

Given half a chance, Hugh will talk on the history of concrete all the way to the reading, be it in Rosemere or be it in Vancouver. Long before that, John will have thrown himself screaming from the car; or will be in paroxysms of hysterical laughter. (Hugh once kept John and self so laughing all the way to Ottawa.) But neither is given a chance: Clark interrupts with an apt quotation from Rilke, Schiller, or Pushkin; someone whose work I have never read. Clark quotes in the original language.

In the back seat, I murmur to Fraser: "Bring out the Argentine brandy."

"Bulgarian this week," says Fraser as he digs the mickey from the inevitable Air Canada bag. "Bulgarian was only 19.6 cents an ounce."

Fraser uses a housewife's calculator to buy his booze. We each take a pull and Ray offers it around but all refuse. Fraser and I are, of course, the only Maritimers in the group.

Hugh and Clark are now fully into the discussion about concrete.

"Those nineteenth-century romantics are ontological arseholes," Hugh is saying.

In rebuttal Clark summarizes Bergson.

Another car comes close to ours. Hugh rolls down his window and yells, "Watch out you stupid fucker, the future of Canadian literature is in this car."

Metcalf says, "Quebec drivers are all either suicidal or drunk. Probably both."

Clark quotes Alberto Moravia on Italian drivers. In Italian.

I remark that I once skimmed a Moravia novel. The cover had promised steamy sex, but the text was a philosophical working out of exquisitely attenuated ennui.

Clark quotes Anouilh on ennui.

Fraser's nerve breaks and we get another pull at the Bulgarian.

"Moravia is a teleological arsehole," says Hugh. In illustration he quotes two pages of a Moravia novel he read in 1947. He quotes in English.

In rebuttal Clark summarizes twentieth-century Italy.

Now John reaches for the bottle. "I saw a great line yesterday in *The High Window* by Raymond Chandler: 'large moist eyes with the sympathetic expression of wet stones.' Superb."

Hugh quotes the next two pages of the novel.

I interrupt to point out a girl standing at a stop light and wearing a see-through top and no bra. Hugh sings a song he has written about lingerie. I never did learn the words, but something like:

Your girdle is a hurdle
I never want to jump
But your garter belts send me
And bikini panties rend me
And black stockings bend me
Into a hump-hump-hump!

47

On the last line Hugh bounces vigorously in his seat. A good thing we are no longer on the expressway, for the car swerves into the next lane and heads for a lamp post. As Hugh nonchalantly regains control, John remarks in tightly controlled hysteria: "Hugh, if I might make a small suggestion. . . ."

Hugh ignores him; he has noticed a fellow in jeans and jean jacket staring in amazement from the sidewalk. Hugh rolls down the window.

"Hump-hump-hump!" he bellows. "Culture!" He guns the car around the corner. "And why don't you get a haircut, you long-haired hippie freak." He rolls up the window. "That's telling him."

Clark quotes Yukio Mishima on lingerie. This time he quotes in English.

Fraser flourishes the bottle. Metcalf grabs it in desperation.

I reflect that whatever Hugh's estimable qualities — and they are many — if he wore a hat it would inevitably bear a card reading: "In this style, 10/6."

By the time we enter the school we are all (save Clark) either half bagged or on adrenalin highs or both. John looks about and remarks, "It reminds me of the borstal in which I used to teach." Everything up to McGill reminds him of borstal. (We read at McGill not at the invitation of the university, of course, but of the Learned Societies which were conventioning there.)

The staff are a bit nervous because they are not sure if we're going to provide a safe afternoon away from the classroom or gang-rape the majorette corps.

The stage with five chairs which we remove at once. Buggered if we're going to sit out there and listen when we can be backstage smoking and working on Fraser's mickey.

The students. Nice kids, on the whole, despite what I'm sure John will say. Earnest, polite girls, pretty girls, plain girls, girls who read and girls who don't. Somehow one never thought of them sexually; I find this rather pleasant, if a bit surprising. The boys also an assorted lot. Everything from the chain-clanking mouth-breathers of mech tech picking their teeth with tie-rods through to the acne-ravaged intellectuals with their dandruff and embarrassing questions:

"Mr. Smith, what do you think of the works of Isaac Babel?"

48

"Ask Mr. Blaise."

We check the timing. A relatively short story will need half an hour. Two and a half hours for the five of us and extra for questions. More likely we have twelve minutes each and are already running five minutes late. A brief discussion on the order of appearance. Metcalf peers around the curtain and says he wants to go first.

"That vice-principal chappie just tossed them a few hundredweight of raw meat, so they'll be quiet for a while."

And it begins again.

I should perhaps include here several finely tuned pages of judgement on the reading styles of the others, but I'll content myself by concurring with John's piece in this; save that I'll add the one thing he couldn't say. John was the best reader in the group, being just better than Clark who, on a good day, was better than John.

By the spring of 1975 I had come to fear readings: the public exposure, the arrogance of it, was like having a layer of skin ripped off. I had already committed myself to a long series for the next winter. I did those, but, although I no longer fear readings, have since let the whole business slip away. In the past two winters I have done three, mostly for sentimental reasons. Until a new book appears, I don't think I have much right to be on a stage. Looking at the friendly faces before me a few months ago at The University of Western Ontario, I found myself wondering, no doubt incorrectly, if they weren't rather surprised at my presence, as I myself had been surprised when, in the early sixties, I discovered that Alexander Kerensky was still alive.

The other day an old friend who works for some trade publication in New York called me with an offer of work. I explained that I was a novelist with, however modestly, a novelist's skills and that journalism involves very different skills. He argued that a clear mind and a clean style are transportable. He then read me a sample of the sort of thing he wanted. It was about a municipal money-saving scheme which involved the harnessing of the methane gas produced by organic garbage.

Is there a message in this? I asked myself.

No, I replied.

I thanked my friend for his kind offer, but regretfully declined.

The roses in my garden are blooming again.

1983

49

Raymond Fraser
THE GUY IN THE WINGS WITH HIS PINT

I've never cared to re-read my finished writings, neither privately nor in public. Wanting to be perfect I'm always afraid of disappointing myself, of seeing need for further improvements; and if I can't draw the line somewhere and call it quits I'm liable to be revising the same page the rest of my life. Even so, when Hugh Hood asked me early in 1971 to be one of the Montreal Story Teller Fiction Performance Group, as it was to be called, I said I would because I figured that was the sort of thing you had to do to promote your name in the writing game. At the time I was approaching thirty and my career wasn't looking too rosy. In fact I was frustrated and bitter at how poorly I was doing. I'd come down with a bad case of shattered illusions, a condition I couldn't sanely deal with. I felt the fates had set me up, because previously everything had appeared to be rolling along so well.

In the fall of 1969 Delta had published my third collection of poems (*I've laughed and sung . . .*) and people seemed to like it, for the most part. Then in February 1970 Chateau Books accepted my latest version of a novel (*The Robin Hood Gang*) and I signed my first contract with a publisher. Shortly after that I completed the rough writing of another novel. And in April I received a Canada Council grant. The day I got the grant was my idea of how a typical day in my earthly kingdom should be. The sun happened to be shining, and I left the post office and strolled the streets of downtown Montreal like a being in a higher dimension than the poor mortals I passed. In my foolish rapture I wondered if those dreary unfortunates could detect by the radiance on my face what a lucky chap was I. I wanted to tell them all, grab them by the lapels and say, "Guess what?" I was filled with a sense of unlimited freedom, a multitude of desirable choices open before me. It

50

was the first time in my life I'd had a substantial sum of money (the grant was $3,500 and return fare to Europe) and it was *all free*... which meant I could spend it as I pleased without feeling guilty. For a fellow with my background, where the pennies were always watched, this was a delicious feeling. I even delayed going to the tavern because it didn't make sense to drink; how could I improve on the high I already had? There would be something morally wrong in drinking now, no excuse for it, so I put off for a half hour. Later I bought a big steamer trunk at a second-hand store (I couldn't lose my habit of frugality all at once) and a tent and sleeping bags and packsacks and champagne and four or five other kinds of fancy wine. First the celebration then so long, Montreal, time to move on. Not that I'd been unhappy the past few years in Montreal, I hadn't, they'd been good years; but there was *more* to be had, more of life's delights.

It seemed clear to me that my train to glory was on the rails and commencing to build up a head of steam. I'd been earning a reasonable living writing for tabloid newspapers (*Midnight, National Examiner, National Spotlite*, etc.), but now I was free to quit this demeaning occupation. My wife Sharon and I packed our stuff and departed for Newfoundland for a summer of camping on Little Bonne Bay Pond with our friends Al and Marilee Pittman. And from there we flew to Spain. Spain in September was like Heaven. The hot sun and the clear emerald Mediterranean, palm trees and walnut groves — writing and swimming and eating out every night, and the booze so cheap it was almost free. Sixty cents for a litre of brandy — like that. A gargler's paradise, as Brendan Behan called it. But my drinking was negligible. I'd work in the morning from eight-thirty to twelve, walk to the beach for a swim and a snack, then back to work until four or five. And only then would I open a beer. It's true that once started I drank steadily until eleven or so, but leisurely. I not only didn't get drunk but didn't want to. I didn't *need* booze — I was content by my standards, I had things my way. I was pretty sure I did. There were moments of doubt; I mean not everything was in the bag, I was impatient, and I tended to create concerns if none were at hand. But working during the day and nine or ten beers and a half litre of wine in the evening kept me fairly tranquil. Most likely my novel would be a spectacular best seller and there'd be wild bidding for the new one. Movie offers, the problems of fame. For the most part I viewed my prospects with complacency, borrowing

51

emotional charges on my future winnings. I practised affecting a personable modesty, which wouldn't prevent me from pronouncing on and straightening out a certain number of unwarranted reputations.

What actually came to pass, and in a quite short period of time, was something altogether different.

Chateau had a change of mind and following assorted inane proposals ("Why don't you try re-writing it into something like *Love Story*, that's what's selling now") they returned my novel. I'd already submitted the new one to three publishers at once and all three rejected it within days of one another. I was informed by the Canada Council that they weren't renewing my grant. Winter was here and instead of the beaches and cafés of Spain I was sulking in an apartment I despised back in cold Montreal. I put out a fourth book of poems and it got one review, in the Sir George Williams school paper (a good review, anyway). My literary magazine, *Intercourse*, which I'd handed over to a poet friend to publish, got into the hands of Tyndale Martin and his cult and appeared as a voice of Buddhism which was a long cry from how I'd conceived the thing. I added that to my list of reasons for feeling badly done upon. I was too proud to go back to the tabloids (I'd told them goodbye for good) so I had no paying work. And then Noise really started to get to me. For a long time I'd been abnormally sensitive to noises, annoyed by them, and often with justifiable reason, but now they began to drive me completely crackers. It was probably a case of something definable to focus my anger on — an anger brought on by frustration and apprehension. I was being threatened with failure, and that scared me. I'd been accustomed to take eventual success for granted. I saw myself blossoming in a certain way, and if it didn't come about, what was I then? The world would be severely disappointed in me. I'd have let billions of people down, the dead as well as the living, and those yet to come. The weight of so much disapproval was horrible to contemplate. I could hardly maintain I was doing everything right if I hadn't the credentials to back me up. The way things were now, and after all the time I'd been at it, could I even call myself a writer? A few books of poetry — what were they? All that white space on the pages.

The blueprint in my head and the reality beyond weren't jibing, which is a common starting point for lunacy, in radical cases. Some manage to alter their vision, others try and shape the world to fit it, like the characters in my novel *The Struggle Outside* (plug), and others let

52

themselves be eaten away inside.

I was already a dedicated tipler at this time. I couldn't stray far from the flagon, I drank every day to feel a human among humans, to ease pressures, face obligations, diminish fears, magnify pleasures, stifle guilts, lessen pains... trying to outwit the Dealer, in other words. I had developed a considerable tolerance for the stuff and rarely got noticeably drunk, and I might have a couple of serious hangovers a year. I thought I'd found the secret to successful drinking. But the recent turn of events had put me into such a dismal state that sobriety wasn't merely uncomfortable, it was intolerable. I was morose and enraged by turns — those were my two moods, my unfailing companions, always one or the other, until I got sufficiently oiled.

Every few days I'd go across the street to a small grocery store for my supply of beer. I was amused when the young fellow who worked there said, "Man, you must have a hollow leg!" The owner of the store asked me one day what I did for a living. I said, "I'm self-employed." He nodded knowingly. "Well, that's all right, I don't knock it. I'd rather work myself but each to his own. You can't blame a guy for taking it if it's there." He obviously thought I was a welfare drunk, or something of the sort. But I had nothing to come back with. I was eking out the last of my grant money and just about all I did was drink.

I didn't write anything to speak of for about eight months. I'd sit at my desk and say what's the use? blaming publishers and editors and the universe. I'd written five unpublished novels in ten years. Why do another one? Why do anything? Maybe I had no talent and had been deluding myself all this time. The possibility made my stomach turn. It was an idea I didn't dare entertain. If I was mistaken there, in something that essential, then I couldn't trust myself in anything. Moreover I hadn't left myself an option to fall back on, all my eggs were in the one basket. So every day I sat around feeling lousy and guzzling beer to change the picture.

That's how I was during most of my time with the Story Teller troupe. So far as I could see the show biz angle was the only thing I had going. But I often felt like a charlatan, pretending to all those people out there that I was a flourishing author.

And I had to wonder about the other guys, what they thought I was doing with them. To myself anyway I was the odd fellow of the five. The rest of them had their fiction in books. They all taught English

Literature for a living. None of them was a poet or a practising drunk. I was not included like the others in the anthologies of stories John Metcalf was editing, and felt kind of uncomfortable when they'd discuss these collections as if I wasn't present. I had the sense of being one of them by accident or mistake. Perhaps I helped make the group unclassifiable, visible evidence that we were an assortment of varied individuals and not a "school," a tag each of us was quick to discredit, being jealous of our unique identities.

The fact was, obsessed as I'd been with writing novels I hadn't written very many short stories. And the novels weren't such hot stuff either. Before long I'd cranked out another, making six in all by the age of thirty, and basically I didn't know what I was doing, it's as simple as that. I wasn't ready, but I was impatient, so I did the things anyway. One I completed in two weeks, 250 pages. The others took no longer than four months. I didn't want to strain myself. I wanted the finished product to come easily. Only later did I learn to take pains.

As for performing, I thought that for anyone to stand on a stage and read to an audience he would have to be half-pissed. It surpassed my comprehension that this evidently wasn't true for the others, for Clark Blaise, Hugh Hood, John Metcalf, and Ray Smith (to get their names in here. . . in alphabetical order). I couldn't understand it. I had to conclude it was because they were all teachers and used to lecturing and reading in front of students. I wasn't. I always packed a pint of rum and settled the butterflies before I went on.

Of the stories I did have in stock, maybe only a couple were sufficiently free of vulgarities and crudities to be fit for reading to high school students, who comprised most of our audiences. But with a few exceptions (which I saved for the universities and general public) I read them anyway. I thought they might prove entertaining, and if I had any honourable idea about the Story Teller group it was to demonstrate to students that literature could be enjoyed as well as suffered as a course of study.

It goes without saying that all five of us wanted to make a good showing, to please the crowd. We weren't above aiming for a laugh, because when you give these readings and people just sit staring you can't tell if you're getting anything across; but laughter is an unmistakeable reaction. And sometimes there were other reactions.

About the only thing I wrote in my arid period was a story called

"Spanish Jack." I'd originally composed it as a newspaper feature and sold it to one of the tabloids. My partner in those days, a photographer, had got hold of a large collection of European medical and wire service photos, and once a week we'd sift through them looking for ideas. We came upon one of an elderly lady who'd had a breast removed surgically, and we matched her up with a bewhiskered old bum in a seaman's cap with a cigar butt in his mouth... *Sex-crazed Man, 76, Bites Off Wife's Breast.*

One day, looking through my collected tabloid works, I thought, now I wonder if I can take this crazy tale and make a short story out of it. Because it was a fact that many of the wild yarns I used to invent for the tabloids sooner or later had their real-life counterparts show up in what's called the legitimate press — which is to say, there's almost nothing you can invent that someone's not going to do somewhere in the world, or hasn't already done. I wrote "Spanish Jack" in a folksy down-east kind of style, and when I used it at a couple of readings everything rolled along quite amusingly, the audience chuckling and grinning, until I got to the *pièce de résistance* where the old chap clamps his teeth onto the missus's breast and bites it off and spits it out on the floor. Well, there was no laughter, but rather a mass retching sound, a vocal consensus of disgust.

I read the story at Sir George Williams and later at the University of New Brunswick in Fredericton, where Alden Nowlan (God rest him) came to the reading. I was on second or third, and he got up and left after my bit, and everyone said, "Alden was so revolted he walked out." But that wasn't so. We were longtime friends and he afterwards assured me that he'd only come to catch my act and when I was finished he left. In fact I stayed at his place that night. The truth is he thought the tale was gross but not enough to drive him from the room.

The first time I read it Ray Smith said to me, "Fraser, you don't refer to a man's penis as his 'knob' in your narration. In the dialogue, okay, maybe, but in the *narration*, for God's sake."

But my narrator was a character, too, so he could call a penis anything he felt like. My narrator is almost always a character. I have to first invent someone to tell the story. I need a consistent attitude, that's the thing, and I don't have enough idea who I am to use myself personally.

I enjoyed hearing the other guys read. Maybe I was wrong, but for the most part considered them better public readers than myself. I hadn't a clue what I was doing, how to use my voice — modulation, emphasis, whatever it's all about. I was surprised, however, that my fellow stars — with the exception of Hugh — would read the same couple of stories over and over. I remember how it disappointed me to learn that comedians performed night after night the one routine, and singers did a set pattern of songs and patter, and politicians delivered the identical speech in different cities. I thought one was obligated to give an original show each time, in case someone was in the audience twice — or for the benefit of the rest of the cast. This was naïve on my part, I realize now; but I expected performers to be always spontaneous and original, nothing rehearsed, no tricks, no gimmicks. Ideally — and for a while — I believed a writer shouldn't revise his work, that to do so betrayed the concept of pure inspiration. I had lots of good ideas in my time.

At all events I tried for a while to read something different every show, and it wasn't easy, because my supply at first was limited. I was forced to use some dubious material: for example a parody of the *High Noon* type of movie. One of the kids during the question period after asked me if I only wrote cowboy stories. I had trouble explaining what I'd done, since the youth had taken my story straight, but I was rescued by Clark Blaise stepping in and lucidly explaining my intent. It was remarkable how my companions could talk on the subject of literature. I rarely talked, about anything — or so I seem to recall. I couldn't be bothered. I saw talk as a dissipation of vital energy, and to tell a story vocally as wasting it on a limited audience. I later took to drunken raving, but it was only later still, at the age of forty-one, that I began discovering how to open my mouth. I've found it's good for me. And I don't mind repeating my stories either. I've been a slow learner in more ways than one.

I had my little successes. One of my stories, "The Newbridge Sighting," required that I do an unusual voice for the principal character. He was based on a person I knew and I could bring him off fairly well, I think. After the performance a teacher asked me if I'd ever considered taking up acting. It wasn't a hint; he confided that he thought my story had gone over the best of the lot. But me, an actor? I was never so flattered. Even in my drunken fantasies I only barely thought I could be an actor. I was the reverse of the type, as I conceived it, self-conscious, nervous, fearful of crowds, outwardly unemotional. Of course with a quantity of rum in me performing wasn't that hard, I might even say I enjoyed my stage appearances, especially if there was a microphone to give me a big voice. But you weren't getting the real me. It was always painful when sober to see people after I'd first met them while drinking. I didn't like them to find me out. I wasn't the free-and-easy chap I'd passed myself off as.

In April 1971 Sharon and I moved from Notre Dame de Grâce — where the nearest tavern was a mile away; I hated the neighbourhood — to a tiny apartment on Esplanade, at the back of a building. She had a part-time nursing job and I was making forty dollars a shot from our readings, and we paid eighty-five dollars a month rent, with furniture, heat, and electricity included. It was called an apartment but it was no more than a medium-sized room partitioned into a bedroom, living room, kitchen, and bathroom. I remember friends staying with us on occasion, and when we pulled the living room couch out to make a bed it filled the whole room — you stepped through the door and onto the bed and that was it.

There was one school where I must have given an inspired performance, because I sold about thirty copies of my new poetry book *The More I Live* after the reading. I was always the one who sold books, mainly because mine had a tag of fifty cents, cost price, while the other guys' novels and story collections were beyond the means of the students. At this school they had their own literary magazine and they wanted to tape an interview with me and print it. I have a feeling they could sense I was emotionally about their age, therefore easier to approach. I said, "Sure, come and see me anytime. I'm always free." Seven or eight of them showed up and it was quite a feat packing them all in, like cramming a football team into an elevator. I produced a big pitcher of homemade beer — with the volume I drank that's all I could afford by this time, seven cents a quart — and poured around, and kept refilling the pitcher as the interview proceeded. When we finished an hour later the youth handling the tape recorder discovered he'd pressed a wrong button and not a word had got taped. I don't think they cared, they didn't appear to, anyway.

I'd read several issues of their magazine, and some of those youngsters had writing talent. But I suspect I dampened their literary ambitions. Because here was I, one of the famous Montreal Story

57

Tellers, and here was the hovel I lived in. I'd noticed the expressions on their faces as they walked in the door, the dismay with which they parted the cobwebs and booted the cockroaches aside, slipping on the mud floor, huddling their coats about them as the wind whistled through the cracks in the wall. Or had the cockroaches been lately exterminated? I can't remember.

But a few writers more or less, what's the difference? There's no shortage of potential talent around. I saw quite a lot of it when I edited *Intercourse*, young writers with ability to burn, they seemed to have the gift, but they'd come and go, they didn't stick with it, they must have found better things to do. There was something missing, the obsession, the need, some factor that precluded their making a full commitment. I've thought at times they merely got wise. But I don't know.

Had I been one of those kids maybe I'd have found an element of romance about how Raymond Fraser was living. I was in favour of fame and riches and so forth, but my daydreams weren't consistent. I also saw myself as a Henry Miller type, living it rough and in disregard of conventional symbols of success... but still getting my books published, there was the *sine qua non*. And after I tired of this role I could shift into the yacht in Antibes and apartments in Paris and Rome and affairs with movie actresses and all sorts of interesting diversions.

But being where I was, and with no guarantee it was the early part of an eventually happy biography, I was bitter about my lot. For all I knew my condition wasn't going to get any better. And because I was *me*, life owed me more, there were no two ways about it. So what was going on around here?

One of the reasons I was so sensitive to noise had to be because my daily heavy drinking put my nerves on edge. But physiology aside, I was incensed that my sacred privacy was being invaded, I was being bombarded and assaulted by that rotten world out there. It was an indication of humanity treating me with indifference, offending me and neither knowing nor caring... an inimical chaos deaf to my complaints — first my orders, then my complaints, and what next, my berserk screams of impotent rage? Something of the kind. Like crossing the street with a crowd and a taxi nosing round the corner blasts its horn and I kick the side of the cab and yell, "*You lousy goddamned bastard! FUCK OFF!*" The other pedestrians move quickly away... a maniac loose on the streets...

58

Every Saturday there were weddings, and lines of cars would stream by on Park Avenue and St. Urbain Street with the drivers leaning on their horns. I actually picked up the phone several times to call the police in order to lodge a complaint. But with the phone in hand I realized they'd think I was nuts, a crackpot. One day a helicopter landed in the park which faces Esplanade; it made a hell of a racket coming down, and again I was about to call the law — it was all I could think of, my only recourse — when I saw it was a police helicopter. What do you do then?

I got into such fits that I felt I needed to retaliate. When I lived in NDG I used to daydream of getting a rifle and firing at the jetliners that flew low overhead in their approach to Dorval. There was a dog that barked every day on a nearby balcony. I wanted to shoot him too. I'd pace the floor and kick the walls. One day when the traffic seemed particularly bad I raced out the door on Esplanade and strode the length of the block snapping off all the aerials on the cars parked along the street. That would show them. It's possible my mind wasn't absolutely sound.

This was a little later on, early in 1972. A year before that I organized a march on City Hall to protest against the tyranny of automobiles in Montreal. There were some sane people took part in this... it was rather the thing at the time. I got into it in the way I involved myself in a number of escapades, while I was three-quarters cooked. A lot of talk, and next day I discovered I'd been taken at my word, and to save face (I always honoured my drunken commitments — I was too proud not to) I found myself in the police station procuring a marching permit. I talked to an assistant chief inspector. He was a calm, fiftyish man, friendly and civilized, a personable executive sort. I felt like an idealistic adolescent in front of him, and I was surprised he took me seriously, or pretended to, and didn't just show me the door. I was hoping he would, because all I could think of was getting to the nearest tavern. It was morning and I'd come into the station with only a few pints of beer in my belly. I really did feel like a fool, some kind of woolly-minded visionary, a dilettante of life, and considered I was being graciously tolerated by a man who had important practical matters to deal with. He asked me my occupation and I said I was a writer. He was interested. He said he liked to read... and what had I written? I told him I had a novel coming out soon, in a few months probably. He said he'd be sure and look for it. I hope he didn't look too hard. That's the type of thing I mean. It was humiliating to have to lie to people.

Finally I got the permit and a couple of mornings later at the scheduled hour the march got under way — in the worst snowstorm of the winter. About a dozen people turned up with placards condemning traffic noise and air pollution and cross-town highways wrecking neighbourhoods, and with an escort of police motorcycles — as many of them as us, just about — we leaned into the driving storm up to our knees in snow, barely able to see one another, plowing along from Philips Square to Old Montreal. The whole scene was ludicrous, a fiasco; it was so ridiculous I couldn't help laughing. I was thankful there were few people out-of-doors to see us. For a climax someone stuck a leaflet in the snow on the steps of City Hall and then we all headed for a nearby bar. Even years later in recalling that experience I'd find myself wincing with embarrassment.

It was during this time that I gave up writing poems. I stopped when the panic set in. Writing for fun wouldn't do any longer, I had to get serious, efficient. Turning thirty made a strong impression on me. I got to worrying about the future. I couldn't stay "promising" forever. I had to concentrate my energies and get some hard results. And yet I didn't seem to *have* any energies. I was in a defeatist stage. But I eventually decided I'd better do something — after eight idle months — if only to keep myself occupied. Thus it was that like a worn-out old man I set myself to write a sixth novel. I kept at it almost every day over the summer months, typing words onto pages, but it was a worthless dispirited effort, I'm sure the worst writing I did in my entire life. I later read it through and saved two sentences out of 75,000 words and threw the rest in the garbage.

Meanwhile Hugh Hood was having his latest book published by Oberon, and he informed me that Michael Macklem, the publisher, was interested in my work... he'd personally liked my novel *The Robin Hood Gang*, even though he'd rejected it on the advice of others. He told Hugh he'd like to see a collection of my stories. I wrote Macklem and got back a nice encouraging letter. Encouragement was just what I needed. So what if I didn't have enough good stories for a book? I soon would have, just watch.

I sat down and in a couple of months wrote "The Quebec Prison," "They Come Here to Die," "On the Bus," "A Cold Frosty Morning," and "The Janitor's Wife," and adding some earlier things and titling the lot *The Black Horse Tavern* I put them in the mail.

And in a while they came back. Rejected again. If I was in a bad state before, and I mean by my reckoning, my crazy inner world, it was mild to how I felt now — because while I was never sure about the other works, I *knew* this was a good book. It was the best I was capable of right then. I hadn't been lazy or self-indulgent, I'd taken my time and revised carefully and objectively. This time I was right for sure, and *they* were wrong. So after all it wasn't me — it really was *them*. That was more than disheartening, it was scary. If I was right and everyone else was wrong, that meant in effect that I *was* wrong — my entire perception was out of whack, my standards were meaningless. To doublecheck I sent the manuscript to Doubleday, and got another rejection. The hell with it.

I wasn't going to throw in the towel, I was too stubborn; but what could I do? A violent frenzy seethed inside me. I couldn't stand it. Naturally I had to drink, if I didn't thoroughly anaesthetize myself I might do something catastrophic. Every day I sat at the kitchen table guzzling beer and going over in my head how I could rob a bank. If I had money... with money I could start a publishing house, put my own books out. I didn't know how to get money any other way. I cased the banks, outlined getaway routes, dreamt up disguises — I worked it out in detail, all the fine points, the plan getting thorough and elaborate. But what if I got caught? I doubted I could handle a long stretch in prison. For one thing they didn't let you drink there. I couldn't possibly survive without drinking. It would be better if I were killed in the attempt.

I couldn't be sure I was only fantasizing because I could feel myself getting nuttier every day, more cornered and desperate. Something had to happen one way or another.

I continued to give readings with the group. The other guys could have had no idea what was going on with me. On the surface I think I acted carefree and cheerful — but that was my pride covering up. I pretended not to take writing too seriously. They only saw me when I was amply fuelled and able to roll. If I drank enough I almost appeared to be a normal human being. Sometimes I felt like one. You might have caught me onstage at Loyola boisterously singing a song I wrote, mixing the verses in with one of my new stories. Did I look like a guy with

61

troubles? A real Maritimer, that fellow, give him a drink and watch him go. You can tell a guy who's enjoying life.

There was another frustrated literary giant in Montreal in those days, Bryan McCarthy, the poet. He was a gifted writer, but a trifle lazy I'm afraid — he didn't write much but had great expectations from what he did. He got the idea to form a performance group of his own: himself, me, and a broken-down alkie and former jazz musician named Art Housten. Bryan was to read poetry, I'd do poems and stories, and Art would do a vaudeville comedy routine — "I stayed in a hotel once, the room was so small the bedbugs were hunchbacked..." Inspired stuff, bad enough that you had to chuckle despite yourself, at least I did. We were billed as The Rank Outsiders, and I have to say we were so much what we were called that despite Bryan's sending notices of our availability to all the schools in Montreal we got no offers. The only appearance we ever made was at the Boiler Room on Crescent Street as part of a larger performance — readings and recitations and songs by a collection of Montreal talents that included Willie Dunn, Ron Lee, Mario Gross, Manuel Santos-Betanzos, Graham McKeen, and the three aforementioned. I guess most of us were of the outsider variety and two-fisted boozers to boot. It was a pretty slapdash affair, followed by a spirited drunkfest, the beer being on the house for the entertainers. (Some scenes come back to me — Bryan looking like George Bernard Shaw striding up and down among the tables and screaming his poems above the disruptive chatter of some drunken patrons... Graham indifferent to modern verse giving a dramatic delivery of "The Shooting of Dan McGrew"... Willie Dunn strumming his guitar and singing his lonesome Indian songs, the highlight of the show... Ron Lee the Gypsy reciting a vicious poetic diatribe against the politicians of Montreal — "Drapeau the fascist!"...)

I knew The Rank Outsiders would amount to nothing, one of assorted wild schemes of Bryan's, but I went along with the idea to please him; he'd have done the same for me. The last I heard from him he was in England; he wrote to tell me, "I'm now a half-assed carpenter who keeps getting fired." This was after belonging to a primal scream commune in Ireland until they kicked him out. His primal scream must have been like nothing they'd heard before.

For reasons unfathomable by me, God, who knows every hair on our heads, has been in the habit of intervening in my extremes to keep me writing, and out of jail, and the madhouse, and the grave. I had made my yearly application to the Canada Council, but my hopes were of the slimmest kind, considering the way I saw my luck as running. But I was hanging in to find out, it was the last card being dealt in that particular hand. I hate to think what the next deal would have been had I not got the grant, but as it happened I did. There was no elation this time, only a grim consciousness that I'd had a narrow escape, miraculously saved at the last instant. A very sober reaction — rare for me. Being crazy, however, a mocking voice in my head kept saying, "Your cup runneth over, your cup runneth over." It wouldn't stop, going on maddeningly. "But it doesn't," I answered. "Stop saying that." I knew what I had now was an opportunity, not a reward. I couldn't act frivolously with this money, in my condition I was convinced my life depended on putting every penny to work.

My first act was to call Kenneth Hertz and ask his advice on getting a book printed. I was aware that doing my own book would involve numerous problems, and lies, and probably humiliation — So nobody else would touch it, eh? Had to put it out yourself. Like some old spinster and her religious verses blowing her savings at a vanity press.

I should say that after Doubleday I hadn't sent *The Black Horse Tavern* to another publisher because I felt it would be a waste of stamps. I was full-up with rejections, no room for any more. But I had given Hertz a copy of the manuscript. He had a small publishing outfit called Ingluvin, and he told me he would do the book, but he didn't know when, he had other commitments, maybe someday... that sort of thing. It could take years and I had no patience; I never had any, but now especially I felt I couldn't wait much longer. Better to see to the job myself, then I could be sure it would get done.

When I called him he said, "I don't know why you want to do that. I said I'd publish it."

"Yeah, but when?"

"Well, I'm almost finished with Pat Lane's book. I can get to yours next."

He sounded as if he meant it. I wanted to believe him, because the way I am, once I consider doing something almost any alternative looks better. I project catastrophic outcomes. Here was an appealing option, the job taken out of my hands. I'd get my book done and have my money too. What more could I ask?

"They're good stories," I said. "You won't be embarrassed."

"I know. I like them."

"You do? You mean you read them?"

"Of course I read them." He was properly indignant. "Do you think I'd publish something I hadn't read?"

"I suppose not."

It must sound strange, but I'd come to believe that what you wrote had nothing to do with a publisher's decision, I didn't know how you could influence those people, if they were people. Maybe they flipped coins or cut cards or threw darts at names on the wall. If it was the case that you had to know one personally, then perhaps it followed that the content and quality of your work wasn't a factor.

Now that I could see some light I thought possibly I'd come around a hairpin bend and was on the way out of the noxious cavern I'd been stumbling around in. But it was an elusive light, a false light actually; things didn't really get any better for the next ten years. The story of how *The Black Horse Tavern* got published would discourage I don't know how many would-be writers. But the book did finally come out, and I'm grateful to Kenneth Hertz. And two novels and a biography followed, from three different publishers. Nothing went smoothly, and none of it was easy, often because of my unrealistic demands and expectations.

It so happens I'm sober — but not solemn, not sombre — these days, thanks where thanks belong, and it's a remarkable experience for me, an adventure no less. I'm writing at a fine clip and while some days are inevitably exasperating I'm generally enjoying it. I feel I'm in the neighbourhood of where I ought to have been all along, where it's the work itself that counts and not what might happen because of it. It's nice to knock off some words every day, do my bit.

As for the Story Tellers, I left Montreal and the group when I got the grant, and I don't know how they fared after, except of course they fell apart. But what could you expect?

I wish them all well, every one of them. It was a pleasure having trod the boards in their company. May their needs be met.

1983

Clark Blaise
PORTRAIT OF THE ARTIST AS A YOUNG PUP

Montreal has a certain genius for spawning poetic movements — from poets like A.J.M. Smith, Frank Scott, and A.M. Klein in the Twenties, down through Louis Dudek and Irving Layton a poetic generation later. And while individual novelists had always existed in English-Montreal — Hugh MacLennan, John Glassco, Brian Moore, and Leonard Cohen — it was my privilege to be associated with the only conscious *gathering* of English language Montreal prose writers in this century.

Time and doctoral dissertations seem to bestow inevitability and distinctive coloration to such groups, as though internal affinity accounts for literary alliance. We were five prose writers in the same city at the same time; we had similar critical standards and very different literary tastes. And in late 1970, under the guidance of John Metcalf and Hugh Hood, we — Hood and Metcalf, Raymond Fraser and Ray Smith and myself — became the Montreal Story Teller. We're now a footnote in the larger history of Canadian literature, but we rate a few paragraphs in the history of contemporary Canadian fiction. The Story Teller is yet another instance of synchronicity and serendipity at work: contemporary Canadian literature was just being born; and we were in a time and place, and possessed the energy and vision, to assist the delivery.

Montreal is a cultured city with many writers. The problem, in those first few years, was with me. The only young writer I knew in town was Jerry (C.J.) Newman. Hood was around, of course, but teaching in another world, l'Université de Montréal. I'd been writing in a vacuum, except for Jerry's critiques, and nearly all the stories I was publishing — despite their Canadian setting — were still being placed in the United States. Nevertheless, I felt hurt and resentful when John Metcalf, another local story-writer I'd never met, published the first significant anthology of the new writing—*Sixteen by Twelve*—and left me out.

(How a pompous young pup can howl!)

I was still discovering the city, or, more precisely, discovering parts of myself opened up by the city. I was respectful if not worshipful of all its institutions. I defended its quirks and inconsistencies as though defending myself against abuse; I was even charmed by things I would have petitioned against in Milwaukee like separate Catholic and Protestant schools, Sunday closings, and male-only bars. "The Frencher the Better" was my motto to cover any encroachment on the aboriginal rights of the English.

I was writing very openly, in the late Sixties, of Montreal. The city was drenched with significance for me—it was one of those perfect times when every block I walked yielded an image, when images clustered with their own internal logic into insistent stories. A new kind of unforced, virtually transcribed story (new for me, at least) was begging to be written—stories like "A Class of New Canadians," "Eyes," "Words for the Winter," "Extractions and Contractions," "Going to India," and "At the Lake" were all written in one sitting, practically without revision. I'd never been so open to story, so avid for context. I was reading all the Canadian literature I could get my hands on, reading Canadian exclusively; there was half a continent out there to discover. My literary community was more on the page than in the flesh. Jerry Newman, George Bowering for a few years, Margaret Atwood for one year, and the poetry readings at Sir George Williams and the parties after them—those were my only contacts with the raucous, boozy, quick-witted writing life I'd known, and depended on, at Iowa.

Those, then, are the pre-Story Teller facts. I knew of Metcalf from the Clarke, Irwin 1969 volume of *New Canadian Writing*. (He'd appeared with Jerry Newman and Doug Spettigue; I'd appeared a year earlier in the same series with Dave Godfrey and David Lewis Stein.) Of course I knew Hugh Hood's work—he went all the way back to my Iowa days when I'd read *Flying a Red Kite* in Dave Godfrey's hand-me-down review copy. Ray Smith I knew through his "Cape Breton is the Thought-Control Centre of Canada" story in *Tamarack Review*—one of the break-through stories in our writing. I particularly remembered it because until its appearance I'd thought my *Tamarack* story "The Mayor" (later retitled "The Fabulous Eddie Brewster") was a shoo-in for The University of Western Ontario President's Medal as best Canadian story of the year. That "The Mayor" actually *did* win is a testimony to the innate conservatism of the judging process.

I know how this must read: I was a posturing little pup — a typical product of American alienation, mixed with Canadian sentimentality. (The portrait of "Norman Dyer" in "A Class of New Canadians" is my own ironic self-portrait.) I considered myself an heir to the Two Solitudes, the uncrowned princeling fated to write the books, discover the new talent, script the movies, teach the secrets, that would move Canadian literature to the cutting edge of the world's consciousness. Canada's duty was to exploit its twin heritage of English and French, its twin tensions of America and Britain. I was ambitious, ruthless, selfish, vain, and arrogant. I was also hard-working, observant, anxious to learn, and even humble.

Then Metcalf called. How he got my name, I never asked. He mentioned the group: himself (whom I resented), Smith (whom I feared), Hood (whom I admired) and Ray Fraser (whom I didn't know). None of us, I suspect, knew that Literary History was knocking — the moment when one's lonely individual efforts have suddenly passed a critical mass and begun to set off other writers' alarms.

Our purpose was admirably eleemosynary. We would charge two hundred dollars a performance — forty dollars apiece. Twice the amount paid by *Fiddlehead* for my stories "Eyes," "A Class of New Canadians," and "Words for the Winter." The Protestants wouldn't have us. (I had assumed, until reading the full story in Metcalf's "Telling Tales," that the Protestants had rejected us because Hugh was so dreadfully Catholic.) But the island was even richer in Catholic schools, and they were agreeable to trying us out.

Money, then, was the first goal. Hugh, as a matter of principle (everything with Hugh is a matter of principle), insists on top dollar for any creative work. John and the two Rays were living hand-to-mouth as free-lancers. Ray Fraser epitomized the word, and the consequences, of "free-lancing." He raised it to an art while writing characteristically Fraseresque stories for the local tabloid, *Midnight*, in the Maritime tall tale genre touched with a bit of the Montreal macabre: DAD RAPES INFANT SON; SERVES HIM FOR DINNER.

Our second goal was a bit more combative. John was tired of the bloody poets getting all the readings and recognition. It seemed to us that the league of warblers had enjoyed their monopoly on the stages of the country quite long enough. Prose was intrinsically more interesting and easy to follow than poetry. There was no reason why stories, if limited to fifteen minutes, should not move, delight, and instruct any audience — and still not betray our own high standards. This, it seemed to me, was a battle worth joining.

The third, and most altruistic, goal was to prove something to, and for, Canada. John had taught in the high schools and knew the attitudes of the boards and most of the teachers. Chesterton and Kipling as moderns. Morley Callaghan or Hugh Garner thrown in just so the students could thrill to seeing descriptions of familiar Toronto landmarks in print. Just think what *we* could do: living, young, funny, sexy, bold, dirty, Montreal writers. We'd begin that great reaming out, the great scouring of all those corroded pipes. We'd have the rarest of all literary privileges — that of creating our own audience.

I remember those drives through unfamiliar but very Catholic parts of the island — a jolly band of prose-troubadours in my car, or Hugh's. We were a hit from the beginning; I couldn't understand it. The bookings were coming three and sometimes four times a week. Every now and then I'd wince at our collective arrogance, inflicting all this shameless puffery, this elevating slobber, on immigrant youngsters whose English needs were for something more rudimentary and whose experience of literature was utterly virginal. And a second later I'd think (like the appalling Norman Dyer) what a splendid, noble thing we were doing. Those kids were our perfect audience, uncorrupted by ghastly good taste, analogues to our purest intentions. Didn't we want to communicate the real, the actual, the tangible *montréalitude*? Didn't we want to present ourselves as serious writers who were also living, imperfect Montreal presences? Didn't we pride ourselves on the accessibility of our stories, that anyone could appreciate them? Our proudest boast was that unlike Chesterton or Belloc or whoever-the-hell, *we were in the phonebook!* Look us up, call us, talk to us. We drink, we fart, we get horny, we make fools of ourselves, our lives are usually in a mess, we're afraid of cops and taxes, and we're not ashamed to show it. Like kindergarten kids with finger paints, we wallow in it! We make art of it!

In a typical reading, John and I did two voices from a segment of his novel *Going Down Slow*, in which a high school teacher is so drunk, rude, and honest that he gets thrown out of a bar. I then read my story "Eyes," about a man who watches Greek butchers popping calf testicles in their mouths, and sucking. Big Ray Smith read a chapter from *Lord Nelson Tavern*, a monologue on the pathos of having been a tall girl in the cutie-pie Fifties, with such intensity that he ended up in tears while the audience laughed. Hugh's "Socks" was about an immigrant from southern Italy who ends up working on snow removal in wet socks. And there was Ray Fraser's unpredictable and never-repeated routine, tall tales of mounting disgust, teetering over a pit (one suspected) of imminent intervention from a hardly-amused administration.

Despite all that (and of course because of it) we became legitimate. We grew out of the ghetto of Catholic schools, to the junior colleges and university classrooms. We were featured in the second issue of the *Journal of Canadian Fiction*. (My two tales in that issue, "Is Oakland Drowning?" and "The Voice of the Elephant," were inspired purely by our ensemble readings, the need for levity, brevity, and surreality. I wanted to be as precise as Metcalf, as witty as Smith, as various as Hood, as irreverent as Fraser.) We read at the conventions of the Protestant teachers. We popped up in Fredericton, Saint John, and Ottawa. We got to be polished, convincing, and even successful in all three of our initial goals.

We were clearly an idea whose time had come. We were a new generation of Canadian fiction, arriving all at once, in all parts of the country. The first book of the movement was Hugh Hood's *Flying a Red Kite*, then Alice Munro's *Dance of the Happy Shades*. There were the two Clarke, Irwin collections, plus the early House of Anansi books — collections by Dave Godfrey and Ray Smith. Peggy Atwood was busy revising *The Edible Woman* during her year at Sir George Williams. Jerry Newman wrote *A Russian Novel*. Then came *Sixteen by Twelve*, the first national collection. Then the Story Teller, the first national performance group in fiction.

We were, however, a group very much of our time and place and class-interests: no French, no women, no unseemly minorities. When I think of our work — as distinguished from Alice Munro's, for example

—I see a line of continuity with the typical French language Montreal *conte*. Our work had a similarity to that of Carrier, Vigneault, Ferron, and Tremblay, though we in no way consciously emulated them. (Carrier and I have both written about hockey sweaters.) It was merely that the structures we accepted — a dramatic appeal to a tangible audience, a firm sense of place and voice and readership, a political and aesthetic intention — differed from those of the printed page. We were performers. We were moving toward compression. We have all written long prose fictions by now, but I wouldn't call any of us as successful in the novel as we have been in our stories. It took me an inordinately long time to write my first novel (if indeed I ever have); John (I suspect) is most at home in the novella form, and what can any of us say about Hugh Hood's giant opus? It seems to me he is writing *one* enormous novel, not twelve separate ones. Or that *The New Age* is the world's longest short story collection.

(I should acknowledge here the influence of Hugh on my work. His ease of delivery, the way he wraps allegorical significance around the keenly-observed realistic core, the variety of his styles and voices, left me feeling one-dimensional. It was Hugh who offered the title for, and could easily have written, "He Raises Me Up"; and it was with Hugh in mind that I attempted my own "Socks"-like casual memoir, "I'm Dreaming of Rocket Richard.")

The Story Teller is now a part of Canadian literary history. For me, it was the public manifestation of inner maturing. I learned in the group that I still needed an ensemble; despite my immodest flights of fancy, I wasn't yet ready to stand alone. I always had the sense that of the five, I was the one the audience hadn't heard of, and I was the one they had to endure after the famous Hugh Hood and the sexy Ray Smith and the satiric John Metcalf and the whack-o Ray Fraser. So I learned to tame myself, to wait.

We are now at the age of the rock stars of the Sixties; we've had to change, or run the risk of becoming absurd. The easy work is all behind us — that fire and passion — but I have to feel our best work is yet to come. We're a little too gray and cranky to give collective readings. We've already proven that prose readings are interesting and profitable; we've succeeded in stuffing Canadian literature into most crannies in the curriculum. But, I fear, we've lived to demonstrate the applicability

70

of Murphy's Law to literary funding. Official money and government money will drive out private money. Bureaucracy will replace individual choice and initiative. The magic, the sense of occasion, the mystery of having a writer in your presence, of words made flesh — that is now taken from our students. The budget for such an extravaganza has all been lost. In the way of benevolent bureaucracies, everyone gets something — a lot *less* of something — and the intangibles that provided a context, and much of the authentic pleasure, have disappeared.

We have lived to see a dangerous corollary to our hardest-won battles. It goes like this: if you're in the phonebook and if you give readings, let's call you up and ask you to read. I've had calls from high school teachers a thousand miles away, asking if I wouldn't mind flying out and addressing a tenth-grade class. I've been at Canada Days and I've had my ticket punched down at Harbourfront in Toronto. Right now, in the fall of 1983, on my first long trip back to Canada in three years, I'm being allowed to give more than my upper limit of eight ''senior'' Canada Council supported readings. I enjoy it. It's part of the whole fabric of Canadian life; it's what I dreamed; it's the literary equivalent of the CBC's own national mandate. But.

But this. Thirteen years ago our Sir George Williams poetry series had an equal mix of Canadian and American poets; now (I'll wager) if it has a series, the writers are all domestic. Very few colleges in Canada have anything but Canadian readings. We've all been everywhere, usually more than once. We used to have a two thousand dollar budget for our readings; we even budgeted our after-reading parties at seventy-five dollars for booze, breads, and meats. I remember the big pre-reading dinners at the best restaurants, and I remember the packed auditorium. I realize times have changed. I'd forego the big dinner and the catered party. But I fear now no one would really *care* to eat with the writer *or* go to a party after his performance. The ''less is more'' philosophy does not work at all in the matter of public readings.

This year I'm giving my readings at one o'clock in the afternoon, in classrooms. At many, with no lunch, no announcements, no audience. I remember the weeks it used to take, designing posters, arguing over lay-outs, cajoling for colours, picking them up at a printer's, and then distributing them to Montreal's bookstores and cafés. Now there is a xeroxed nine-by-twelve sheet of typing paper with a Magic-Marker announcement of my reading, taped to the door and pinned to a cluttered bulletin board. There are thirty students for my reading — the same attendance as the regular class. It *is* the regular class. The last well-attended evening reading I've given, significantly, was not at a university, but at the Jewish Public Library in Montreal. What does it all mean? Simply that the general public will no longer come out at night for a Canadian reading.

And, I fear, we suffer too much exposure of too much Canadian talent. Alice Munro is an estimable writer and probably only second to Mavis Gallant as a writer of prose, but it's wrong that she alone should be the model for all short story writing by women in this country. When I teach writing in Canada all I need are her books, Atwood's novels, and maybe works by one or two others (Kroetsch or Wiebe) depending on the region. There's something wrong when a Chinese-Canadian woman has never heard of Maxine Hong Kingston, or, perhaps even worse, when a Jewish-Canadian woman concerned with her background has not plunged beyond the sensibility of Mordecai Richler because she has not discovered the larger world of Jewish *women* writers.

I once had the bizarre experience of being told that I could fly Audrey Thomas — a writer I admire greatly — to Montreal from Vancouver at Canada Council expense, but couldn't offer John Gardner a fifty dollar busfare from Bennington, Vermont. By that time, you see, Sir George Williams had given up its private budget for other exigencies, and the Canada Council was picking up the tabs, and the Canada Council cannot fund anyone from outside of Canada.

Good sense and maturity will eventually triumph. Excess is never a cure for deficiency, and a less-charged time will permit both generosity and cosmopolitanism. Our little revolution of the Sixties needs to be protected from too much success. Canadian literature should not substitute for world literature. We need to redirect a fraction of the honoraria and travel expenses now paid to keep a hundred or more Canadian poets and fiction writers constantly airborne, and give it to the dozens of world-stature authors out there in Europe, Asia, the Caribbean, Latin America, and the United States who would be excited by the prospect of reading in Canada and instructing our students. Otherwise, our little revolution will die of boredom.

1983

Sam Tata
A DARNED COLD DAY

Some months after meeting me at an exhibition of Seymour Segal's paintings at the Mansfield Bookmart in Montreal, Hugh Hood called. He wanted me to take photographs of him up on Mount Royal to be used for his forthcoming book of short stories *Around the Mountain* as well as for his novel about Hollywood *The Camera Always Lies*. "Just another job," I thought, little realising at the time that that December day in 1966 would lead to a warm, lasting, and cherished friendship. In acknowledgement of that long chilly session "around the mountain," he made me a gift of his *White Figure, White Ground* over a cup of coffee at his home, inscribed it rather conventionally, dated it, and then as an after-thought added "and a darned cold day, too."

Some years later, circa 1971, I met most of the members of the Montreal Story Teller Fiction Performance Group at John F. Kennedy High School for a reading which Hugh had urged me to attend in order to document the event with a brief photo essay. He had liked the portraits I had done of him and felt I might do justice to the evening. Recently I told Hugh and his wife, Noreen, an anecdote connected with those portraits that might bear repeating. After publication of the two books, my former wife Rita, who is still one of my sharper critics and who at that time had thought that I had only done Hugh's photograph for the jacket of *Around the Mountain*, airily pronounced it "not bad" but wished that I had been able to do something "really good" like the portrait of Hugh for "that Hollywood actress book." It was rather an abashed lady critic therefore, who, having at my insistence taken a closer look at the credit, found my name therein.

That evening's reading as well as the photography went off very well. I am glad I was there; besides gaining friends, I some time later substantially added five new portraits to my growing portfolio of photographs of writers familiar to readers of the Spring '79 issue of Geoffrey Hancock's *Canadian Fiction Magazine*.

I clearly recall the story that Hugh read that day, as it is dedicated to me and is titled "Whos Paying for This Call." I knew it well of course, but it took on an entirely new dimension with Hugh's rendition, the changing rhythm, pacing, and gusto giving it a life beyond my personal realisation of it. It was a great experience for me; it should have been taped. An added unlooked-for fillip was provided by Hugh introducing me to the young audience as the dedicatee of the story as well as the recorder of the evening's doings.

Clark Blaise, if I remember, read a story called "Eyes"; he reads skilfully and persuasively, lingering for effect in the right places, varying the pace tautly where required. I have photographed Clark a number of times with much success. He is married to the writer Bharati Mukherjee, with whom he co-authored *Days and Nights in Calcutta*, and has visited India on different occasions. During one photographic outing at their Montreal home, remarking Clark's manner and fluid gestures, I mentioned that were I to come upon him without preintroduction on a street corner in Bombay or Delhi dressed in Nehru jacket and tight Indian trousers and wearing a Gandhi cap, I would easily take him for a Kashmiri Brahmin.

In an essay that Hugh once wrote he talked of my "pantheon" of friends. Into this pantheon I have long ago warmly welcomed the very talented John Metcalf with his great gifts as a writer of rare craft and barbed humour. He has an eclectic taste in Western painting and an acute appreciation of African and Chinese art, the latter fascination especially intriguing to me as I was born in Shanghai. The average Western eye is inclined to view Chinese art with a jaundiced look.

Once, delighted by one of his stories, I told John that I would give much to be able to write, especially the short story; not merely write but to write like him. He countered in kind: "I'd give much too," he said, "to be a bloody good photographer." I got the message. Incidentally, John wasn't at the reading I covered and the accompanying photograph was taken in 1979 at York University during a symposium on the work of Hugh Hood organised by Jack David and Robert Lecker.

Ray Smith imposingly wrapped in a magnificent serape looks twice his height, especially on a stage; perhaps it is well that he doesn't further the effect by affecting a sombrero. He punctuates his readings with dramatic gestures, actor-like, dominating. I suspect he was always a favourite with the females in the audience, a serape-suited ladies' man.

A portrait that I did of Ray in 1973 is among my favourites for it is a definitive portrait and essentially Ray Smith. The function of a portrait photographer is to act as a mirror; a self-conscious photographer will only produce self-conscious portraits, his sitters ill at ease. The secret is relaxed confidence to attract absolute trust; the friendly confrontation has to be completely free of antagonism. Ray on his part became sufficiently relaxed to do a creditable turn-about photograph of me.

Of the five Story Tellers I got to know Ray Fraser the least. Hugh told me that they all had time and again impressed on Ray most carefully that the prime commitment of their group was *story telling*; just plain prose, *no poetry*. For it seems that Ray Fraser, a fervent poet, could be quite devious; he would artfully insinuate poems spoken by the protagonists of his fiction into his performance, even to the extent of having those characters occasionally burst into song accompanied by a guitar that seemed to be mysteriously plucked out of thin air. I never did find out if he managed to hold out to the bitter end.

Some days after that memorable reading at John F. Kennedy High School, Hugh had the happy inspiration of gathering the four others in order that I might photograph them as a group. It was decided that historic Old Montreal serve as a backdrop against which the Five were to be immortalised. Following a brief stab at photographing them clustered around an ambiguous lamp post amid a good bit of ribaldry and clowning reminiscent of the Keystone Cops, I called for a change of venue. We finally settled on a sedate spot with the required steps and stately columns more in keeping with the occasion, so that pictured in this august manner the Montreal Story Teller Five could pass into the history of Montreal's literati legitimately. After which we all hied ourselves to a nearby tavern on McGill Street to warm up, because as it turned out that was a darned cold day too.

JOHN METCALF

RAYMOND FRASER

CLARK BLAISE

HUGH HOOD, RAY SMITH, RAYMOND FRASER

HUGH HOOD

RAY SMITH

THE MONTREAL STORY TELLERS. (Standing, l. to r.) HUGH HOOD, CLARK BLAISE. (Front, l. to r.) RAY SMITH, RAYMOND FRASER, JOHN METCALF.

Lawrence Garber
RAY SMITH'S *CAPE BRETON IS THE*
THOUGHT-CONTROL CENTRE OF CANADA:
THE DIAGNOSTICS OF THE ABSURD

You can't trust people with pens.
—Ray Smith, "The Dwarf in His Valley Ate Codfish"[1]

They definitely should have seen it coming and certainly should have
recognized it when it arrived. If labels were needed, there were labels to
guide them—Dadaism, the Theatre of the Absurd, the Existential
Novel, the Language of Revolt—obvious niches and movements trail-
ing back to the 1920s. It thus seems incredible that a collection of short
stories published in 1969 and borrowing from these traditions should
have been viewed by many as incomprehensible, incompetent, or even,
alas, "experimental."[2] But it was Toronto and, worse than Toronto,
the deep suspicion of the non-narrative was in full force; radicalizations
of language and form were being received as a sort of exotic trickery, as
the random, adolescent playfulness of authors who would soon (God
willing) lose their literary acne and begin producing the smoother-
complexioned realism of their maturity. In the meantime (we were
warned with patronizing grace) boys being boys, they had launched
themselves into tom-catting enterprises without visible controls, sensed
motivations, or recognizable precedents.

One doesn't require extensive readings in the literature or criticism
of the Absurd[3] to recognize some of its basic tenets: its diagnostic and
often satiric attitude towards the human predicament, its parody of the
very forms by which it expresses that predicament, its conception of a
disharmonious world, its consequent abandonment of logical reasoning
and construction, the aggressive irreconcilability of its vision of chance

and chaos with more traditional assumptions and structures. Such *conventions* of the type were hardly startling news in the late 1960s, one would have thought, and any writer moving instinctively into that literary venue some forty years after its first fruits should have been looked upon as an artist more at ease with a specific, continuing custom than as a venturer into maddening, profitless, mischievously self-indulgent exercises. But looking back upon contemporary reviews of Ray Smith's first book of fiction, the complaints and bafflements on just that score seemed the rule: and, so, reflected an insistent recoil from Absurdist literature, indeed from the very aesthetic genuineness of the Absurdist movement in Canada — a critical constant which was one of the despairs of that golden age in our literature.[4]

It is not the explicit purpose of this essay to defend Absurdist or Fantasist art in Canada (although the targets, strengths, and influences of such enterprises in our literature certainly deserve closer attention than they have thus far received), but to explore Ray Smith's *Cape Breton is the Thought-Control Centre of Canada* on its own immediate terms, *at its word*, so to speak, and in doing so to provide some notion of the author's intentions and mediations. It should be added that since I myself published a collection of three novellas, *Circuit*, at about the same time, placed approximately within the same camp, brought out by the same publisher, Anansi, and indeed benefitting from the astute and sensitive stewardship of the same editor, Dennis Lee, my critical excursion into Smith's festival of treats is not without a certain proprietorial interest.

II

They definitely should have seen it coming, should have diagnosed the symptoms and submitted to the cure: because the first story of the collection contains the whole. Viewed in that context, "Colours" establishes a pattern of attitudes, subterfuges, and architectures that each succeeding story will somehow modify, subvert, or comment upon in any number of glorifying or reductive procedures. It represents, in this sense, the vestibule of the entire construct that *is* the collection proper, an arena of its first principles, and is well worth studying closely both for what it effects and what it anticipates.

For those requiring a theme, some sort of narrative walkway, Smith himself has provided one in an "Author's Commentary" accompanying "Colours" in John Metcalf's anthology *Sixteen by Twelve*. "Smith was concerned with searching," Smith writes in the secondary guise of a naïve reader:

> He writes about a man who goes about asking questions. To us these questions seem idiotic.... But Smith is using extreme exaggeration to show us that we may not always understand the searches of others, the reasons behind their lives....It is this failure of understanding, failure of sympathy that Smith was concerned with; so this is what the story is about.[5]

But, as Smith himself quickly qualifies, that "is not the whole truth"[6] about "Colours"; and, indeed, if "Colours" is about searches, they deal in a more central way with the very nature of language and arrangement as the means at hand for projecting identities, patterns, ideas, sensations, colours, textures, moods. "My story," Smith thus concludes, in his own voice,

> is about many other things...titles, plots, England, a dictionary, make-up, casualness, set pieces, soft lights, accuracy ... the use of the semi-colon...the use of "he"...the naming of characters...contrasts... and so on and so on.[7]

In an essential way, the story is even more significant for what it is *not*, for what it resists in the way of received wisdom, for its narratively contrived dead-ends, and for the refusal of its language to offer up the usual linears of meaning. There is throughout *Cape Breton is the Thought-Control Centre of Canada* a great deal of challenge, anger, and revolt: challenge and anger in the face of a reader's easy expectations, revolt against the assumptions which any reader automatically seems to make in regard to the short story genre. Accordingly, throughout "Colours," preconceptions concerning narrative order, character-identity, composed scenes, compartments of thought and feeling are met with devastating reversals. These reversals, in turn, serve as primers for the collection itself, schooling us quickly in those variables, confusions, and literary acrobatics which are yet to come.

"Colours" is a mine field of such subversive elements. Ostensibly about a search for an individual to whom the seeker, Gerard, can address the Big Question — as if some resolving truth were at stake in the success of this venture—Smith chooses the most classic of structures upon which to effect his subterfuge: the grail journey. But instead of a tight, causal logic, an irresistible continuum by which each defined stage is gained through suffering and test, with the questor propelled forward towards some redemptive insight, the five parts of "Colours" have a kind of lateral self-sufficiency and are connected only by a series of failures to resolve even the simplest issues. Of course, we are warned immediately that a certain rational element has already been removed. Part I of the story begins with a telling aphorism: " 'Port is the wellspring of anecdote' " (p. 1)—a caution which alerts us that the thinning wedge of intellect has just touched the point where imagination is freed. Moreover, the initial search by our questor, Gerard, involves a seventy-six year old Englishman named Pillsbury whose first anecdote "concerned a little girl rather like Alice" (p. 1)—a further announcement that we cannot rely on the usual gravities and relationships here, not in a fictional wonderland where topsy-turvy laws prevail. This leads to the nature of Pillsbury's second anecdote, which was "almost neat enough to be fiction," and thus to his third, which "while amusing, was incomprehensible" (p. 1). Thus forewarned that the common comforts of "story" will prove useless, we are subjected throughout "Colours" to similar reversals of this sort. Pillsbury is, after all, "a fellow of some Royal Society" (p. 1), an aging upholder of "tradition" (p. 2), and it is precisely the traditional which Smith means to find ineffectual, if not delirious. It should come as no surprise then that Pillsbury can be of no help to our questor, who has, in any case, mistaken him for someone else: " 'I've never been to Tibet,' " Pillsbury replies; " 'I fancy you're thinking of old Philbrick the occultist...' " (p. 2). It is similarly at our own peril that we allow ourselves to misjudge the narrative curves that lie ahead.

The problem of mistaken identity, in terms of both the means available to tell a story and the failure (of narrator and participants) to classify character accurately, is continued in Part II, where Patchouli the Passionate turns out to be a stripper and not the exotic belly-dancer as advertised. " 'My agent bungled the bookings' " (p. 3), she explains. Indeed he did: another artist booking us into deceptive practices. Nor is Patchouli what she seems in either dress or facial appearance: " 'I don't have the costumes to be an exotic,' " she states; and Gerard observes too that "her make-up did not coincide with her features" (p. 4).

88

Obviously, then, not being very integrated herself, she can be of little help to Gerard in his search for the man whom he must confront with the Big Question. Gerard thinks that the colonel whom he is seeking had long toe-nails; but Patchouli says that the colonel had big ears. (By their extremities ye shall know them, tradition tells us.) Then, in a deft act of creative subversion that mirrors her own multiplying identity, Patchouli disintegrates the very image of the colonel that she first offered: " 'You know, I'm not sure now that he *was* the one with the big ears. It's been two years now since...' " (p. 5).

If "Colours" is here smashing our assumptions about categorizing individual character, or about the sanctity of information, or even about the reliability of perception itself, it goes a long way towards examining its own shaping techniques as well:

> Gerard disliked thinking about the big questions; he liked particular things, like that jar of cold cream. Surely if one considered a particular jar of cold cream one could ....
> Episodes: that was it, that was how Gerard lived.
> Episodes. Take an episode and understand it one way or another. Take it. Belief exists only in action.
> ....
> ...Or, say, let us examine the pearls one by one and surely we shall know of the string? Pearls are more interesting than string. (pp. 2-3)

Separate units, disparate parts, proceeding indirectly towards stark irresolution: these represent the little disturbances by which "Colours" operates. For the episodic pearls, the disguising jars of cold cream, all the immediate, intoxicating, and compiled items are far more significant in what they portend than the whole, indeed take precedence over the more conventional impulse to arrange them in a formally cohesive order. Smith's suspicion of the over-view, the governing idea, the neatly buttoned fabric of "meaning" which all such details are usually made to serve, is reflected in Gerard's very impatience with his own quest: for each time he contemplates the *raison d'être* of his journey, he yawns.

And in Part III, Gerard interviews a young, bearded painter who, like Smith himself, has pitted his energies against conventional format:

> 'See, a painter is a few steps ahead of the law because he travels light and fast and the law is big — like an elephant — and goes slowly. This has to be, because the painter is alone and can take chances on unknown ground and narrow trails while the elephant has to be careful or he will

trample things under foot and wreak havoc and so on.' (p. 8)

While the painter, like the story that here contains him, has freed himself from slow-footed, ponderous conventions (though to what advantage we are characteristically left in doubt since the canvas that he is working on faces the other way and the rest of his paintings are turned towards the wall), Gerard is no further ahead. Not only does the artist refuse through diversions and deceptions to co-operate in the matter of identities — " 'I can say without fear of contradiction that I have never used a model named Charlene or Virginia or both with possibly thick ankles' " (p. 8) — he compounds the refusal by refusing to sign a statutory declaration which would at least confirm his own denial. After all, even Virginia " 'after a while . . . decided [her real name] was inaccurate' " (p. 6). There are just no prescriptive guarantees in Smith's universe of floating variables.

In Part IV, which concerns "an expensive woman of the world called Aspidistra, by friends, Asp" (p. 9), Smith challenges the demands of formal composition in another way. Observing two figures at a game of chess, each placed symmetrically at either side of a bay window, the narrator comments:

> They would have made a pretty picture for Poussin because of the light, but Poussin was not there; the formalized composition did not allow for more than two people. (p. 9)

The chess set itself — created for Asp by a sculptor who subsequently attempted suicide when humiliated by her prowess as player — comes to represent the very symmetries which, in their prohibitions, seem so deadly to the artist. The formal beauty of the pieces, the acute precisions of the game, Asp as its brilliantly exacting death-dealer, are by analogy attached to all other measured tableaux.

> Nothing disturbed the pastel light. In fact, the reach of a hand to move a piece was illusion; nothing moved for fear of destroying the composition. (p. 11)

Throughout this section, Smith continues to challenge the sanctities of spatial order, the grooves and prohibitions which formalism throws in the way of the artist, narrowing his options for the sake of pretty

90

balances. For, as Smith remarks in his "Author's Commentary," "The jungle is the world that goes on far below Asp's peaceful penthouse . . . it is what we glimpse behind Asp's veneer."[8] Thus, when Gerard confesses that he once ate a (Wordsworthian) daffodil,[9] and Asp recounts the tale of Z--- the violonist who at the age of seven " 'ate an orchestration of Mozart's Symphony No. 40' " (p. 12), we are given hints of the voracious, passional alternatives to precise geometries of composition, alternatives that obviously cannibalize the sacred design. No wonder, then, that Asp detested the jungle elements of flowers and passion. And so, while Gerard loses his game of chess with the deadly Asp — answering her deceptive sacrifice with his own — he can avoid the suicidal urgency of Asp's lamented sculptor. "Gerard was not interested in motives" (p. 12) and can therefore dismiss the claims of the well-rounded story, composed tableau, or smoothly-finished artifact. Rather, it is Asp who finds herself a captive to the narrows of formalism:

> Asp, fragile light above the chess table, pondered the game a while. Then she began to brood. Some time after that tears filled her eyes and the wonderful pieces of inestimable value upon their table of great value shattered in the tears. She did not know why she was crying. She was crying because the composition was broken and would not anymore have made a pretty picture for Poussin. But then. Poussin preferred outdoor scenes and was long dead. (p. 12)

The formalist tableau has indeed been cracked, the radical alternatives to the symmetries which Asp and her chess set represent have indeed done their work: the focus has indeed shifted, and shatteringly so.

In each of these first four sections of "Colours," Smith has deftly called into question a number of story-telling conventions having to do with narrative continuity, character identities, formal design, philosophic over-view — all the familiar elements of the well-made story. In the fifth and last section of the story — in a climax which is, of course, comically anti-climactic (another bird shot on the wing) — the search ends in death and insignificance. Here, ultimately, both imposed over-view and narrative resolution are — whatever frail hopes remain — denied us. Mr. Rufulus is dying; Gerard waits in a hospital corridor for admittance to his room; the Big Question has yet to be asked. But can the legitimacy of any such summing-up be allowed? made reasonable? rendered effective? As Gerard sits in his chair, he leafs through "a pictorial magazine'' and discovers ''a black and white photograph of a man sitting in an alcove in a hospital reading a magazine'' (p. 13). Although he cannot see the man's face,

> Gerard recognized the hat and the trenchcoat, however. They were his own, or very good copies. On one finger Gerard wore a ring; the man in the picture also wore a ring, though it showed indistinctly due to the modish graininess of the print. Gerard was, it seemed, living inside a rather stale joke. Fortunately he had a rather stale sense of humour.
>
> Here I am looking at myself looking at . . . obviously, myself looking at, etc. That old one. (p. 13)

He begins to test the reach of this image-reflection: ''Now, if I look at the camera, will he also look up?'' (p. 13) But he immediately realizes that ''if I look up I can't see if the picture man is also looking up'' (p. 13). The urge to test the illusion, however, concludes in a telling way:

> At last he realized that he need only move an arm or leg and see if the photo-man did it too. The muscles in Gerard's leg had just tensed for the action when he chuckled: no, I shall not do it. This is either miracle or mundane coincidence. If I let it alone, I can always believe it was a miracle.
>
> So he closed the magazine . . . . (p. 13)

In ''Dinosaur,'' an essay accompanying two of Smith's stories in John Metcalf's anthology *The Narrative Voice*, Smith has confessed a certain suspicion of coincidences as a kind of narrative ''crutch,''[10] an author's stacked-deck attempt to impose a preconceived design upon events. Gerard prefers the miracle of the imagination's performance, the found phenomena and free quirks of its image-making processes that defy easy, manipulated explanation and yet are able, in their very mystery, to offer perceptions that move us ''behind [the] veneer.''[11] It is this alternative operation which is opted for here, through Gerard's wilful act of choice. The artist, after all, is free to choose, revise, or retrench before our very eyes. That too is the miracle of composition. At any rate, as Hesse's Harry Haller also discovered in the magic theatre, a subjectively created universe mirrors only the selves to infinity.

Eventually Gerard is allowed to enter the dying man's hospital room. The narrator momentarily intercedes: ''All searches are the same. Utter success and utter failure are both perfection and perfection is denied man'' (p. 15). The hopes of resolution have been withdrawn within a hair's breadth of the ultimate moment itself. Nevertheless, the Big Question is at last asked and answered—and in a curiously comic inversion of the Fisher-King's impasse in Eliot's "What the Thunder Said": " '...in your long and honourable life, sir...did you like parsnips?' " (p. 16) The question, naturally, finishes off Mr. Rufulus who manages only a horrified " 'ArrhrrhrrH' " (p. 16) at the end. Neither his correspondence nor his widow's word on the matter of parsnips can possibly substitute for Mr. Rufulus' own unguarded opinion, since

> Mr. Rufulus might have been forced during the first month of marriage to say he did [like parsnips] and never have had the chance to tell the truth all these years. More serious deceptions exist in every marriage. (p. 17)

No matter how insignificant the question put to Mr. Rufulus (in itself, perhaps, the artist's revenge on the Big Question he detests), no matter how trivial the inquiry now seems, it is, like all searches and seizures in Smith's universe, absolutely unanswerable, unverifiable, irresolvable. Gerard "would never know now, not directly, at least" (p. 17) the narrator informs us. As Smith observes in his "Author's Commentary," "the death of Mr. Rufulus ... is also the end of whatever suspense the reader has felt over the hidden significance of Gerard's questions: there is none."[12]

The over-view is thus denied us as a directly accessible satisfaction; but that does not mean that these searches have been for naught. If language, composition, perception, character (and each section of the story has strained their resources) have failed to surrender up a neat meaning, an envelope of tidy truths, fortune-cookie answers, there is still a powerful function at work here. The tale has assembled and nourished its own found fabric, its random unfolding has mirrored its pattern as Gerard was mirrored in the photograph. And that pattern, which only reflects back itself, has been the search alone—and more, the *impulse* to search, a *modus operandi* which for Smith is as central to our experience as our most essential needs. The narrator concludes by drawing our attention away from the irresolution of his construct and towards its possible values:

> But the pattern was there, it was there and it was the truth and all you needed was to look hard enough and long enough and you could find it.

> ...Ah well, the details did not matter. In the end there was only the
> search and, with luck, the pattern. It sure made you think. (p. 17)

As if to demonstrate the inescapableness of this premise, the search as means and end, Gerard is placed once more *in medias res*, launched again on the trail, about "to meet a woman named Culver who might or might not have had a great-grandfather with the middle name of Jonathan. Or was it Nasturtium? Or Bicycle?" (p. 17) Forget the triviality of this newest excursus, it's the imagining of the trail that counts and always has. But as for the now-tired possibility that this one might provide at last the truth, the key, the philosophic cement, fear not: we are assured once more that "Gerard yawned" (p. 17).

Colours are the artist's tools, and "Colours" introduces us to them. In every aspect of the story — in its indirection, resistances, narrative interruptions, subversions, and refutations — a series of radical principles has been demonstrated that alerts us to the range, bankruptcies, and freedoms of the text as a whole. "Colours," in this way, operates as an aesthetic primer for what is to come: and possibilities which have been proffered here are to be played out in a variety of ways in all that follows.

III

Addressing each story in order of appearance is not essential to its organic health. Since each story on its own terms tends to challenge the tyranny of the consecutive, to break down our assumptions concerning aesthetic and conceptual order, it follows that *taken together* the stories should afford us no available conjunctive order. Rather than any logical growth of focus from tale to tale, what we experience, as readers, are variables on the kind of non-narrative literary enterprise at which Smith is engaged, a compilation of effects, strategies, and forms that is represented in microcosm by the title story itself. To mix the stories up, to re-arrange their grouping, is only to demonstrate that *variables* on attitudes to language and form are just that. And while "Colours" offers us the primary pigmentations, the same service might well have been performed by any number of alternates — say, the title story or "Peril" — oscillations initiating us via their own peculiar impact.

In "Dinosaur," Smith has attempted to provide his readers with a context for dealing with his particular approach to fiction:

> ["A Cynical Tale" and "Peril"] are part of a body of work called 'speculative fiction.' Generally ironic in tone. Aesthetic in approach; which means, I suppose, an indirect approach to the many social and political problems of the world around us. This is in clear contrast to the other rising body of writing which includes things like revolutionary writings, the new journalism, documentary novels and the like, all of which try to grapple directly with the aforementioned soc and pol problems. I should emphasize, or repeat, that spec fic doesn't ignore the world, but approaches it somewhat indirectly.[13]

This indirect and ironic focussing of materials can produce a surprising boldness in its address to contemporary events and situations or in its evocation of strong emotions. As variants of what Smith also calls "compiled fiction" (p. 21), both the title story and "The Dwarf in His Valley Ate Codfish" provide us with fine working examples of how these qualities operate with interesting effect.

Early in "Cape Breton is the Thought-Control Centre of Canada" (whose very title contains the ironic, bitter-sweet attitudes played out in the text proper), Smith's narrator states:

> Recently a friend cornered me into explaining my interest in compiled fiction, an example of which you are now reading.
> '. . . the technique isn't new at all. I got it from Ezra Pound and he got it from some French poets. Other precedents might be Francis Bacon's essays, the Book of Proverbs . . . the whole *Bible* . . . .' (pp. 21-22)

Smith might well have added T.S. Eliot's *The Waste Land*, even such non-fictional compilations as Pascal's *Pensées* or La Rochefoucauld's *Maximes*. The seemingly random arrangement of luminous details, the selective piling up of illuminating literary fragments, statements, analogies, anecdotes, images, aphorisms, can, when well-managed, elicit amazingly sharp emotional responses, establishing in their interplay highly charged circuits. Manipulative, deliberately abusive at times, yet playing up and down the full scale of feelings and values, these frequently analogical structures or compilations are capable of performing—by a sort of literary calculus—on several levels simultaneously. "Cape Breton," for instance, addresses itself to at least six essential subjects: Love, Revolution, Innocence, Dislocation, Art, and Nationalism. The numerous panels, fragments, or sections of which it is composed (31 in all) are integrated, drawn towards some unannounced centre, by a twofold method. Conceptually, the six subjects project similar crises, cast enveloping shadows of likenesses which bind the compilation. Tonally — whatever the ease of its comic surface — resonances of anger, despair, and bitterness expand and contract throughout, submitting finally to the full centripetal force at the centre. Thus, specific crises of dislocation or love-hate relationships at the most personal levels are played off against alternating attitudes towards Canada; scenes of revolution, resistance, and guerrilla warfare in the face of American exploitation interweave with passages on the loss of innocence, both sexual and idealistic; the dignity of Polish resistance to Russo-German occupation and plunder is juxtaposed with specific instances of our own solipsistic nature as a nation; the progress of the "Canadianized" artist whose subject becomes the maple leaf itself and whose achievement of a cultural identity is met by sudden critical rejection is undercut by the single felicitous slogan "Visit / ez EXPO 67" (p. 29). This cumulative vision of a country / personality confused, immobilized, and fragmented by its mixture of languages, of cultures, of self-loathing and complacency is brilliantly captured in the following Platonic image:

> The internal walls of an octagonal room are covered with mirrors. In the room stands a man naked. He is an ordinary-looking man; other people . . . cannot get in to see him because they do not know where the entrance to the room is, or, if they did, how to open it. Likewise the man does not know where the exit is nor how to open it . . . .
>
> In any case, the man is ordinary looking; but at times he thinks himself surpassingly beautiful and at times surpassingly ugly. The man acts out these conflicting feelings, all the while watching himself in the mirrors. With one hand he strokes his beautiful body; with the other (it holds a whip) he lashes his ugly body. The times when he does these things are, it would seem, all times, and they run concurrently. (pp. 34-35)

Yet compare this image of passivity, narcissism, incarceration, and loathing to the following activist injunctions:

> Of course, you can always kick [Joe Yank] first. (p. 34)
>
> Well . . . uhhh . . . thought of blowing the Peace Bridge? (p. 19)
>
> For Centennial Year, send President Johnson a gift: an American tourist's ear in a matchbox. Even better, don't bother with the postage. (p. 35)

This struggle at the personal and national levels to resolve the dilemma of exploitation, displacement, plunder, and partition is worked out structurally by just such a confederation of differing elements, contrary drives that enlighten us through the elaborate cross-referencing of the form itself, and that lead us towards a single, disturbing recognition of our state. This state, too, is reflected in the very fragmentations of the structure, in its perceived lack of integration, where the jarring poles of anger and acceptance, resolve and apathy, can only *compile* their evidence.

"The Dwarf in His Valley Ate Codfish" is compiled fiction of another sort where the familiar rhythms of story-telling are attempted, scrutinized, and abandoned, where the very artifacts of passion and memory refuse to yield up their fuller meanings. The narrative voice, constantly shifting its identity, can only establish an ambience and can do so only by stages and accumulation of details. "Is it a sense of loss we feel? Yes, I believe so, for we are weak" (p. 99), the narrator remarks in the opening paragraph, and then proceeds to define The Great Man, Gladys, and The Shadow People in terms of association, anecdote, talismans. Throughout, the narrator offers us only tentative vistas, constructs-in-process:

> Make a vista for yourself; I will not disturb it; I am going round to the back of the house to the trees. Come if you wish, or not as also you wish. I will not trouble you. (p. 99)

The deep suspicion that little redemptive order resides in these slivers of detail is allied to the welling mood of bitterness and loss which obtains in all three sections of the story. "History lacks sincerity; so I have always thought" (p. 100) leads to the resigned sense that "Revelation is the bread of fools, the bane of merchants and the salve of kings. So much for bloody journeys" (p. 104), and ultimately to the conviction that "Process is horrible" (p. 105), that "there's nothing more meaningless than connections" (p. 106). So the details fail to cohere, fail to shape themselves into a controlled structure. "The memory of them is sharp but it is only a few pictures and the colour is too bright for truth" (p. 107). Thus we are left only with the bitter taste of that disjunctiveness:

> So the time passed and passes. One wonders how long it can go on.

97

It's the happiness that goes first, and it matters damn little what goes
after that. We pick up daisies and dream of train rides. Hate sneaks in
like juice into a grapefruit. One day it leaps out at your eye. Something
will snap somewhere. Somehow it will get at them sooner or later, the
Great Man, Gladys and The Shadow People. (p. 107)

While the story begins and ends with the same images of "Long noses
and petulance" (pp. 99, 107), this circularity only confirms that the
revelations have accomplished little in the way of salve, strength, or
understanding, and that, unlike the compilations of the title story, the
centre has been lost rather than discovered.

"Cape Breton is the Thought-Control Centre of Canada" and "The
Dwarf in His Valley Ate Codfish" display the resourcefulness of compiled fiction in achieving very different ends; and they demonstrate how
Smith's techniques of indirection, narratorial ambiguity, and piled
fragmentation can be made to serve more than one version of our
predicament.

IV

Ray Smith's comments on and typical aggression towards the traditional story form raised red warning lights for me; he directed my attention towards dangers I'd never really seen . . . .
Ray probably isn't aware of his influence on me—possibly because
it's a largely cautionary one. Ray prevented me from perpetrating yet
more gauche stories of sensitive youth. Ray has a thing about sensitive
youth. Show Ray a sensitive youth in literature or life and he will don
his leather coat and stride towards the Royal Pub on Guy Street, muttering.[14]

These comments — first published in John Metcalf's hilarious, moving, and delicious *Kicking Against the Pricks*, a series of pieces on what it
is to be a writer in Canada—may serve as an introduction to one of
Smith's favourite literary pastimes, the genre-satire. One way of melt-
ing down the rigidities of the traditional is to sap their generic energies
at the source, shrink them into something akin to Oldenburg's soft
forms. In four of the nine stories, Smith accomplishes this siphoning
tactic with telling results.

Like "A Cynical Tale," which immediately follows it, "Passion"
constitutes a satire on its subject, Smith's fresh look at the bankruptcy
of genre—in this case, gothic romance. In his own specialized execu-

tion of its generic rules, Smith comically reduces conventions to self-mocking exercises while cleverly retaining the flint if not the fire of the original. "Passion," then, is a recycling of the passional abstracts of *Wuthering Heights*, whereby all the staples of Emily Brontë's novel — nourishment/starvation motifs, death-wish, obsession, cosmic forces, fetishism, betrayal — are filtered through an absurd network of puns, word-plays, double-takes, and crazy logic. Thus, the destructive, semi-incestuous passions of Heathcliff and Catherine are reduced to

> Oh you do love me love you do don't you?
> Yes love I do love you love
> And I love you love
> And you do love me love you do. (p. 38)

The central nourishment/starvation motifs of the original become

> Watermelon? For me? Oh! Sweetcliff!
> Eatit.
> She rushes all over the plates for each of us: Actually no, Catchy, I've just had a gigantic supper and really, no, I, couldn't, no . . . . (p. 40)

And Catherine's tragic, suffering demise is rendered as

> Rhadhe didn't ate her.
> You mean . . . .
> Mean and nasty, yes. I, Eatcliff . . . the remains are packaged here.
> A tradedgy! Horrors! Ghastlys! Terribles! Uncouths! (p. 41)

In "A Cynical Tale," the English lament ballad "Bonny Barbara Allen" is transformed into a kind of absurdist minute waltz. In Smith's version of this most moving of verses, Barbary Ellen, "an ultrafeminist of undeniable beauty" (p. 43) and "*latent Lesbian*" (p. 44), triggers a swift series of byzantine intrigues in which the homosexual paradise of Sweet William and his lisping lover George is shattered, Russian spy and counter-espionage agent contend for microfilm, and all ends in the semi-tragical passing of the three principals. Mimicking the legend-like, ineffable sadness of the original, poisoned briar and rose take root in the bodies of Barbary Ellen and Sweet William (these being the weaponry they have turned on each other) "& flowered & intertwined *(symbolic of the love which might have united them in life had not nature*

99

played a cruel jest upon their hormonal balances before birth) & mingled..."
(p. 45).

All the ingredients of the ballad are here—betrayal, lament, rejection, and double-death. Yet Smith not only recycles these abstracts into a comic frenzy of spy-thriller action, but also announces his distance from the original by drawing our attention to his own satirizing focus; and that satiric impulse becomes itself a subject for scrutiny:

> (Note: *a frail swoon approacheth*.) (p. 44)
>
> Ah! Irony! (p. 45)
>
> ...thus adding a piquant touch to this gruesome tableau, etc. (p. 45)

In these two stories, Smith demonstrates again how freedom from conventional story form can multiply the means available for rendering ideas, situations, characters. Once the necessity of obeying standard rules of composition has been dismissed, the author is free to satirize, compile, juxtapose, cross-reference, and liberate his materials from strict spatial or temporal realism. Thus, in "Raphael Anachronic," a third genre-satire—this time of the *künstlerroman*—Smith illustrates how, once we have dispensed with the demons of historical accuracy, chronological continuum, the field is open for any number of absurdist confrontations. Accordingly, Raphael Santi, the " 'well-rounded Renaissance man' " (p. 110) transported to the twentieth century, reads Walter Pater, delivers a lecture on virtue to a group of hippies, rides in an airplane which he insists "had been invented by Da Vinci and would therefore not work" (p. 114), reads *The Times* in imitation of an Englishman, watches television, argues with Andrew Wyeth, and passes modern judgements on his rivals past and present:

> 'Leonardo is a scientist with a good pencil sharpener. He has a great future ... programming computers.' (p. 109)
>
> 'A great feeling for form has Buonarotti. A great feeling for sculptural effects. With practice he might become a first rate cartoonist for the sports pages.' (p. 109)
>
> 'Dali has a facile touch with a brush. He would do well illustrating medical textbooks.' (p. 110)

This broad anachronistic comedy of artistic judgements and temporal

100

dislocations has for its primary aim the unsentimentalizing of our attitudes towards the artist-figure; this is rendered especially effective in Smith's choice of Raphael, the consummate Renaissance man, whose only abiding interests, it turns out, are money, women, and self-promotion. The modern spirit, for sure!

"Smoke," the last of the four genre-satires, begins with an epigraph out of Tolstoy, the famous first sentence of *Anna Karenina*: "Happy families are all alike; every unhappy family is unhappy in its own way."[15] What follows from this is Smith's own absurdist version of a Domestic Tragedy, the attempts by the children Milton and Mildred to do away with their respective siblings, Gould and Rachel, having earlier framed Gould's father for the murder of his wife. Each attempt at elimination increases in zaniness (a rocket, dead woodpeckers as missiles, etc.); while behind these extravaganzas lurks the artist Paleologue, a strange, forbidding manipulator of their destinies, whose own comments once again direct us to the controlling dispositions of the artist (Smith) himself. " 'I'll construct an ending for you' " (p. 132), he assures Gould and Rachel, then proceeds to describe the scene of their triumph over the pernicious duo with figures " 'standing in an artful arrangement. I'll see to that' " (p. 133). But the very arbitrariness and freedoms of the non-narrative form are stressed even here, for as Paleologue comments:

'What does it matter? If you don't like it, construct your own. Mine's probably no better than the next.'
. . . .
. . .'It hasn't really happened, you know. That was just one ending. . . .' (pp. 133, 134)

V

The two longest stories of the collection, "The Galoshes" and "Peril," are indeed deceptive, for they seem to demonstrate something approaching narrative continuity. "The Galoshes," in particular, likely brought a breath of relief to those critics hungering for "a real story,"[16] and yet, despite its nominal resemblance to the well-made narrative form, it too diagnoses the state of the art though in a subtler way.

"The Galoshes" has a certain Gogol-like ambience — reminding one perhaps of Gogol's "The Nose" or "The Overcoat" in its concentra-

101

tion upon a single article as the depository of our dreams and the symbol of our status. But, comforting as its extended form seemed to those less taken with Smith's more obvious radicalizations, "The Galoshes" contains a powerful surrealistic strain which regulates its entire progress. Thus, Black Angus — under whose sway the protagonist Jasper finds himself — is a fabulist, a figure out of legend, and a precursor of those magical creatures in Smith's *Lord Nelson Tavern*;[17] the zodiacal mysteries which seem to determine the lives of those irresistably under their spell signal both "the deepest pit" of Halifax in February and March's "promise of rebirth" (p. 65); the newly-bought galoshes themselves take on a cosmic significance, become the very genius of place and circumstance and a strange guarantee of their intactness: "Jasper knew intuitively that if he wore them everything would end, for he had acquired them the same day he acquired a friend and a beloved. So the galoshes sat in the corner" (p. 81); the spectre of Halifax itself is attached to Jasper's off-centre sense of unreality and tentativeness: "February in Halifax destroys vision with a peculiar sort of illusion. With all colour grey and all light dim, the viewer sees every edge slightly blurred" (p. 83); the libidinous women in Jasper's building who lie in wait to seduce him, "those crazy women who wanted him, those frenzied bacchantes hunting out a victim" (p. 91), resemble some absurdist vision of the great Canadian wet-dream; and Jasper's final escape (wearing two left-footed galoshes) becomes the comic fulfilment of the prophecy that has haunted the story from its beginning. So while the narrative form appears to be more standardized than elsewhere in the collection, Smith has actually liberated *its interior* by impressing upon its causal progress the mysterious, the fabulous, and the talismanic, none of which are accountable to mere common sense, or even to the linear construction that contains them.

In "Dinosaur," Smith discusses the patterns which work to unify his story "Peril":

> Three incidents which each contain a hidden peril. Three youngish men, rather similar, rather different, take a walk. They meet a stranger or strangers and converse about one thing and another, then go on. In the graveyard walk the peril is in the necromancer's sanity . . . . The peril in the park is in the question: Is either of them sane? The peril of the beach is that, if everything is as it is presented, then Purlieu has lunched with a god and goddess.[18]

But at the level at which literature explores its own boundaries and escapes—and here the story recalls the similar explorations of "Colours"—the perils of "Peril" reside in the demesne of identity, language, direction, perspective, and assumption.

In the first part of the story, Passquick encounters a necromancer in a graveyard whose pride of craft in conjuring the dead leads to a discussion of the role of the artist himself:

> 'But what is a poem? Dead scratchings on dead paper. And a painting? Dead paint on a dead canvas. Dead: *no life*. But your necromancer, now, he's a different kettle of fish. Give him dead matter, and he puts life into it, real guts, spirit....' (p. 50)

Yet the perilous fate of the necromancer is to be spurned by society, rejected:

> 'We have no artistic freedom; we are scoffed at, humiliated, hunted down...you just don't realize what it means to be forced to live outside society...most of us are warm human beings who need love, who want to love in return, to be accepted....' (p. 50)

This is both a lament for the artist and a satire of his complaints, a by-now-familiar feature of Smith's re-doubling ruminations on his craft. As for the new breed of necromancers:

> ' ... I think their work is pretty hollow. They've got no style, no elegance, no ... beauty in their work. Rebels, that's what they are, rebels. And ... they don't even know what they're rebelling against, you know what I mean? This new stuff, it's all shallow ... so shallow ....' (pp. 50-51)

Here, Smith has ironically shifted the view, representing his own rebellions through the diminished perspective of a crusty, conservative critic, exposing his own suspect status to the perils of reverse scrutiny.

In the second part of "Peril," Period sits in a park observing a carousel, attempting to create some compositional unity out of what he sees:

> The scene was like a painting in its serenity; yet the figures were too small. It was like music in its harmony; but music was too demanding. Light hung everywhere; the shadows were blinding. The little toddlers

toddled roly-poly short distances and their cries and laughs came lightly
on the breeze, shattered, the sequence jumbled, random, like a volley of
arrows shot by little painted soldiers. (pp. 51-52)

He is joined by the ghost of G.K. Chesterton who, however, seems a
little shaky on the particulars of his own *oeuvre*. While Period, in turn,
assumes the identity of a Pierrot — '''You're a bit happy for a
Pierrot' '' (p. 54), observes G.K. — they test each other's identities,
concluding that they would never have gotten on had Chesterton been
Cecil Rhodes and Period the young Goethe. The attempt to compose
one's identity and surroundings comes to a head when Period refuses to
revise his first impression of the object before him, which G.K. has
identified as a bandstand:

> 'I know, but it has the same shape as a carousel and "carousel" has a
> better sound to it.'
> . . . .
> 'It's a carousel,' said Period. 'And damn the consequences!' (pp. 53,
> 56)

The subjective view has been enforced, its penalties accepted and its
pleasures accounted for.

In the final and most evocative part of the story, Purlieu visits a
mysterious beach and encounters an old man in a wheelchair, a table,
and a naked girl. Naked himself (for how else shall we encounter the
gods), he seems to have entered a realm of mythic dimensions where the
landscape has shaped itself into a harmonious exactitude:

> The girl took a tray for herself and sat on a log on her side of the old man
> and as far forward as Purlieu so that the three formed an isosceles tri-
> angle, broad-based upon the sea. (p. 60)

Suddenly, a horseman, soundless, his horse's hooves not visible behind
the dunes, gallops to light the lighthouse and the mysteriously salva-
tional force of his mission, its redemptive illuminating of the landscape,
attaches itself to the very light of the sun: "the horseman was gold now
and he gleamed against the dark sky beyond" (p. 62).

In each of these encounters — as indeed in the entire collection — the
perils ultimately have to do with the risks of perception itself; with
how through language, form, and focus, we diagnose, re-build, and
render malleable the world around us. And these perils of myth-

making, of reinventions of the self, of exploding time and space, of invoking, expanding, questioning the very freedoms which absurdist art allows itself, are perils that each artist faces at the very risk of his equilibrium: dangers into which he puts himself as a mortal god who must always pay the price for his creations, establishing fatal edens at each contrivance of his fancy.

Notes

[1]Ray Smith, *Cape Breton is the Thought-Control Centre of Canada* (Toronto: House of Anansi, 1969), p. 101. All further references to this work appear in the text.

[2]See John Reid, "Turning Fiction into Fiction," rev. of *Man in the Glass Octopus*, by J. Michael Yates, *Cape Breton is the Thought-Control Centre of Canada*, by Ray Smith, and *You Used to Like My Pies*, by Barry Charles, *Canadian Literature*, No. 44 (Spring 1970), p. 79; Kent Thompson, rev. of *New Canadian Writing, 1968: Stories by David Lewis Stein, Clark Blaise and Dave Godfrey, Cape Breton is the Thought-Control Centre of Canada*, by Ray Smith, *Dance of the Happy Shades*, by Alice Munro, and *The Fire-Dwellers*, by Margaret Laurence, *The Fiddlehead*, No. 82 (Nov.-Dec. 1969), pp. 70-71; and Douglas Barbour, rev. of *The Streets of Summer*, by David Helwig, and *Cape Breton is the Thought-Control Centre of Canada*, by Ray Smith, *The Dalhousie Review*, 49 (1969-70), 591, 593.

[3]See Martin Esslin, *The Theatre of the Absurd*, rev. ed. (Garden City, N.Y.: Doubleday, 1969); and Arnold P. Hinchliffe, *The Absurd* (London: Methuen, 1969).

[4]See my article on Ray Smith's *Lord Nelson Tavern*, "Exploring Ray Smith's Labyrinth," *Books in Canada*, June-July 1974, pp. 12, 15-17.

[5]Ray Smith, "Author's Commentary," in *Sixteen by Twelve: Short Stories by Canadian Writers*, ed. John Metcalf (Toronto: Ryerson, 1970), p. 219.

[6]Smith, "Author's Commentary," p. 219.

[7]Smith, "Author's Commentary," p. 224.

[8]Smith, "Author's Commentary," p. 222.

[9]Smith, "Author's Commentary," p. 223.

[10]Ray Smith, "Dinosaur," in *The Narrative Voice: Short Stories and Reflections by Canadian Authors*, ed. John Metcalf (Toronto: McGraw-Hill Ryerson, 1972), p. 205.

[11]Smith, "Author's Commentary," p. 222.

[12]Smith, "Author's Commentary," p. 223.

[13]Smith, "Dinosaur," p. 206.

[14]John Metcalf, "Telling Tales," in his *Kicking Against the Pricks* (Downsview, Ont.: ECW, 1982) p. 78; rpt. (revised) in *The Montreal Story Tellers: Memoirs, Photographs, Critical Essays*, ed. J.R. (Tim) Struthers.

[15]The wording of this quotation was corrected in the second, 1971 printing of *Cape Breton is the Thought-Control Centre of Canada*.

[16]Douglas Barbour, rev. of *The Streets of Summer*, by David Helwig, and *Cape Breton is the Thought-Control Centre of Canada*, by Ray Smith, 593.

[17]Ray Smith, *Lord Nelson Tavern* (Toronto: McClelland and Stewart, 1974).

[18]Smith, "Dinosaur," p. 207.

Louis K. MacKendrick
A VOICE WITHIN THE TAVERN CRIED:
CROSSING THE BAR
WITH RAYMOND FRASER AND RAY SMITH

There is no convenient comparison between Raymond Fraser's *The Black Horse Tavern* (1972) and Ray Smith's *Lord Nelson Tavern* (1974), but rather radical differences of milieu, personnel, and fictional technique. Fraser's collection of stories is essentially the work of a raconteur and anecdotalist. Smith's novel, or story sequence, is the work of a literary impresario. Fraser's tales are often familiar in voice, but consistently observe the traditional qualities of the realistic story; Smith's narratives throw considerable emphasis on the literary construct *per se*, and employ a distinctive range of technical presentation. In one sense, Fraser writes stories and Smith writes fictions. Fraser's principal interest is in getting a story told in clearly demarcated episodes, whereas Smith is less concerned with conclusions than he is with reverberation, association, and stylization. Their respective emphases are upon localized realistic environments and self-contained narrative units as opposed to a creative fictive world, not as specifically placed, where the characters' interrelationships and social evolution are often balanced against the writing act itself.

Though the stories of *The Black Horse Tavern* have several settings — Newbridge, Montreal, and Quebec City — Newbridge's tavern, and its *habitués*, are most frequently cited. Fraser's collection varies in its degree of seriousness and in the completeness of its effects. Several stories are a story-teller's oral presentation and, as John Metcalf has recalled of Fraser's unique contribution to the Montreal Story Teller Fiction Performance Group,

Ray's stories were less stories than anecdotes or tales. They were typed on yellow newsprint and heavily influenced in style and subject matter by his former employment at the tabloid *Midnight*. Most of these yarns seemed to feature massive insobriety, murder, incest, mutilation, rape, anal crime, and genital abnormality.[1]

Fraser writes of only certain kinds of people; even in his comic pieces, his characters are often the aimless or dispossessed, the victims of their own constricted circumstances despite any pretense to the contrary. Though *The Black Horse Tavern* is not deliberately crafted as a series of related stories, it is reminiscent of James Joyce's *Dubliners*, where a local paralysis or inertia traps the individual, each with his own compulsion, without much hope of advancement. Fraser's stories answer to no strict classification, but they may be individually considered as ranging through the general modes of comedy and realism.

"Spanish Jack," one of several stories associated with the Black Horse Tavern in fictional Newbridge (modelled on Chatham, New Brunswick[2]), is a chronicle of good-natured scurrility. The colloquial narrator of elderly Jack McIntyre's gulling and misadventure is frequently present, using the familiar words "I," "you," and the storyteller's informal "well"; though he plays the bystander with slight irony, his tone becomes more objective in presenting Jack's activities away from the tavern. Jack, who believes that " 'my skinnin' days is over,' "[3] is not at first persuaded of the alleged aphrodisiac effect of powdered cantharides ("Spanish Fly") in his beer, but becomes so randy, perhaps only at the suggestion of his drinking companions, that he mutilates his wife. The account of his arousal is slapstick, but the narrator controls the details and pacing of this extended vulgar joke, and his ingenuous conclusion is deliberately assumed naïveté: "Many people now, the guys around town, they don't call him just Jack now, or old Jack, they call him Spanish Jack even though he's not a Spaniard" (p. 125). The story is at heart a barroom jest, with no pretensions beyond.

Another figure of fun, in "The Newbridge Sighting," is railroadman Alec Mooney, "a conversationalist of some renown" (p. 89). His alleged sighting of a UFO at a ballpark is counterpointed by the genial scepticism of Paul Ryan, who uses Mooney as an unconscious butt: Paul perpetuates Alec's delusion for the press and quietly makes landing marks to confirm the sighting. The narrator is again first-person, but the story's real achievement is Alec's rapid, repetitive gabble:

107

"Got to check the field, that's what I was doing, eh, check the field, might coach team. Saw flying saucer, came down, whooosh, came down, it did, just out of nowhere, all bright and shining, whooosh, down on the field, almost scared me to death, I was." (p. 93)

The incessant excited rattle combines with Alec's inflated self-importance — he claims familiarity with "Mr. CNR" — in a pleasant inconsequential tale which only wishes to tell an amusing story. The overreacher, however, is a recurrent figure in *The Black Horse Tavern*.

A related pretender narrates the collection's longest story, "The Quebec Prison," a character of promise rather than of achievement. His style can be modestly self-conscious:

> I like to pretend I'm creative and a man of great potential. If you have never produced very much in the way of art it's important to believe in your poetential. Observe. I made a typing error and produced a new word, "poetential". By accident I have just described myself perfectly, since I have for some time considered myself a poet and have been meaning for years to write some very good verse. (p. 22)

The "for years" is characteristic of the narrator's overestimation of his possibilities, even as "a musically creative person" (p. 26). In a review of *The Black Horse Tavern*, Linda Shohet has treated Fraser's technique severely:

> He uses the artistic self-consciousness so fashionable in "literature of exhaustion," but he does it so ineptly and with so obvious a lack of necessary erudition that the reader feels mainly pity and occasional anger.[4]

However, this view exaggerates inappropriately both the consistency of Fraser's intention and his unnamed character; even the division of "The Quebec Prison" into individually-titled subsections gives the structural impression of related anecdotes, not of a reflexive aesthetic construct such as John Barth describes in his essay "The Literature of Exhaustion."[5]

Fraser's unwearied melodist, petulantly escaping the noise of Montreal, joins with an anti-automobile guerrilla in Quebec City whose single-entry "combat journal" and grand talk produce only childish and unimaginative actions. The narrator is infected by his associate's rhetoric about personal law, but his own natural romanticizing excess and tendency to generalize about conditions — including a whimsical man-to-man discussion with a magistrate — are dropped when he is imprisoned. Like other Fraser personae, he has exaggerated his own role, but his foolishness passes; the details of gaol that he presents are virtually documentary, his style becomes less self-serving and his embarrassment and loneliness are apparent: "I hardly have to say I felt very little romance about my situation" (p. 46).

Much of the remainder of the story, in yet another key, is a verbatim recording of the exploits of a fellow internee, in the form of anecdotes about imposture. Dan Kiley's language has at times a gentlemanly formality, and he sees himself as " 'an intelligent man of cultivated tastes' " (p. 57), but his chief talents are passing bad cheques and inveigling the charitably-minded. Yet Dan is an engaging rascal who admits, " 'I'm an unrepentant alcoholic and a bum and I wouldn't be anything else. I'm one of the few free men in this country' " (p. 56). While the narrator's eventual release technically ends the story, it is in essence a sequence of portraits and episodes with little apparent cohesion as a literary artifice — despite the fact that Fraser pays joking tribute to certain literary artifices by titling the last two subsections "The End of the Sentence" and "Footnote." The demands of social law on the free spirit may be considered a theme of "The Quebec Prison," but this overblows the tale: Fraser's focus is not on neatly structured narrative but on eccentric and self-indulgent character.

Physical eccentricity is at the heart of Fraser's human comedy "Bertha and Bill," set in Montreal. Bill Lewis, from Glace Bay, Nova Scotia, is a tall, thin, and acned poet-presumptive who drunkenly makes love to the armless poet Bertha Northrup. The guilt, self-recrimination, and fear of responsibility which follow his initial awe at her accomplishments are treated with gentle amusement by Sam McCarthy, the first-person narrator:

> He went away, as disconsolate as ever. As he left I recommended that his experience might prove valuable as material for a few good poems later on, but he just looked at me. He wasn't in a poetic frame of mind. (p. 185)

Still, the unlikely one-time relationship leads to an ironic reversal. Although Bill's "morning-after" reaction to Bertha, as related to Sam, is that she is "a freak" (p. 184), Bertha tells Sam that she pities Bill's

109

shyness and unhandsomeness:

> "Well, how would you feel if you looked like him and had to walk down the street? I'm sure people stare at him. He's probably very sensitive. He must be or he wouldn't be a poet. I probably sound like a mother hen or something but I'd like to help him along if I can."
> (p. 187)

The story of these incongruous characters is told with sympathy, not with a leer; Fraser is not satirizing the poetic nature, and his narrator is privy to both sides of the situation. It is perhaps as well-rounded, controlled, and pointed a fiction as Fraser can achieve within the parameters of the conventional short story. "Bertha and Bill" is the final story in *The Black Horse Tavern*; its compactness and understated pathos are indications of Fraser's real ability with the story form.

The narrator of "On the Bus," also set in Montreal, is a proudly self-confessed "flop" (p. 102), a dreamer of no particular talent who loves losers. With narrative self-centeredness he purposefully plays with the traditional objectivity of narrative outlook:

> I don't want to get too far astray. Aside from establishing an ungainly writing style I've written a paragraph that has little or nothing to do with what I want to say — and I would like to make *more* irrelevant remarks. (p. 102)

He is arch and intermittently self-conscious, awkwardly drawing attention to several of his gratuitous and humorous artifices, as when he stops in front of an art gallery:

> My reason is that I am going to use a literary device. As I stood there before the large window I saw a reflection of my own person .... Now that you have my description I can walk away from the windows of the Gallery Martal. (pp. 105-06)

His language and manner are affected, or mannerist; the character's whole style largely reflects his proposed dilettantish attention to champagne, music, and painting. On a bus, however, he is vilified as a hippie by some elderly fellow-travellers, his smugness is challenged, and he loudly counteraccuses his critics of personal uncleanliness. This is an incident of admitted "minor significance" (p. 101); Fraser's comic pretender to leisured ease does not move out of a precious limbo, and

110

what he believes is his moment of triumphant reversal is not given substance beyond his posturings. The ending is a weak, implicit joke rather than an explicit resolution — not the conventional rounding-off of the short story but the more open form of an oral narrative. Significantly the narrator has described his artistic capacity as merely "would-be" (p. 103), and this story's blurred ending exemplifies this absence of tidy artistry.

Fraser's realistic stories have a more identifiable social context than his comedies and, appropriately, an ultimately serious, even bleak, outlook. In "The Actor," Frankie, a last-minute replacement in a minor dramatic role, is a pretender who is confused by wine and by a conviction of his talent for improvisation:

> He had crammed desperately, then gone to bed feeling the role would flow freely from him, given the old Roman atmosphere of the stage setting, and his own complete release, his intuitive feel for the part, once on stage. (p. 172)

Frankie is an overreacher for recognition who shares the delusion of many of Fraser's characters: "He told himself, it was the price of fame to take perilous risks" (p. 174). He fails miserably, paralysed. His subsequent refusal of a drink after this humiliation shows his greater self-awareness, no longer prey to fantasies of success. The story manages to generate a degree of sympathy through its completely objective and uninflected manner, and the foolish confidence which gives way to befuddled terror and shame is accurately rendered and complete.

"A Cold Frosty Morning" represents the ultimate extension of the kind of situation in which Fraser's creative aspirants stand in conflict with an unforgiving social reality. Brennan, the narrator, is a poet called from his creative self-communion to act selflessly in the larger imperfect urban world. In his stream-of-consciousness monologue, the cold and inconvenience provoke his truculent self-pity and a rationalizing unvoiced argument with the supposedly self-righteous friend who has recruited Brennan to paint a needy arthritic's apartment. The story's implicit theme is a contrast between the demands of the real world and those of the personal artistic routine. Brennan's " 'pursuit of perfection' " (p. 131) does not extend to his present social obligation; his goal is elsewhere.

> ...I'm up to four pages now the longest poem I've done yet I try to
> avoid thinking about outside things like and I wouldn't admit this to
> anyone but when you get that far along and you think it might be a ma-
> jor work little thoughts creep in and you have to keep them out until the
> work is finished because they might interfere with the flow like I'm
> thinking of well I suppose I would submit this for the President's Medal
> that is if I get it published....(p. 131)

Finally, the stench from and imagined squalor of the old man's apartment, and a delayed assistant, repel Brennan absolutely. Though he sees
himself as " 'the slow but certain sure worker like some other good
poets If I'm slow I'm sure my poems are tight and taut' " (p. 131), he
has just received a rejection slip and his present circumstances have little
poetry about them. He bolts from an image, from a projection of what
he imagines. Brennan's flight is, in effect, a vivid creative moment,
more authentic than what he might create in a closeted artistic labour.

The realistic content of "A Cold Frosty Morning" to a great extent
outweighs Fraser's attempt to create interior monologue; his technical
practice is considerably more adroit in "College Town Restaurant,"
which has a reportorial quality. Its content and its manner of observation are complementary. The story shows a country-girl waitress and
her husky down-home admirer; she is distant with him, perhaps indicating her exposure and attraction to even a modest urban life. The
first-person narrator is impassive, and his account is a slice of life whose
essential pointlessness is underscored by the suitor's awkward, unreci-
procated overtures and by the narrator's own final comment:

> I revolved around on my stool and looked down at the booths for a few
> minutes. When my cigaret was down to a butt I stepped on it and paid
> my bill and went home. (p. 144)

The story captures an incident cleanly in its complete realism, without
any apparent subjection to theme or resolution.

"They Come Here to Die," the first story in *The Black Horse
Tavern*, introduces much of the pathos — a product of the characters'
illusions — that characterizes both the comic and the realistic stories in
the collection. Comedy and pathos mix in this story with an odd effectiveness, though here as elsewhere Fraser's reader is never wholly sure
where the borderline between deliberate literary arrangement and an
accidental complement of elements falls. Newbridge's Ralph Ramsey is

an amusing, articulate alcoholic, but his true condition is shown in his accusing his fellow Black Horse regulars of being nobodies. In the first part of the story the sympathetic narrator, his friend, presents the comic, thirsty, and anecdotal Ralph; in the second, which is largely a dialogue, it is apparent that Ralph and his companion Danny Sullivan are rejects from both the tavern society and from life's feast. In metaphoric confirmation of the story's title, Ralph lives in an old men's rooming house: his figurative death is social, economic, and spiritual. This milieu, overcast by wind-whipped rain, acts as a symbolic externalization of his dreary life and prospects. Ralph's treasured trumpet and the railroad to Toronto represent a better life but for his and Danny's inertia. As Ralph says, in a startlingly apt image,

> "I can't stand being alone in this room anymore, I'd rather be in jail. At least you'd know why you're there. I'm serving a sentence and I haven't been arrested yet. Solitary confinement." (p. 15)

The two men have a perverse pride in being outcasts; but when they head for a boxcar to drink the last of their money, the conflict between the ambition to escape and the Newbridge prison is subtly underlined. The succession of comic alcoholism and crippling futility is convincingly dramatized in this story of delimited circumstances, and the duality of its tones is not incongruous.[6]

"The Janitor's Wife" is the most brutally realistic, or naturalistic, story in *The Black Horse Tavern*. It features another Fraser protagonist convinced of his social ineptitude, while his basement room, cockroach-ridden and associated with previous tragedies, seems a squalid counterpoint to his inexperience. Frankie Walsh's self-deprecation and self-doubt are specifically activated when he assays a date with Irene, a desirable co-worker:

> Could I handle it, was I capable of pulling it off, would she not realize that a mistake's been made, that I had outreached myself, that I was bluffing? I'll be cool, I instructed myself, I'll act cool and possibly a little superior. (p. 155)

However, at the aptly named Catastrophe club, Frankie gets brash with drink, and surlily resentful at a party above his social experience where Irene's former beau is overly attentive: "I had, I suppose, a kind of envy of them all out there. They weren't selfconscious about their movements or the expressions on their faces'' (p. 164). A thaw of his cooling relationship with Irene is temporary.

This chronicle of nervousness, over-confidence, resentment, and isolation is remarkably true to life in its emotional registers. It is interrupted and concluded by italicized episodes which highlight Frankie, his unpleasant surroundings, cheap wine, and the tenement janitor's wife. The woman is sluttish, with *"a face scarred all over like a pincushion"* (p. 149), and her invitation is clear; the story ends with a passionless coupling of the two. The woman's parting promise, *"'I'll come see you again'"* (p. 170), emphasizes the lovelessness of this actual scene which contrasts so strikingly with Frankie's fantasized sexual success with Irene. The contrast is between sordid, unappetizing erotic achievement and young love's moon-calf, frustrated hesitation. At opposite extremes, both women are associated with drink, with parties, and with earlier claims on their affections — the janitor's wife, momentarily absent from a raucous gathering, has a sottish husband. The contest of blowsiness and a rather hollow sort of beauty and propriety is clear: one party is in a tenement, the other in a highrise. Indeed, the parallels and contrasts speak well for Fraser's implicit sense of structure, which seems consciously but not pointedly striven for in the story.

Linda Shohet has commented of *The Black Horse Tavern,*

> Unfortunately the language and technique are not equal to the vision. The process of narrative is often clumsy and appallingly naïve; Fraser's narrators work themselves into technical corners from which there are no exits. There are errors in the sentence structure to be found only in elementary composition classes, and time-worn clichés intrude at regular intervals.[7]

Fraser, however, cannot be taxed with deficiencies of literary formality when his range is far from ''literary''; a demand for conscious artistic form does not strictly accord with the forms his stories take. His slight loosenings of linear narrative are unpresumptuous and uncomplicated, and few characters achieve a demonstrable amplitude. Fraser's rendering of situation, emotion, and expression is similarly unpretentious, and becomes pretentious only as suits particular characters. Clare McCulloch's remark that ''Fraser's voice comes through too strongly and his puppet-glove is too visible,''[8] if not actually confusing author and personae, also does not allow for his modest accomplishments in the realm of stories being told. The frequent absence of definable formal material in *The Black Horse Tavern* has to be accepted on its own informal and vernacular terms.

Ray Smith's fiction is quite the opposite: it in many ways focuses on its own technical elements. From one perspective *Lord Nelson Tavern* is a sequence of composite accumulating portraits of its principals. While each of its seven independent stories usually concentrates on one or two characters, the totality of any individual and his development over time is represented by the sum of all his major or incidental appearances. Halifax's Lord Nelson Tavern has a merely occasional function in the sequence; it is, however, a locale where the characters behave as a social group, responsive to each other, and from which they move out into a wider world where various relative forms of self-realization and achievement can occur. Arnold and Cathy Davidson suggest that "the novel is structured as a montage";[9] Barbara Godard has referred to its "modular concept";[10] and Douglas Barbour has observed that "each new story, read in order, builds upon all the previous stories an edifice ever more rococo in its intricate and barely balanced extensions...."[11]

In Smith's first story, "Two Loves," two kinds of relationships are contrasted: the temporal and irregular found in the real world of accident, and the eternal, perfect, fairy-tale romance or myth. This contrast begins a pattern in *Lord Nelson Tavern* identified by Lawrence Garber, who sees Ray Smith as "an explorer of shadows and substances, of hard realities and fabulous conducts."[12] The pattern is more exactly described by Godard:

> Just as the female characters are separated into romantic stereotype versus emotional reality, so too the males are divided into two groups, those artists who have rich inner lives, the others who live stereotyped ones.[13]

Francesca, whose academic faculty is ironically science, cannot be specified by her peers: her origins are mysterious and she becomes the stuff of rumours and myths. The poet Paleologue says, " 'Perhaps she's just the sort of girl legends get told about,' "[14] unlike his own Lucy, a down-home girl and compulsive monologuist whose earlier broken engagement signals her subjection to the imperfect world of error. Francesca is " 'unreal, like a vision' " (p. 18), and believes that " 'Nothing matters but love' " (p. 20). The painter Ti-Paulo sees her as a mirror, a reciprocator of others' gestures with no distinguishing characteristics in her unreachable unassailable perfection. As the narrator comments, "Her beauty, grace, elegance was of that sort that is at the very limit of our experience" (p. 19).

The incongruous friendship of Lucy and Francesca is built on their respective musical tastes. Lucy's addiction to Tammy Wynette's song "Stand by Your Man" epitomizes her ideal relationship — never achieved — but more properly signifies what will become true for Francesca and her elegant, Adonis-like lover, Dimitri; Francesca's fondness for Chopin's "Tristesse Étude" and the bittersweet love story *Tristan and Isolde* strictly applies to Lucy's relationships. Yet these pieces suit Francesca admirably; as Grilse notes, " 'I figured she must be a person like everyone else and perhaps being so beautiful maybe she was lonely . . . ' " (p. 19). Dimitri, in a similar "desolation of loneliness" (p. 25), is as remote as Francesca; once they meet, in a succession of deliberately and romantically clichéd situations, they will live happily ever after in ephemeral moneyed sophistication. The imagery associated with the fantastic couple is suitably lyrical:

> The lemonade summer poured around them; and their days and nights were days and nights of beaches, endless beaches of curves into endless spirals of white sand, foam-edged on the inside of the curve, spirals up into the lemon sky. (p. 29)

This passage, with its dreamy repetition, points up the distinction between the styles consciously applied in the story. Lucy's long monologue clearly reveals her informal, gossipy character through language and pacing, while the Dimitri-Francesca episodes are almost hieratic in tone and formal graciousness — a contrast initially reflected in the girls' favourite music. Dimitri and Francesca's "accomplished union" (p. 28) and conventional romantic appointments cast an aura of purification over the other characters who nonetheless, in an extension of the story's contrasts, must return "back to their imperfect selves" (p. 29). Back in the Lord Nelson Tavern, they are all too human, and engagingly so.

The narrator, too, is sometimes present, given his familiarity with the characters: "Probably Grilse was going with someone, but with Grilse you never knew" (p. 10). There are observations removed from traditional narratorial objectivity, including "As is always the case, the soul recognized things the mind refused to see" (p. 17), "Nothing makes a goddess human like seeing her tipping back a bottle of beer" (p. 19), and "Of course he was right" (p. 20). Here as elsewhere in the novel the narrative point of view can be objective, intrusive, or participating in an indirect discourse appropriate to the character in point. As Arnold and Cathy Davidson remark, "The shifting I-voice and the playful omniscience of the narrator results in a continuous counter-pointing of oblique views."[15]

The break-up of Lucy and Paleologue, after he has sold his first poem, has its own style, an over-romantic fevered immaturity: "A kiss good-night, good-bye oh my pale Lucy, pale Lucia, light and airy, brave love, from the doorway she lifts her head and gazes into my eyes . . ." (p. 30). Paleologue's resolution that "I will not perform for them any longer" (p. 30) suggests his turn to maturity and self-containment, despite his conventional spurned-lover gesture, "I will sleep in the harbour" (p. 30) — from which, we learn in a later story, "Were there flowers in the hair of the girl who danced on his grave in the morning?", Grilse rescues him. Paleologue's is the final romantic excess in a story of opposites, where the love of Gould and Rachel — as related subsequently in the novel — is, with their understanding of each other and their disagreements, a model of the ordinary.

The next story, "Nora Noon," focuses on the self-realization of Nora, a grey girl in dress and personality whose "metabolism was too low to let her see high frequency colours" (p. 33). She is gentle and torpid; but Naseby, whose activities with pornographic films are here anticipated, buys her sexually fetishist garments and makes her popular as the epitome of "poignant prurience" (p. 34). Nora is made into what she is not, but still her identity is passive and undifferentiated; she has a curiously dissociated existence, even when being raped by Gould. Her inner life is limited to a cryptic image of three figures in a cave, which may be seen as her unrealized potential; when, much later, she sees a drawing by Henry Moore, "Figures in a Cave," her reaction — blinking and shrugging — shows her distance from her younger absence of firm individuality, from any externalization of personality. Significantly, her inner figures have lost their obsessive hold as she has become engaged with the world.

Nora has met Roger Portable, a well-spoken devotee of politeness, perhaps the substance of Nora's figures as monitors or super-ego.

117

Moreover, as "the man who had forgotten his own name" (p. 41), he suited her in that she only fully finds her own identity at a later time. The narrative treats the eccentric Portable jokingly, and the story, advancing to the present of Nora and Paleologue, also ends with a corny joke:

> "It's funny how time passes," she said.
> "You can say that again."
> "It's funny how time passes," she said. (p. 43)

Such banality and literalism are the life Nora has achieved: full, acceptable, unharried, and ordinary.

Paleologue, meeting Nora on a train (on a visit subsequently mentioned in "Break-up: From the Journals of Ti-Paulo" and in "Were there flowers . . . ?"), sees that she is now "calm and touching in repose" (p. 39), a woman who has assumed a full rightful identity. The time of her life is no longer poised at midday; it is now Nora's after-Noon. She has taught in Africa, though feeling incomplete; she has studied with Ti-Paulo, who has promised that " 'you will learn solutions' " (p. 40). The training was important to Nora, for she was taken seriously by the painter, and she appreciated his practicality and the reality of his life. The day after encountering Paleologue on a train, Nora visits him and Ti-Paulo, and, in a hint of her own recent success as a painter, is said to admire "Ti-Paulo's work in a way that showed she knew about it" (p. 43). Her full, confident, and assured identity is complete.

Nora's story is continued, in time, in "Were there flowers...?", the life story of Grilse, another character with an intangible identity. Nora, we are now told, is a celebrated artist, and one of her works is a metaphorical self-portrait: "a lyrical yellow painting with a hard corner in it" (p. 79). This is what she has developed into: she has found herself, having always been the creature of others and having never been at home with herself. Though as seemingly cryptic as Grilse himself, while as ever she speaks, paradoxically, in banalities, Nora turns out to be his only true intimate and confessor. Nora is an important measure of other characters in the novel, particularly those like Paleologue and Ti-Paulo who gain self-realization, an accommodation with their world.

"Break-up: From the Journals of Ti-Paulo" is a sequence of entries that, like a later diary written by his daughter, "Sarah's Summer Holidays," breaks up the narrative format of *Lord Nelson Tavern*'s other stories. To the painter the sequence memorializes a "woman period" (p. 44) in his artistic career. Each entry has its own title — the purely descriptive, the joking, the private allusion — and the entries suggest a series of portraits, of arrangements. The story of Ti-Paulo's relationship with his model Odile recounts their break-up and his own consequent breakdown; Ti-Paulo is not, apparently, the sexual pirate of his younger days. The vernissage he is having in actuality, when "painters would slap on a new coat of varnish to make the garbage look fresh for the public the next day" (p. 45), describes both his one-man show and his journal, for in both respects "A show is an exhibition of the most painful failures, the ones closest to being successes" (p. 45). As Arnold and Cathy Davidson comment in their attention to this story, "Indeed, the real 'show,' in the chapter, the true vernissage, is not the art show, but the journal itself, self-consciously literary with its numerous references to Shakespeare, its exhibition of love's labours lost."[16] An ambiguity remains: is Ti-Paulo's vernissage or his journal the true gloss on his life?

As an artist Ti-Paulo has an essential purity of commitment and direction; he rejects the logistics, the confusing associations, and the details required by the external world in which his work takes place. He is "getting to painting again by the back door" (p. 48) of drawing. One journal entry, "The thing itself," reveals the fundamental excremental Naseby — " 'Repulsion is his big line' " (p. 49); the title of another entry, "Painting the town red," is a clichéd expression for an evening with Paleologue and Gussie, but from a painter the entry is a self-contained portrait. "After 1.P-K4, White's game is in its last throes" (p. 53) is a conscious metaphorical analogy. Ti-Paulo's "crippled notes" (p. 55) contrast with the epiphany he experiences of Odile's total harmony and presence: "I saw the perfection of her and saw also that it was not for me" (p. 54), he admits, knowing his game has been checkmated by her furtive involvement with Naseby. In "An incident with my father" each man — and the father's new inamorata, Lucy — enacts what are performances, actions that protect the individual from a full range of feeling.

As the loss of Odile preys on him — "Ti-Paulo in the old days: Mean. Tough. Proud" (p. 61) — he recognizes in "Quiddity" that his

119

feelings are competing with logic, and that his work is balked by Odile's imminent departure. "Good time to get back to pattern, design, simple colours, lay off the metaphysics. Good basic stuff" (p. 65). He realizes that he cannot replace a human being, and that the aftermath is his self-lacerating emotional punishment. Ti-Paulo's journal records his change, some loss of self-centeredness, through this relationship, a profound involvement with another and with himself, as a self-portrait; it reflects the personal influence he had on the life of Nora Noon and looks forward to his relationship with Rachel in the story "Family Lives."

In "Were there flowers in the hair of the girl who danced on his grave in the morning?", which Douglas Barbour has studied in some detail,[17] John Grilse only achieves a belated identity, like Nora Noon, and many of the episodes that structure this story insist on his featurelessness. He is "a master at dealing with curiosity" (p. 74); his peripatetic existence and mysterious activities in the drug trade — which result in his being murdered twice — reduce Paleologue and Gould at one point to drawing arch literary parallels. Grilse is seen in terms of both Shakespeare's "Sonnet 129" and Conrad's Lord Jim, thereby establishing the central problem of Grilse's 'real' or fabricated life. Paleologue considers "the problem of meaning in action" (p. 73) which is essential to the character of Grilse, for neither specific meaning nor action can be attributed to him. Paleologue concludes with the equal impossibility of assigning even an archetypal status to him: " 'Quest . . . Traveller . . . Haunted Man . . . Bah!' " (p. 73)

Grilse is the man who wasn't there. Institutions lose or erase his identity; and he himself, though knowing, is minimally responsive. In Paris he lives with a girl surrounded by mirrors, is gunned down, and nonchalantly reappears, claiming to have managed the apparent slaughter " 'with mirrors' " (p. 79) — a familiar allusion to the traditional explanation for a magician's expertise but also, through Smith's typical narrative play, to Grilse's former lover's fetish. The narrator here blithely highlights the whole thriller atmosphere of this stage of Grilse's life: his supposed murder is strongly reminiscent of Graham Greene's *The Third Man* and the elusive drug-dealing Harry Lime, whose first death was also fabricated; the murderers' abandoned car was registered to "J. Maigret," Georges Simenon's famous detective.

Ironically, it is the formerly characterless and now famous Nora

120

Noon to whom Grilse, in self-deprecating understatement, unburdens himself as " 'just a quiet nobody, same as the next man' " (p. 80). Nora responds in clichés which capture Grilse's central ambiguity:

> "But it's funny, isn't it, how you start things expecting one thing and you get something else from them. You really can't tell, can you. Things just work themselves out. This way for some people, that way for others." (p. 81)

When in the story's next episode Paleologue says to Grilse, " 'You are a wreck, you look ready for the grave' " (p. 83), it is to become less a figure of speech than literally true. Grilse's own concern is with Paleologue's achieved life, after they eulogize Nora; he envies the other's certainty of place, and bitterly condemns his own life. Just prior to his real death Grilse snarls, " 'Famous people: what do you have to do with life?' " (p. 87). Yet in these scenes with Nora and Paleologue, in these two moving instances of confession and true reflection, the character of Grilse achieves through his voice a real dimension of personality that had never been his.

In this story, too, the narrative acquires an unashamed degree of literary play. For example, at an early stage in the fiction Paleologue imagines, as a jest, Dimitri, Francesca, and Grilse conversing by saying nothing:

> The truth is that as Paleologue was having his joke, Grilse was with Dimitri and Francesca and what was going on was much as described. *This could not be true! People must talk, surely?*
>
> Indeed yes . . . . (p. 69)

Smith takes complete liberty with the form of the fiction: invention and life are treated as identical, an anonymous voice is allowed an interjection, and the narrative voice responds and puts the truth in another literary form, a brief dramatic scene with few words or sounds and mostly stage directions. Similarly, in the description of Grilse's appearance when Paleologue attempts a romantic suicide, the narrator's rhetorical question and intrusion dictate the language of the character's response:

> What was to be the explanation of the time he would turn up on the wharf at five in the morning to pull Paleologue, gibbering and sputter-

ing, the silly bugger, from the harbour?
        "Come out of there, you silly bugger." (p. 70)

As a result, any illusion of the objectivity of fiction is interrupted.

There are related instances of freedoms with conventional narrative practice. The provocative title of the story is answered affirmatively — "Yes, there were flowers . . . " (p. 89) — as Dimitri and Francesca, whom Paleologue sees as "Poetry girl, for sure" (p. 89), perform their affected, ritualistic farewell to Grilse with dance, champagne, and a cigar. But this rhetorical answer is counterpointed by Grilse's previous acknowledgement of Nora: " ' 'Damn it, P., she was a real woman, not some girl in flowing robes running through the fields with flowers in her hair, not some damn poetry girl' " (p. 87). Francesca and Nora, here joined only superficially by poetry and flowers, remain radically contrasted, the unreal perfection of the one balanced by the successful struggle to become truly individual in the other. The perspectives of Paleologue and Grilse on the girls are also in direct contrast, though this, to further the irony, offsets the beginning of the story: "Paleologue wrote a sonnet sequence around John Grilse and the poems were counted among the best of his early work" (p. 68). This work "pleased him immensely but . . . did not really catch Grilse, had not tried to catch him though he was the subject" (p. 71): in this way the permutations of real, possible, or ambivalent identity multiply. Grilse's final death is his real one; like his confession to Nora, the first evidence of real feeling in him, his life at its end becomes authentic. And yet, as a final irony, Grilse is ultimately celebrated as artifice, through Dimitri and Francesca's graveside ceremonial and through Paleologue's artistic rendition.

Like "Break-up: From the Journals of Ti-Paulo," "Sarah's Summer Holidays" is a personal literary form, a diary which records the visit of Rachel's pubescent daughter to Paleologue and Gussie's farmhouse. The story considerably precedes Grilse's death, part of what Douglas Barbour has called "the shifty nature of time in these stories,"[18] as Smith continually advances, reverses, or conflates the linear order of conventional narrative time. Sarah's diary is a self-conscious medium; she is appropriately strong-willed, precocious, articulate, and a precisionist: "I said I thought it was mean of Paleologue to make up things and not say they were made up. I mean, it makes a difference whether something is true or not'' (p. 94). Sarah's summer experiences are a learning process; she is a literalist who begins to succumb to the imprecision of the country. She learns that there are distinctions of story and truths in fictions. She beings to draw away from her scornful deprecation of her schoolmates and parents, particularly Rachel, who is dismissed as ''a sentimental fool'' (p. 109). Sarah's waspish analyses are cool; even her bare-breasted temptation of Paleologue commences as ''a limited experiment in human biology'' (p. 108). Her continual testing of her own reactions has some intellectual distance: ''I notice I am becoming quite amusing about it all: it was not amusing at the time'' (p. 111). Her sophistication, however, can be cruel, and her inability, unlike Ti-Paulo in the earlier journal-type story, to suffer the too-human is at once likable and pitiable.

The last entry of Sarah's diary, recording what she believes to be her seduction of Paleologue, is addressed to Sarah's thirty-three-year-old self, wishing her frequent happy copulation. More importantly, through her experience of the natural and unaffected Gussie and Paleologue, Sarah grows into something less forbiddingly academic and more female, much as she has absorbed the natural environment. Her thirteen-year-old sexual enthusiasm — ''Fucked till my eyes rolled and I'm not even regular yet'' (p. 119) — will, however, have an inverse effect in the next story, ''Family Lives'': one of her diary observations, ''Any psychology book will tell you about the dangers of sexual precocity'' (p. 108), is ironic before the fact of her defloration, and more so in the light of her forthcoming indiscriminate sexual career.

''Family Lives'' ranges from before Sarah's conception to her becoming, at thirty-three, the person she never has been. The family in point is that of Gould, Rachel, and, after Rachel's impregnation by Ti-Paulo, Sarah. What in effect Sarah will learn from Paleologue and Gussie is anticipated in Rachel's confession to the painter, '' 'It feels so wonderful to be here, the swimming, the sun, it feels like my body is. . . breathing again' '' (p. 124). Rachel's long monologue, a confession of schoolgirl suffering until her physical style came into fashion, stresses the idea of self-realization that is repeated throughout the novel.

An apparently disconnected episode in this story begins with Paleologue's junked poem ''about the predictability of individuals'' (p. 134) and Gussie's silent mouthing of his predictable lecture on paradox and its refutation. The amusement, however, does not conceal the operation of these concepts in the fiction: characters behave predictably as the reader now expects them to behave, but their interactions, in general terms, also may become paradoxical when such expected behaviour is not forthcoming. The paradox in "Family Lives" is centred on Naseby's predictably gross nature, his lack of effect upon the grown and jaded Sarah, and the conventional resolution of the family's disharmony.

Sarah's marriage at nineteen to Boden Rastuble permits the introduction of a purely zany detail: "Rastuble was the sole issue from a marriage between a Bombay brothel keeper and an eight-foot-tall Arizona cowgirl named Mickey" (p. 138). But Rastuble represents Sarah's notorious "weakness for poets" (p. 138), an obsessive legacy from Paleologue that requires resolution. The dangerous results of Sarah's sexual precocity are realized in her loose behaviour, her loneliness, her abuse of Rachel, and her complaint that " 'nobody has ever understood...' " (p. 140). Her confrontation by Naseby symbolizes the depth to which her spirit has sunk. He vulgarizes Sarah's and Rachel's sexual qualities, and exposes Sarah to an absolute devaluation of herself. He poisons her idea of Paleologue, his supposed informant: " 'Yes, it was one of them told me about you, gave me the low-down, can't get much lower than you've been...' " (p. 143).

The splendidly vile Naseby, however, acts as purgative and catharsis for the prodigal daughter: Sarah becomes momentarily insane and has a symbolic vision of a crumbling cathedral. The collapse of what she had worshipped and what she had constructed about herself is complete: "Every excuse, every evasion disappeared" (p. 145). In an extension of her vision Sarah inadvertently kills Naseby and then goes to her apartment where she takes out the diary of "Sarah's Summer Holidays." It becomes the talisman, the touchstone of a more innocent uncorrupted girl, and Sarah subsequently returns home, chastened, to Gould and Rachel, their child really for the first time. The story's final scene represents just that sentimentality which her life has rejected, caring and feeling; one might say that this dramatic reversal is predictable, as fiction of sentiment, and paradoxical, in that Naseby's foulness ultimately cleanses.

In "Were there flowers . . . ?" Grilse enviously commended Paleologue on

"The virtue of your acts. You've been too good to be true. Good artist, good husband: when do you find those two together? You have been the

124

best of several people. You have no faults. And the horrible thing is you're still human. It's disgusting." (p. 83)

Such is the premise of *Lord Nelson Tavern*'s final story, "Walk" — "an idyllic coda,"[19] as Lawrence Garber terms it — which features the true and enduring love of Paleologue and Gussie. As the elderly couple walks across "the fields of light" (p. 148) in winter, the range of their humanity is accented almost lovingly. Even Paleologue's careful work on his property is a metaphorical extension of his role as poet — the story is almost consistently parabolic — despite his disbelief in any sort of permanence. For Gussie, "Together, he was the landscape in which she walked and all the people she met there" (p. 154). Their existence is liberal, mature, and generous; they are completely harmonic individuals. They can talk profoundly and metaphysically, and this is a benefit of their life-core understanding. In their leisurely and sure stroll across their landscape the narrator, here unobtrusive but respectful and sympathetic, translates their activity into metaphor: "Gussie and Paleologue kept moving; in their lives they always kept moving. No one had ever locked either of them in a closet" (p. 156).

The living success of this couple, its human ideal, is directly contrasted to another reality:

> Get up in the morning, pull on yesterday's clothes, instant coffee in a dirty cup, smoke a cigarette. In other times, other places, Gussie's acting, his poetry, failed: she became a whore, a druggie, he died young of disease and failure. But those were other places, other times.

This is the other side of the conventional, perhaps fictional, coin; while the passage toys with both social reality as well as with imagined types, the whole tone of "Walk" and the extraordinary depth of its characters counters this unpleasant imagining. The story's last scene on a train — Ti-Paulo noted earlier that "P. has some sort of fascination with train trips. I suppose that says something for him" (p. 45) — reveals the undying romance of Gussie and Paleologue, who delivers an under-table stimulation to her, a private experience in public. This final image is not simply erotic; it is rather one easily appreciated as standing for their lives, never still, fulfilled in every respect.

Such a commentary as the preceding can only hint at Ray Smith's control of character, of detail, and of narrative styles — as Stephen

Scobie has written, "one's primary response to Smith is to the glittering surface of the writing."[20] His gallery, in its depths and shallows, is carefully arranged beneath the novel's stylistic freedoms and narrative familiarities — to Douglas Barbour, "fictions which participate in the chaos of life rather than offering an ordered vision of it."[21] Yet the artistic orderliness is unmistakable. The most extreme of Smith's individuals, if lacking in dimension, are memorable through the quality of their eccentricity or excess; the others achieve a range of personality through a process of incremental addition and development. And — it must not be overlooked — Ray Smith, like Raymond Fraser, is a story-teller; Fraser achieves his effects through the fundamentally aural appeal of identifiable, uncomplicated types, while Smith's fictions interrelate in the mind's ear through overlays of different perspectives. It is the manner of these voices within the tavern caught that is their true measure.

Notes

[1]John Metcalf, "Telling Tales," in his *Kicking Against the Pricks* (Downsview, Ont.: ECW, 1982), p. 65; rpt. (revised) in *The Montreal Story Tellers: Memoirs, Photographs, Critical Essays*, ed. J.R. (Tim) Struthers.

[2]In a Letter to J.R. (Tim) Struthers, 6 June 1984, Raymond Fraser explains, "Newbridge is Bannonbridge is Chatham, a town six miles down the Miramichi River from Newcastle. The Black Horse tavern on the cover of the book of stories is in Newcastle, but I wasn't writing about it. The tavern in Chatham is called the Ambassador."

[3]Raymond Fraser, *The Black Horse Tavern* (Montreal: Ingluvin, 1972), p. 117. All further references to this work appear in the text.

[4]Linda Shohet, "Maritime Mishaps," rev. of *The Black Horse Tavern*, by Raymond Fraser, *Canadian Literature*, No. 62 (Fall 1974), p. 108.

[5]John Barth, "The Literature of Exhaustion," *The Atlantic Monthly*, Aug. 1967, pp. 29-34.

[6]"They Come Here to Die" was incorporated into Fraser's novel *The Bannonbridge Musicians* (1978), where the narrator and the narrative were more consistently informal and coarse, though the fundamental distinction of tones was preserved.

[7]Shohet, p. 107.

[8]Clare McCulloch, "Writers, Pearls and Oysters," rev. of *The Black Horse Tavern*, by Raymond Fraser, *Journal of Canadian Fiction*, 2, No. 4 (Fall 1973), pp. 106-07.

[9]Arnold E. Davidson and Cathy N. Davidson, "Vernissage: Ray Smith and the Fine Art of Glossing Over," *Canadian Literature*, No. 92 (Spring 1982), p. 60.

[10]Barbara Godard, "Ray Smith's Tavern," rev. of *Lord Nelson Tavern*, by Ray Smith, *Open Letter*, Ser. 3, No. 2 (Spring 1975), p. 121.

[11]Douglas Barbour, "Ray Smith: Some Approaches to the Entrances of *Lord Nelson Tavern*," *Open Letter*, Ser. 3, No. 5 (Summer 1976), p. 55.

[12]Lawrence Garber, "Exploring Ray Smith's Labyrinth," rev. of *Lord Nelson Tavern*, by Ray Smith, *Books in Canada*, June-July 1974, p. 17.

[13]Godard, p. 122.

[14]Ray Smith, *Lord Nelson Tavern* (Toronto: McClelland and Stewart, 1974), p. 10. All further references to this work appear in the text.

[15]Davidson and Davidson, p. 67.

[16]Davidson and Davidson, p. 61.

[17]See Barbour, pp. 57-62.

[18]Barbour, p. 56.

[19]Garber, p. 16.

[20]Stephen Scobie, rev. of *Lord Nelson Tavern*, by Ray Smith, *The Dalhousie Review*, 54 (Summer 1974), 372.

[21]Barbour, p. 58.

Barry Cameron
POINTS OF REFERENCE:
APPROACHING CLARK BLAISE

"I'm a kind of tropical tree with an awful lot of shallow roots and I can easily be blown over. On the other hand, I can survive a lot of changes. I adapt very easily to just about anything around me"[1] — Clark Blaise speaking of the double-edged legacy bequeathed to him by his wandering parents: a sense of ultimate rootlessness coupled with a positive ability to adapt, a sense of vulnerability coupled with an instinct to survive. Blaise was born on 10 April 1940, in Fargo, North Dakota (from which he moved six months after birth), to Canadian parents — his mother, English Canadian from Manitoba and his father, French Canadian from Quebec — who had come to the United States in search of the American ideal of success.[2] Because his father's career as an itinerant furniture salesman took him there, Blaise spent a part of his childhood in the Deep South of Alabama and Georgia, but most of it in central Florida.[3] According to the dust-jacket of *A North American Education: A Book of Short Fiction* (1973), Blaise's first book, he "attended twenty-five schools" during this period of time. That fact alone, if one were seeking direct autobiographical influences on Blaise's work, might account for the predominance of alienation and dislocation as psychological and metaphoric motifs in his fiction.

Blaise's childhood, particularly in Florida, gave him his first apprehension of "a continuity between the moral and the physical,"[4] a perception that would be re-experienced and deepened when he moved to Montreal. Landscape and cityscape are, as John Metcalf has said (Metcalf, p. 77), moral landscapes in Blaise's fiction. Setting in a Blaise story, down to the minutest detail, is consistently metaphoric, often synecdochic, correlative in a variety of ways to the human "action" of

128

the story. For Blaise, as for many other writers, the South as a region and Montreal as a city " . . . are places where setting is not merely an excuse, but where setting is in fact the mystery and the manner" (Metcalf, p. 78). In an interview with Geoff Hancock, Blaise speaks revealingly of the formative quality of his Florida experience:

> . . . Florida was physically, morally and historically an apt place for me: I exploited it ruthlessly and it exploited me in turn. It was a location (thinking back now to the still-rural, Deep South Florida of the mid- and late-40's) that was made for the hounding out of some central worm-like creature in myself.
>
> Florida was foreign to everything in my nature. It was a brutal confrontation, but it was physically so interesting and physically so unforgettable that it linked up forever a notion of nature, of water, of solitariness, and a kind of harshness that I lost myself in for hours every day.
>
> . . . in Florida. . . you literally passed through a wall at seven in the morning and came back at dusk and were out in it all day walking through jungle and water and you never felt as though you were in particular danger. Yet you were always seeing things that were dead or dying, or crawling up from the mud or down from the trees. You saw putrefaction, you saw the tropical world in which all the processes are speeded up and [in] which the chain of exploitation is just so much more vivid than it is up here.
>
> So I was the beneficiary of that and later on. . . I came to see the social and historical and economic analogues to that kind of nature. The myth was laid down for me pretty early, and it was a matter of feeding into the myth with plots and psychologies and characters.[5] (Hancock, p. 48)

After spending 1950 and 1951 in Winnipeg, to which he had moved from Florida, Blaise moved to the American Midwest, living for some time in Springfield, Missouri, and Cincinnati, Ohio, and then in 1953 settling in Pittsburgh, Pennsylvania, where he attended high school.[6] In 1957 he went to Denison University in Granville, Ohio, where he first majored in Geology and then, after eight months out of university, switched his major to English. It was during this period that Blaise first began to write intensely and to read "serious" fiction:

> In the eight months I was out of school I read never less than a book a day, and often two or three. Nothing heavy; I was still courting facts, and the only writers I really valued were those who described experiences, appearances, or states of mind that I knew to be true. Theodore Dreiser, Sinclair Lewis, and Thomas Wolfe were obvious

early favourites; they reaffirmed the helplessness I felt; the venality of my petty-bourgeois surroundings, and the noble calling of "writer." At the close of that period I discovered the French: Flaubert (not of *Madame Bovary*, but of *The Sentimental Education*), Alain-Fournier's *Le Grand Meaulnes*, Zola, Céline and Stendhal. I even liked Camus, something I would now avoid. . . . Lawrence and especially Faulkner became even more important. . . "influential". . . since I had begun to write by then, out of the same desire to capture moments of myth acting through nature, as Lawrence had, and to capture as intensely as Faulkner did the palpability of time-passing in a geographical and historical milieu that I too knew very well. Thomas Mann had been with me from the beginning.[7]

After graduation from Denison with a B.A. in 1961, Blaise went to Harvard, where he attended Bernard Malamud's class in creative writing.[8] In February 1962 he moved to the University of Iowa Writers' Workshop. At Iowa, he met in 1962 and married in 1963 (during their lunch hour on the first day of the academic year) Bharati Mukherjee, the talented Bengali-Canadian novelist of *The Tiger's Daughter* (1972) and *Wife* (1975). The Iowa experience was important for Blaise, for, like others who attended the Workshop in the sixties,[9] Blaise learned "a sense of obligation to craft and community and standards and articulateness about aims" (Metcalf, p. 77).

After graduation from Iowa in 1964 with an M.F.A. — his thesis for which was a story collection entitled "Thibidault et Fils" — Blaise taught at the University of Wisconsin in Milwaukee; but because he had "dreamed restless dreams of Canada, especially of Montreal," and because "he felt it was the place that would let him be himself,"[10] he emigrated to Montreal in 1966 and became a Canadian citizen in 1973. Except for sabbaticals in India in 1973-74, and 1976-77, Blaise remained in Montreal for twelve years, teaching modern fiction and creative writing at Sir George Williams University (subsequently Concordia University). In 1978, he moved to York University to become a Professor of Humanities; in 1980, he left Toronto to share a teaching position with his wife at Skidmore College in Saratoga Springs, New York;[11] and in 1983, he moved on again to join his wife and two sons — with interruptions for short stints of teaching and reading tours — in Iowa City.

In Montreal, Blaise became part of the "Montreal Story Teller Fiction Performance Group" — to use its official name — which also included John Metcalf, Hugh Hood, Ray Smith, and Raymond Fraser. Metcalf and Hood formed the group in the winter of 1970-71 "to promote Canadian prose to as large an audience as possible by bringing the writers into direct contact with students in high schools, colleges and universities."[12] Because neither the media nor the publishing industry itself seemed to be promoting Canadian literature and because of the "paucity of Canadian literature in high schools and university English courses," Metcalf believed that writers themselves would have "to create and educate an audience for Canadian fiction."[13] The group was forced to disband after a few years[14] but not before it had implicitly proven to the Canada Council, through highly entertaining and instructive performances, that prose readings as well as poetry readings should receive financial support. The struggle to create and educate an audience for Canadian fiction, alas, continues.

The continental range of Blaise's personal history, its culturally disparate quality, is the framework or "shell" — at least until very recently[15] — of his fiction. "Canada, America, French, English, north, south, and a kind of reflective, observant, fat and phlegmatic child" (Hancock, p. 58) — into these "frames" Blaise places his "totally invented" plots:

> If you have a basically passive and observant, fearful child, then you can create vivid, lurid nightmares for him to fall into. If you create the tension of a responsible and respectable mother and irresponsible, unrespectable father, you can create confrontations between them . . . . If you're talking about such vast geographical compass points as Manitoba, Quebec and Florida, you can talk quite legitimately about North America. So I've been quite happy accepting the givens of my life autobiographically but I have not been dependent upon the contents of my own life. . . . if all the things that I've written about had actually happened to me, then I would obviously be a very different person than I am. They are merely all within me. (Hancock, pp. 58-59)

> I've only written of three characters really and that's my mother, my father and myself. I am utterly dependent upon the family situation and the family conflicts as the source of my fiction. Now the "myself" character is sometimes female, sometimes male and the myself character is sometimes acutely analytical and cynically intelligent, and sometimes it's reflectively and passively intelligent, sometimes it's only cynical and worldly and abusive, but all those are within myself and I can as easily be one of them as another. The father character stands as all males, older,

131

with authority, with physical power, with experience, with sexual charm, with confidence, with a fearlessness before the law, with a kind of lawlessness, people who *define*, or, who are continually pushing out against definitions. And my mother-figures are always the ones who are pulling in within definitions, anticipating, so acutely aware of restrictions and anticipating rebuffs, anticipating them so sensitively that you internalize them before you ever do anything. So that is my landscape, my moral landscape.... (Hancock, p. 60)

Blaise began publishing stories in the early sixties in various academic and literary quarterlies, but his most important short fiction (some of it previously published in literary journals) appears in two deliberately constructed "books of short fiction": *A North American Education* (1973), which won the Great Lakes College New Writers' Award, and *Tribal Justice* (1974), which won the St. Lawrence Award for Fiction.[16] *Days and Nights in Calcutta*, a journal based on the experiences of the sabbatical year in India, the first part written by Blaise and the second part by Bharati Mukherjee, with an epilogue by each author, appeared in 1977 and won the "Asia Week" Award. Blaise's fourth book, a novel entitled *Lunar Attractions*, was published in 1979 and won the *Books in Canada* First Novel Award.[17] A second novel, *Lusts*, appeared in 1983. All these books were published simultaneously in Canada and the United States, and *Lunar Attractions* was also published in England.

In a remark quoted earlier, Blaise speaks of the early influence Lawrence and Faulkner exerted on his writing. Like Lawrence, Blaise often attempts "to capture moments of myth acting through nature," or — to expand this notion — as the epigraph from Sartre for "The Thibidault Stories" in *A North American Education* has it, "... to condense into a single mythic moment the contingencies and perpetual rebeginnings of an individual human history."[18] Like Faulkner, Blaise — especially in his fiction set in Florida of the mid- and late-forties — tries to capture "the palpability of time-passing in a geographical and historical milieu."

Several other literary, philosophical, and aesthetic points of reference suggest the directions from which Blaise's fiction is moving. Early in his life, for example, Blaise was affected by the twelve-volume *Collier's Encyclopedia*, especially the biographies, which he read through perhaps twice a year: "... even at nine or ten I could not imagine living a life that would not someday be glorified in the encyclopaedia."[19] Even more significant as a biographical context for such works as *Lunar*

132

Attractions, "The Thibidault Stories," and the story "Grids and Doglegs" in *Tribal Justice* is the atlas:

> There was only one book in my life, at least up to the age of twelve, and that was the Atlas. From it I typed out, at the age of eight and nine, a 120-page compilation of all the salient descriptive facts about the surface of the earth. By six I had known all the state and provincial capitals (thanks to maps my mother had always hung in the kitchens of our Florida apartments); by seven I'd added the world capitals; by eight all cities in the world (1930 census, alas) with over fifty thousand, with their exact population; by nine I knew all the U.S. counties in every state and their county seats, and by ten I had abandoned the known world for world maps and country maps of my own invention, hand-painted with invented mountain ranges, cities, and rivers, all very precisely named in languages of my own invention, with appropriate altitudes and populations. Of course I think of it now as a writer's natural evolution, from passionate but passive observation and unconscious mimicry, through to the creation of a personal mythology.[20]

Yet the literary and philosophical tradition to which Blaise feels the greatest affinity is neither Canadian nor American but what he has called "the discursive tradition," "literature compounded of cold observation *and* subjective passion,"[21] in sensibility if not completely in fact a French tradition: Pascal, Flaubert, Proust, Céline, Mann, and Kerouac, among others.

Blaise feels a strong philosophical-religious kinship with Pascal: Pascal's existentialist tendencies and Jansenist sympathies; his emphasis on the wretchedness and anguish of man without grace, without God; his awareness of the random, accidental quality of life and his sense of the inevitable; and his belief that the ambiguously irrational in man is in fact his "essence" and that reason can only end in doubt and leave unsatisfied our deepest concerns:

> Pascal, that old *Québécois*, would insist that infinity suspends reason and that to cope with the "infinity of things" lying beyond reason requires grace. And if faith or grace is not forthcoming, silence and fear alone are possible. No one raised in the shadows of French Canada is immune to Pascal, no matter in what form or language he might have absorbed him. . . . It is the hint of unfathomable complexity, the insolent infinity that defeats our humanity, that interests me . . . .[22]

Flaubert and Proust appeal to Blaise first of all, I think, because they are romantic paradigms of the dedicated writer: men to whom art seems more valuable than life itself or to whom life is incapable of meaning unless it be in some way transformed or shaped by art. But Blaise also shares much with Flaubert emotionally; and his sensibility is essentially Proustian, albeit in a minor key. In many ways, too, Blaise is just as preoccupied as Proust with the ways in which the past permeates the present and with the implication in Proust's distinction between "voluntary" and "involuntary" memory that we live mechanically in the present, tragically unaware of the essence of our lives. Consider, for example, Blaise's choice of epigraphs from Pascal for "The Montreal Stories" and "The Keeler Stories" in *A North American Education*, epigraphs which function as thematic directives for reading each group of stories, though their application need not be restricted to those groups:

> *So we never live, but we hope to live; and, as we are always preparing to be happy, it is inevitable we should never be so.*
>
> We do not rest satisfied with the present. We anticipate the future as too slow in coming, as if in order to hasten its course; or we recall the past, to stop its too rapid flight. So imprudent are we that we wander in the times which are not ours, and do not think of the only one which belongs to us; and so idle are we that we dream of those times which are no more, and thoughtlessly overlook that which alone exists. (*NAE*, pp. 1, 39)

Blaise has said he would like to be "a dirty saint," a Céline, to smudge his minor Proustian sensibility in a Célinesque way, perhaps to portray, as Céline, the vileness of humanity.[23] Mann is attractive to Blaise for several reasons: Mann's preoccupation with "the other side," with dualities, with antitheses — discipline and passion, spirit and matter, civilization and the primitive, art and life — and with convergences. In addition, like Flaubert and Proust, Mann represents for Blaise a type of the dedicated artist.

Jack Kerouac is in many ways, I think, both Blaise's alter image and his ironic *doppelgänger*: Jean-Louis Lebris de Kérouac, born an American of French-Canadian parents; Kerouac, perversely precocious as a child; Kerouac, sports fan, athlete, and inventor of sports games; Kerouac, that "strange solitary crazy Catholic mystic"; Kerouac, that "madman bum and angel,"[24] another dirty saint of sorts. Kerouac's innovative use of a personalized narrator in *On the Road*, in which he presents himself unequivocally as the one who observed it and wrote it all down, is also a technical tradition out of which Blaise writes. Kerouac's subject-matter in such books as *The Town and the City*, *Dr. Sax*, and *Satori in Paris* reflects some of Blaise's concerns too — Kerouac's search for his roots in Brittany in the last work, for example.

Because they are "texture-workers" like himself, Blaise is attracted to the fiction of John Hawkes, Richard Yates, Tillie Olson, Cynthia Ozick, and Bernard Malamud.[25] Implying "both vitality and unevenness," texture is, for Blaise, "... detail arranged and selected and enhanced. It is the inclusion of detail from several planes of reference: dialogue, fantasy, direct passive observation ('I am a camera'), allusion, psychic wound, symbol, straight fact, etc. etc. — the sum of all that is *voice*" (Metcalf, p. 78). For Blaise, "to present texture and design without distortion" is "the job of fiction";[26] he wants "to view life through a microscope so that every grain gets its due and no one can confuse salt with sugar" (Metcalf, p. 78). Voice, for Blaise, refers to "... the control, what is commonly referred to when we mention the 'world' of a certain author; the limits of probability and chance in his construction, the sanctions he leaves us for our own variations, what we sense of his own final concerns and bafflements" (Metcalf, p. 78). A concept not unlike Wayne Booth's notion of "the implied author,"[27] voice "allows the reader a confidence that he is in a shaping vision with a tone coloration that is different from the actual 'character's'" (Metcalf, p. 78). This distinction is particularly important in Blaise's fiction because so much of it is first-person narration, autobiographical in mode and framework if not, as Blaise has said, in fact. Indeed, voice allows for "the *suggestive* space between quite ordinary facts" (Hancock, p. 52) that distinguishes fiction from other sorts of writing.

Blaise's concern with voice, however, does not imply an interest in "character." The "construction of 'character'" is "an honourable but not necessarily compelling occupation" (Metcalf, p. 78). For Blaise, character is really nothing more than "that force which tries to maintain balance" between the "delicate interplays of action and description"[28] that constitute the essence of story: "The centre of my stories is not in my characters. The centre is elsewhere and so I do not set out to create character. I do not set out to write a psychological case study. I am really trying to talk about ... the world, the nature of event, happenstance, accident, beauty, permanence, change, violence . . . '' (Hancock, p. 59).

It is a matter of texture to select details, then, and a matter of voice to allow for a wider interpretation. To render the texture of a situation, to make the reader experience details in all their particularity and cumulativeness so that a larger and deeper life may be revealed, Blaise must himself experience the depth of that situation, must see, in fact, ''the other side of it'' :

> Unless I feel that I have seen behind the stage (so to speak) or grasped the texture of a given situation, I won't be content simply to say, here's a street, a house, a car, an attractive young couple. . . . I have to have some *other* sense about that street: what is the last thing I can say about this place? Until I've come to that point I'm not interested in rendering any of it. But once I have come into that awareness, then I can't stop from writing it. It simply grips me and that's it, I'm in its full power.
> The first-person narrator is a way of controlling its power by limiting the world outside the self. (Hancock, p. 51)

It is this power and Blaise's unwillingness to let anything intrude on voice that account for the sparseness of dialogue in his stories: ''Dialogue is a terribly inefficient way to set up anything or to impart information. It only works for me as an instance of inadvertence, or pressure released'' (Metcalf, p. 79). He is, however, moving more and more away from first-person; in recent stories Blaise uses third-person: ''Third-person opens up many, many aspects because the tone of voice can be varied'' (Hancock, p. 51). In these new works, Blaise wants ''to link up an individual life with many things outside that life'' (Hancock, p. 51). The most appropriate point of view for this task is third-person because it represents ''a mode of community'' — unlike first-person, which is ''the voice of isolation'' (Hancock, p. 51). Yet language is essentially visual for Blaise: ''Only the word . . . is truly visual''; and consequently when he writes a story, in either first-person or third-person, he *sees* the story ''. . . in terms of its images and situations, the tone and texture and discovery that seems immanent in that situation. . . '' (Metcalf, p. 78).

Given Blaise's aesthetic of texture, the most appropriate way to read any of his stories is according to what he calls ''the slow approach'' : through ''its associations, its 'world' and its minute details'' (Metcalf, p. 77). A Blaise story should be viewed essentially as ''a single metaphor and the exfoliation of a single metaphor through dense layers of submetaphors" (Hancock, p. 56), and in this respect Blaise's stories show their kinship to poetry. As John Metcalf has observed, "The 'plots' of [Blaise's] stories are carried [along] by an unobtrusive chain of images much in the manner of poems" (Metcalf, p. 79), and for Blaise "plot is the revelation of inevitability, the slow disclosure of something beautifully obvious, though hidden" (Hancock, p. 61).

The sense of a Blaise story as poem is reinforced by his theory of the function of first paragraphs and first sentences in fiction. No matter how skilful or elegant the other features of a story may be, the first paragraph should give the reader "confidence in the power and vision of the author."[29] Genesis is more important to Blaise than apocalypse, for a Blaise story is often, if not always, its beginning amplified or expanded:

> The first sentence of a story is an act of faith — or astonishing bravado. A story screams for attention, as it must, for it breaks a silence. It removes the reader from the everyday.... It is an act of perfect rhythmic balance, the single crisp gesture, the drop of the baton that gathers a hundred disparate forces into a single note. The first paragraph is a microcosm of the whole, but in a way that only the whole can reveal....
>
> It is in the first line that the story reveals its kinship to poetry. Not that the line is necessarily "beautiful," merely that it can exist utterly alone, and that its force draws a series of sentences behind it. The line doesn't have to "grab" or "hook" but it should be striking.[30]

Premature first sentences begin where they should end, and casual and *in medias res* openings are just as damaging. An effective first sentence in a story should, as in poetry, imply its opposite:

> If I describe a sunny morning in May... I am also implying the perishing quality of a morning in May, and a good sensuous description of May sets up the possibility of a May disaster. It is the singular quality of that experience that counts. May follows from the sludge of April and leads to the drone of summer, and in a careful story the action will be mindful of May; it must be. May is unstable, treacherous, beguiling, seductive, and whatever experience follows from a first sentence will be, in essence, a story about the May-ness of human affairs.[31]
>
> A writer is always trying to suggest the *other* side of things. He's trying to create a subject and an object, not only the centerpiece but the frame, and sometimes he feeds the frame first and withholds the picture. Other times he gives the picture and withholds the fact that he's going to hang it in the garage next to an old nudie calendar. Sometimes it may be a very beautiful thing to be deliberately destroyed.... It's always a matter of

137

working by indirection and by surprise and by suggestion, which means that everything you state directly has a shadow meaning, implied. (Hancock, p. 54)

Finally, a good first paragraph should tell us, "in effect, that 'this is how things have always been,' or at least, how they have been until the arrival of the story," until the point when "plot intrudes on poetry."[32]

Notes

[1]Geoff Hancock, "An Interview with Clark Blaise," *Canadian Fiction Magazine*, Nos. 34/35 (1980), pp. 47-48. All further references to this work appear in the text.

[2]Blaise's father added an *e* to his name when he moved to the United States. Blaise's parents divorced some twenty years later, and his mother returned to Winnipeg. In 1978, his father, who had remained in the United States, died in Manchester, New Hampshire, while Blaise was writing his novel *Lunar Attractions*. According to Blaise, that novel is indirectly dedicated to his father.

[3]Leesburg, Florida, where Blaise lived for a time, is the fictional Hartley of several of his stories.

[4]John Metcalf, "Interview: Clark Blaise," *Journal of Canadian Fiction*, 2, No. 4 (Fall 1973), 77. All further references to this work appear in the text.

[5]In another interview with Hancock, Blaise says: "The Florida I knew as a child was very wild and untamed, full of nature, poverty, illness, violence, and terror for me" (Geoff Hancock, "Interview: Clark Blaise on Artful Autobiography: 'I who live in dreams am touched by reality,'" *Books in Canada*, March 1979, p. 30).

[6]Pittsburgh is the fictional Palestra of *Lunar Attractions*.

[7]Sandra Martin, "The Book that Changed My Life," *Saturday Night*, May 1976, pp. 34-35.

[8]Malamud's *The Assistant* offered Blaise "a fresh way of telling a story" ("The Book that Changed My Life," p. 35), and *Lunar Attractions* is dedicated to Malamud and his wife.

[9]Among other Canadian writers who have attended the Iowa Writers' Workshop are Dave Godfrey, W.D. Valgardson, Rudy Wiebe, and Kent Thompson.

[10]Bharati Mukherjee, "An Invisible Woman," *Saturday Night*, March 1981, p. 36. 36.

[11]Blaise's move to Skidmore was a complicated issue, but some of the reasons are suggested in his wife's essay cited above. In a letter to me, he says: "I want to go into an eccentric orbit around Canada for the next few years, wobbling in, and out, of focus..." (Letter received from Clark Blaise, 9 June 1980).

[12]Douglas Rollins, "The Montreal Storytellers," *Journal of Canadian Fiction*, 1, No. 2 (Spring 1972), 5.

[13]*Ibid.*, p. 5.

[14]Only Hood and Smith have remained in Montreal. Blaise continued his association with Metcalf by co-editing Oberon's annual anthology *Best Canadian Stories* from 1978 to 1980, and he also co-edited with Metcalf an anthology of short stories for classroom use, *Here & Now: Best Canadian Stories* (Ottawa: Oberon, 1977).

[15]One of Blaise's most recently published fictions, "Man and His World" (*Fiction*

International, No. 12 [1980], pp. 80-90), written in the third person, is a significant stylistic departure from his previous fiction. Another story, "Prying" (*Toronto Life*, March 1982, pp. 38, 87-92), has a woman as its central character and is also in the third person.

[16]One story in *Tribal Justice*, "The Fabulous Eddie Brewster," originally entitled "The Mayor," had won The University of Western Ontario's President's Medal on first publication in *The Tamarack Review* in 1967.

[17]Blaise was justifiably disturbed by the *Books in Canada* judges' grudging recognition of the merits of *Lunar Attractions*. (See "Blaise of Glory: Breaking from a strong field, Clark Blaise gallops home to win the $1,000 purse for the best first novel of 1979," *Books in Canada*, April 1980, pp. 3-4.) Their apparent "passionate embrace of mediocrity" and "distrust of an admittedly professional and (just possibly) a distinguished, or at least accomplished, novel" Blaise sees as a symptom of a larger cultural malaise in Canada:

> The deeper forces hurt anyone who writes seriously in this country, be
> he or she honored or forgotten. The enemy out there is (to be kind) the
> amateur spirit, which translates to a love of mediocrity. And I mean as
> well its necessary corollary: a fear of ambition, an embarrassment with
> excellence. Layton would have called it constipated and masturbatory;
> I'd call it a decayed gentility, others might excuse it as a neo-colonialism.
> The point is, no one escapes it. (Clark Blaise, "The Truth Is: We Are
> All Laytons," The Mermaid Inn, *The Globe and Mail*, 3 May 1980,
> Sec. 1, p. 6)

[18]Clark Blaise, *A North American Education: A Book of Short Fiction* (Toronto: Doubleday, 1973), p. 131. All further references to this work appear in the text.

[19]"The Book that Changed My Life," p. 34.

[20]*Ibid.*

[21]Clark Blaise, "Author's Introduction," *New Canadian Writing, 1968: Stories by David Lewis Stein, Clark Blaise and Dave Godfrey* (Toronto: Clarke, Irwin, 1968), p. 67.

[22]*Ibid.*, p. 68.

[23]Barry Cameron, "A Conversation with Clark Blaise," *Essays on Canadian Writing*, No. 23 (Spring 1982), p. 14.

[24]See Jack Kerouac, *The Dharma Bums* (New York: Viking, 1958).

[25]There are other affinities between Blaise and Malamud: both, for example, focus on alienated protagonists and the unfulfilled life.

[26]Clark Blaise, *Days and Nights in Calcutta* (Toronto: Doubleday, 1977), p. 18.

[27]See Wayne Booth, *The Rhetoric of Fiction* (Chicago: Univ. of Chicago Press, 1961).

[28]Clark Blaise, "To Begin, to Begin," in *The Narrative Voice: Short Stories and Reflections by Canadian Authors*, ed. John Metcalf (Toronto: McGraw-Hill Ryerson, 1972), p. 26.

[29]*Ibid.*, p. 24.

[30]*Ibid.*, p. 22.

[31]*Ibid.*, p. 23.

[32]*Ibid.*, pp. 24-25.

Michael Darling
THE PSYCHOLOGY OF ALIENATION: CLARK BLAISE'S "THE SALESMAN'S SON GROWS OLDER"

Clark Blaise's "The Salesman's Son Grows Older" was collected in his first book, *A North American Education* (1973), and subsequently chosen by Blaise and John Metcalf to represent his work in their well-known anthology *Here & Now: Best Canadian Stories* (1977). The story is indeed typical of Blaise's best work in its sensitive use of the double narrative voice, in which the speaker's point of view is simultaneously that of adult and child. More importantly, the story is also typical of Blaise's work in its precise and often disturbing exploration of the psychology of alienation. In attempting to come to terms with his adult self, the narrator, Franklin Thibidault, reviews the major events of his childhood which have led to his present state of exile, immaturity, and paralysis. His inability to free himself from the dubious heritage of a salesman's son is indicated by the powerful force of memory that draws him inexorably back into his past.

The narrator's recollections are prompted by sensory impressions that link present and past situations. Sounds in the present remind him of sounds from twenty and five years ago, bringing them to life again:

> This long afternoon and evening, I closed my eyes and heard sounds of my childhood: the skipping rope slaps a dusty street in a warm southern twilight .... *Slap, slap*, a girl strains forward with her nose and shoulders, lets the rope *slap, slap, slap*, as she catches the rhythm before jumping in ....
> All day the slap, slap. The rope in a dusty yard, a little pit between the girls who turn it. As I walked today in another climate, now a man, I heard boots skipping on a wet city pavement, a girl running with her lover, a girl in a maxi-coat on a Montreal street. *Tschip-tschip*: I'd been listening for it, boots on sand over a layer of ice. A taxi waited at the cor-

ner, its wipers thrashing as the engine throbbed. And tonight, over the shallow breathing of my son, an aluminum shovel strikes the concrete, under new snow.[1]

Even though these images are not mentioned until near the end of the story, it is these visual and auditory memories which actually begin the narrator's journey backward in time. The snow and the sound of the shovel on concrete take him back five years to a time when he received a summons and a twenty-dollar fine for having an unshovelled walk. The policeman of that five-year-old memory leads him back to the policeman of twenty years ago, whose message led to the narrator's first return to Canada, the land of his birth. The similarity of the *slap, slap* and *Tschip-tschip* sounds links the present with the past of five years and twenty years ago and provides a rationale for the sensory memories that have been evoked throughout the narration:

> The smell of a summer night in Florida is so strong that twenty years later on a snowy night in Canada I can still feel it. (p. 143)

The ending of the story neatly ties up the threads of memory and provides the reader with adequate reasons why a particular summer night in Florida should be recalled twenty years later on a snowy night in Montreal. This strategy also encourages the reader to look for a parallel or contrast between the narrator's childhood and that of his son, over whose sleeping form he broods as he tells his story. If the meaning of his narration is that for him many things have gone for good, then the reader might expect the option left to his son to involve better possibilities, that certain failures or unhappy experiences of the narrator's childhood have given him the knowledge that will prevent their repetition in the life of his son. But if the narrator is aware of the obvious parallel between his son's fate and his own, he seems powerless to prevent the recurrence of the pattern of exile and return that has left him straddling the borders of identity.

The first thing that Franklin establishes about his childhood is his precocious maturity. As a salesman's son, he differs from other children in that his privileges can also be seen as responsibilities: "staying up late, keeping my mother company, being her confidant, behaving even at eight a good ten years older" (pp.142-43). When the policeman arrives with the news of his father's car accident, the boy takes over from

141

his mother, opening the door and windows, and turning on the lights. He knows that when the neighbours leave, his mother will require his support:

> She would cry as soon as they left and I would have to pretend to be asleep, or else go out and comfort her, bring her tea and listen to her; be a salesman's son. (p. 147)

Being a salesman's son also enables him to acquire an unchildlike knowledge of maps and atlases, the mileage and the time required to drive from one city to another. It is not surprising that the old atlas holds such fascination for him, as it is a refuge from the real world in which he has no chance to distinguish himself in the ordinary children's games like kick-the-can or in the performance of chores on a farm. The constant uprootings occasioned by his father's profession have made him a perpetual alien. As the child of northern parents, he has nothing in common with his Floridian playmates, yet his accent and mannerisms also separate him from his Canadian cousins. Even the climate is unkind to him: in Florida, he sweats; in Saskatchewan, he suffers from the "dry, burning heat" (p. 153).

Two parallel incidents function as "signs of foreignness" (p. 151) for the narrator, each establishing an apparent link between death and sexuality.[2] While staying at the home of a neighbour, Miz Davis, Frankie develops a cough in the night, and when Miz Davis comes to tend to him, her breast works free of her robe. As she forces a mixture of sugar and kerosene down his throat, he reaches for her breast, the first one he has ever seen:

> I knew if I was dying there was one thing I wanted to do; I brought my open hand against the palm-numbing softness of her breast, then, for an instant ran my fingertips over the hard, dry nipple and shafts of prickly hair. She acted as though nothing had happened and I looked innocent as though nothing had been intended. (p. 148)

Some time later, in a Saskatoon classroom, a similarly bizarre incident occurs. Frankie has special permission to use a fancy ball-point pen which is the envy of all his classmates. It features "the head and enormous black hat of Hopalong Cassidy" (p. 156). It is this strange object, prone to leakage, that Frankie is sucking on when his teacher notices

142

blue saliva smeared over his face and thinks he must be choking:

> I was thrown to the floor and when I opened my mouth to shout, the surrounding girls screamed. Then the teacher was upon me, cramming her fingers down my throat, two fingers when the first didn't help, and she pumped my head from the back with her other hand. (pp. 156-57)

The narrator himself associates this incident with his previous encounter with Miz Davis: "What was her name — that second woman who had crammed something down my throat?" (p. 157) In both cases, Frankie imagines that he is dying, and in both there are clear sexual implications in the pattern of the 'assault'. In both, death proves to be an illusion, a romantic promise unfulfilled, and sex, something furtive and grotesque. And both are related to his father's car accident, the first occurring while his mother is visiting her husband in the hospital, the second immediately before Frankie runs home to learn that his father did not die in an accident, but that he had been with another woman. Again, a romanticized death is denied, and the reality of sex proves to be illicit and secretive.

What kind of man would juxtapose such memories as important events in his life? Only a man painfully aware of his inability to live free from guilt, self-consciousness, and alienation. But what Franklin Thibidault wants from life, he tells us, is not just a secure identity; he also wants power and the respect of others. His assumption that his father is dead gives him a temporary superiority to his southern playmates, who treat him "for a day or two with a deference, a near sympathy... that I'd been seeking all along and probably ever since" (p. 149).

When he is unable to keep up with his Canadian cousins, the Blankenships, Frankie finds his security in old magazines, his identity in isolation, his happiness in shooting defenceless animals:

> During the summer I spent hot afternoons firing at gophers as they popped from their holes. Fat boy with a gun, squinting over the wheat through July and August, the combine harvesting the beaten rows, months after believing my father dead, and happy. As happy as I've ever been. (pp. 153-54)

This is no more than an illusion of power, of course. Frankie's resentment of his cousins is at least in part an acknowledgement of his failure to wield any kind of power in the real world or to show any signs of conventional success. It is his aversion to hard work rather than any moral principles he holds that has made it impossible for him to be ''a bloody Blankenship with crinkles and crow's-feet at twenty-five'' (p. 155).

As a professor, the narrator might have valued his heritage of bilingualism and biculturalism, but instead he deplores his lack of a stable identity:

> What calamity made me a reader of back issues, defunct Atlases, and foreign grammars? The loss, the loss! To leave Montreal for places like Georgia and Florida; to leave Florida for Saskatchewan; to leave the prairies for places like Cincinnati and Pittsburgh and, finally, to stumble back to Montreal a middle-class American from a broken home, after years of pointless suffering had promised so much. (p. 155)

The narrator concludes that it is far better to be a professor's son than a salesman's son. But the benefits he imagines his offspring to possess seem relatively trivial—skiing or swimming at a summer cottage. In fact, the narrator is depriving his son of his rightful heritage by repeating his parents' pattern of flight and self-imposed exile. The parallel between his son's life and his own is clearly set out by the narrator; but although he apparently understands how he has predetermined his son's fate, he is unable to break the pattern imposed by his own parents:

> Five years ago, when he was six months old, we left to take a bad job in Montreal, where I was born but had never visited. My parents had brought me to the U.S. when I was six months old. Canada was at war, America was neutral. America meant opportunity, freedom; Montreal meant ghettos, and insults. And so, loving our children, we murder them. Following the sun, the dollars, the peace-of-mind, we blind ourselves. (p. 155)

By the end of the story, we realize that the reasons for the narrator's move from Wisconsin to Montreal are similar to those of his parents, though the direction is reversed. This time, America is at war, Canada neutral. Franklin has been abused as a ''known agitator'' and harassed by the police. Suddenly, it is Canada that beckons as the land of opportunity. Having taken the option left him by his parents, he imagines that his son will someday exercise a similar option. In fact, he has given his son no choice but to accept an exile imposed upon him or to repatriate himself to a country no longer his own.

The narrator's conclusion, indicating that "many things have gone for good," apparently works with the story's title to reinforce the idea that his failure is a direct result of his father's choice of profession. As a salesman's son, Franklin Thibidault is a displaced person, neither American nor Canadian. At a young age, he has learned the rules of the game, and the mastery of a role. But from whom has he learned the rules? For whom is the game played? No one else but his mother. Despite his self-portrait as a "salesman's son," which tends to deflect the blame for his own failures onto his father, Frankie might be more accurately described as a "salesman's *wife's* son," for in his role as "salesman's son," Frankie says and does little that would reveal the influence of his father's presence. It is the *absence* of the father that has thrust the boy into this role, and in it he functions not as a *son* but as a *confidant* to his mother. It is symbolically appropriate then that the father's French-Canadian name should be metamorphosed in America to T.B. Doe — Mr. Doe, the unidentifiable shadow-figure who has no influence at all on his son.[3] It is from his mother that Frankie has inherited his role-playing ability. When the policeman arrives, she seems to know what has happened and is prepared for the shock. Talking to the neighbour women, she preserves an outward calm and composure, just as she does for much of the exchange with her sister-in-law concerning her husband's infidelity. Her decision to retain the name of Thibidault and to return to her husband is as much an acceptance of the role of salesman's wife as it is an affirmation of her love for him.

Although Frankie implies that his interest in geography is part of the code of the salesman's son, it is significant nonetheless that the atlas he reads belongs to his mother, not his father:

> That had been my mother's childhood world and it became mine too — cool, confident, and British — and now it seems to me, that all the disruptions in my life and in Mildred Blankenship's have merely been a settling of the old borders, an insurrection of the cool gazetteer with its sultanates, Boer lands, Pondichérys, and Port Arthurs. (p. 150)

Thus, his vision of the world, "distorted by Edwardian lenses" (p. 150), is also a legacy from his mother, and the security promised by the gazetteer is as illusory as its "sultanates" and "princely states," which would have disappeared long before the boy ever began to learn their names. Like the outdated articles he reads in ancient issues of *Collier's* or *National Geographic*, the atlas offers only misinformation — delusions of grandeur past, promises of a future that will never be realized.

The two parallel incidents in which Frankie has something crammed down his throat can now be seen as symbolic representations of the relationship of mother and son. In the first incident, Audrey Davis is a clear surrogate mother, having volunteered to look after Frankie while Mrs. Thibidault goes to visit her husband. As Miz Davis acts out the role of the nursing mother, so Frankie plays the innocent child, a role which he is never allowed to assume when alone with his own mother.

The second mother-substitute in his life is his teacher, a respectable middle-aged lady who seems like a monster to him when she tries to come to his aid:

> For fifty years she had been pale and prim and ever so respectable but I remember her as a hairy-nostriled and badly dentured banshee with fingers poisoned by furtive tobacco. (p. 157)

If the first scene illustrates Frankie's acceptance of a nurturing never given him by his own mother, the second scene emphasizes the horror and repulsion he feels towards the mother-substitute who does violence to his person in attempting to extract from him what he has just been sucking in. Frankie's bewilderment at this attack is suggested by the duality of his rage, directed against both the Canadians who torment him and the "stupid Yank" (p. 157) he sees himself to be. In both scenes, his claim to maturity and independence is undermined by the actions of the older female guardian or teacher, as if to confirm the ability of the mother, through her avatars, to direct the life of her son, to reinforce his position as an actor with no identity of his own, an alien without patrimony.

As further confirmation of the mother's power over her son, it should be noted that his role-playing prevents him from learning the truth about his father's accident until he chances to overhear the conversation between his mother and his Aunt Valerie. At the time, Frankie had not dared to ask his mother what had really happened: "Her mood had been grim and businesslike, the mood a salesman's son learns not to tamper with" (p. 149). His mother can ignore his position as confidant whenever it suits her to do so. By not telling her son the

146

truth, she keeps him from ever really knowing his father, and thus gaining a true sense of his own identity. It is no wonder then that the narrator is able to feel sorry for Aunt Valerie and to say that he understood her better than he did his mother. He seems to recognize that both he and Aunt Valerie have been deceived by Mildred Thibidault.

With a shadowy father and a mother who will not allow him a normal childhood, Frankie cannot move from innocence into experience. His innocence has not been permitted; his experience is second-hand, derived from back issues and defunct atlases. The real experiences of life —love and death—have been denied him by his mother. This interpretation of the text makes clear the paradox with which the narrator ends his story: "I'm still a young man, but many things have gone for good" (p. 161). What has gone for good is not his role as the salesman's son, but the possibility of playing that role without having to acknowledge that the responsibility it confers is illusory. As an adult, he has new responsibilities to face, but his ability to face them has been effectively limited by the circumstances of his upbringing. Thus, to any problem he confronts, the only possible solutions are play-acting or flight, as both confirm the only identity he has—the identity of otherness and alienation. The "salesman's son" may grow older, but the "salesman's wife's son" never grows at all, remaining in the same state of immaturity forever—always unsure of himself, always on the point of fleeing, an exile from his nation, his heritage, and his manhood.[4]

Notes

[1]Clark Blaise, "The Salesman's Son Grows Older," in his *A North American Education* (Toronto: Doubleday, 1973), p. 160. All further references to this work appear in the text.

[2]For a perceptive analysis of the relationship of sex and death in another of Blaise's Thibidault stories, "The Bridge," see Robert Lecker, *On the Line: Readings in the Short Fiction of Clark Blaise, John Metcalf and Hugh Hood* (Downsview, Ont.: ECW, 1982), pp. 30-31.

[3]It is worth pointing out here that the mother's maiden name may have similar connotations of anonymity. As Robert Lecker has pointed out to me, 'Blankenship' is a portmanteau word for 'Blank citizenship'.

[4]I am grateful to Robert Lecker and J.R. (Tim) Struthers for their helpful comments on this essay.

Kent Thompson
JOHN METCALF: A PROFILE

This "Profile" of John Metcalf is something of a fiction, and you shouldn't expect anything other.[1] Fiction is my trade, and most writing which purports to be biographical is as much fiction as anything else. That's because in any account of "a life" a writer starts with facts and then interprets and evaluates them — as he does with the subject's statements about himself, with the letters and other documents which are available, with anecdotes. What a biographer creates is a person to fit the facts he happens to have.

These are some of the facts about John Metcalf which he has given to me.

He was born in Carlisle, County Cumberland, in the north of England, in 1938. His father was a Methodist minister whose family had farmed in Cumberland for at least three centuries. His mother was a school-teacher before her marriage. He has one older brother.

The family moved to Keighley, in Yorkshire, then to Bournemouth, on the south coast of England, then to Beckenham, in Kent, in the southeast.

John Metcalf attended grammar schools in Bournemouth and Beckenham and in 1957 went to the University of Bristol (on a scholarship) to study English. His subsidiary subject was theology. In 1960 he received his degree (II,2) from Bristol. It was a respectable degree — better than a simple pass, but neither excellent nor outstanding. The next year he returned to earn a Certificate in Education.

He then taught in the Bluebell Secondary Modern Boys' School in Bristol for a year, and next held a temporary post as a teacher at a boys' reformatory on the outskirts of Bristol. He was fired from that job and came to Canada in 1962, at the age of 23.

148

He began to teach in various Montreal high schools for the Protestant School Board of Greater Montreal. About this time, also, he began to write stories. In 1964-65 he went to Cold Lake, Alberta, to teach at the RCAF station there. He returned to Montreal in the summer of 1965, married, and went back to England where he intended to spend his time writing. A shortage of funds, however, forced him back to teaching — this time in the St. Thomas More Comprehensive School in Bristol.

John Metcalf returned to Canada in 1966. He taught at Ross High School in Montreal, marked essays for the Protestant School Board, and began to assemble and write textbooks. In 1969 five of Metcalf's stories were published in Clarke, Irwin's *New Canadian Writing, 1969*. In 1970 *The Lady Who Sold Furniture*, containing a novella and five stories, was published by the same firm. In 1970, too, Metcalf became a Canadian citizen — by giving the correct answer, he says, to a single question: "Have you ever been committed to a lunatic asylum?" In the winter of 1970-71 he and Hugh Hood formed the Montreal Story Teller Fiction Performance Group.

From 1969 to 1976 John Metcalf held various teaching positions and writer-in-residence posts at Loyola College in Montreal, the University of New Brunswick, the Snowdon Campus of Vanier College in Montreal, McGill University, and the University of Ottawa. In 1972 he published his first novel, *Going Down Slow*, with McClelland and Stewart. His first marriage ended that same year. In 1975 he published a collection of eight stories, *The Teeth of My Father*, with Oberon Press, and married again.

In July of 1976 John Metcalf moved to Delta, Ontario, where he lived in an old stone farmhouse with his wife and her son and their two adopted children and sometimes more for the next five years.

With poet John Newlove he published *Dreams Surround Us* in 1977. This was a limited edition of 150 copies, published under the imprint of "The Bastard Press," and it contained Metcalf's novella "Girl in Gingham" as well as Newlove's poem "The Green Plain." The next year Metcalf's "Private Parts: A Memoir" and "Girl in Gingham" were published by Oberon Press under the title *Girl in Gingham*.

In 1980 Metcalf published his second novel, *General Ludd*, with ECW Press. In 1980-81 he served as writer-in-residence at Concordia University; and in June of 1981 he and wife and children moved to

149

Ottawa. In 1982 his *Selected Stories* was published in McClelland and Stewart's New Canadian Library series.

In 1982 John Metcalf reflected upon his career and related matters in a book of eight essays and an interview entitled *Kicking Against the Pricks*, published by ECW Press.

Of course the bare facts demand explanation and evaluation. We can't stand to see them left naked as they are. Why was John Metcalf fired from his job teaching at the reformatory? Because, he has told me (and no more than this), he allowed an entire cricket team to escape. The incident was put to use in a story entitled "The Eastmill Reception Centre," but of course a piece of fiction is a writer's use of an incident and not fact, and probably all the more valuable for that.

Feelings are important. Metcalf is proud that his father's family can trace the possession of a family farm in Cumberland back to 1660 — and he is not happy that the family farm went to a cousin as a result of his father's beliefs in the principles of Christian charity. Metcalf regrets the loss of that farm, that place. He has referred to it as "a very real sort of Eden."

He did not care much for school. His older brother — now the Keeper of the Heberden Coin Room in the Ashmolean Museum and an internationally known historian — had preceded him with such brilliance that invidious comparisons were made. He confesses that although now he admires his brother, there was hostility between them when they were younger.

He says that he preferred fishing, snake-hunting, and bird-watching to school. His mother had to catch him and confine him to the house to make him study for the dreaded 11/plus examinations. However, he did well enough on the 11/plus to be accepted into the Bournemouth Grammar School, which he hated. He has said that the family moved from Bournemouth just in time; he was about to be expelled. He had injured another boy who had been standing too close to a brick wall when John hit him. There was also the matter of the revolver: John was taken in possession of a .45 calibre Smith & Wesson — without ammunition, but in working order.

He describes the Beckenham Grammar School, where he next attended, as "rather like a minor public school." He didn't like it much there, either. He enjoyed English and History and found everything else tedious. He studied Biology chiefly because it required no Mathematics. But to please his parents he worked hard enough to pass his O-level examinations.

He expected to leave school at that point to become a boxer. However, he had done so well in the English portion of the O-level examinations that the headmaster of the Beckenham school insisted that John prepare for the A-level examinations which were required for university entrance. This preparation involved Latin; and the headmaster, Mr. White, taught him Latin during the lunch hours.

John has written me that "every day after that I sat for an hour with that dread figure translating and wincing at each flick of his tongue until I realized that I looked forward to that hour more than anything else. It was there I learned to read and write. Mr. White would spend an hour on a line or even on a word until every possible nuance had been wrung from it. The terror gradually vanished and we would argue and these sessions sometimes sped on for two hours or three — both of us forgetting our supposed roles."

At the University of Bristol John Metcalf did well enough at his studies to earn a respectable degree, but he was more interested in "friendships, sex, drink, rock-climbing, travel in Europe, and being generally disreputable." He says that he hung around with the Bristol underworld and "spent a lot of pub time with criminals and near-criminals and a certified psychotic known as 'the President' who carried an iron bar in a special leather pocket."

He attended the Bristol Old Vic, where Peter O'Toole was then the leading man. "We made a point of going to performances after he'd been at parties with us in the hope he'd still be drunk or very badly hung over," says John. And he recounts that he once saw a prize performance of *The Tempest* which O'Toole entirely wrecked and another of *Hamlet* "where in the grave scene with Laertes he jumped down into the grave and caught his knee on the edge of the block and spent the rest of the play hobbling about and rubbing it and telling the audience that it wasn't funny."

And he spent a great deal of his scholarship money on books, paintings, and antiques — a habit which he continues. "I spent a lot of time with painters, too. Still a preoccupation."

He didn't like his first job, teaching in a secondary modern school. "Awful," he says. "Boring. Above all, boring." So when the Protestant School Board of Greater Montreal came to recruit teachers, John signed on.

In some ways teaching in Montreal was a pleasant change. "After a British secondary modern school it was like being in a rest home. Children called one 'sir' and stood up and sat down and didn't light fires in their desks or threaten me with sheath-knives." But he found the standards in Canadian high schools disconcertingly low, and says that he wished Canada would develop some intellectually elite institutions.

After the year in the RCAF station, he decided to return to England for good. Once there, however, he found himself saving money for tickets back to Canada. "England irritated me all the time. Its class attitudes, after the easiness of Canada, seemed more rigid than ever. It was inefficient and parochial in its attitudes and made me feel very cramped." So he returned to high school teaching in Montreal.

As early as 1964, two years after first arriving in Canada, Metcalf began to enjoy a little literary success: Earle Birney accepted eight of his stories at one time for publication in *Prism International* under the series title "The Geography of Time." Later in the decade Metcalf received encouragement from Earle Toppings, who was then fiction editor at Ryerson Press, and decided to find a part-time job so that he could concentrate on his writing. He became the one-person English department at the "famous/notorious Ross High School... a cram school for dense or emotionally disturbed students." He had been preceded in the post by such people as Bryan McCarthy, John Mills, and Irving Layton — or, as Metcalf puts it, "Any poor bugger without a valid teaching certificate." He was happy there, however, and formed a sincere admiration for Harry Ross, who often brought him breakfast in the classroom when he'd overslept. He was also marking essays for the Protestant School Board — "as many as 200 per week at 25 cents a shot."

And he began to prepare textbooks. "They were simple enough things to do, but no one else seemed to be doing it." He co-authored five books called *Wordcraft* for J.M. Dent and Sons between 1968 and 1977. These were followed by anthologies. *Rhyme and Reason* (1969), *Salutation* (1970), and *Sixteen by Twelve* (1970) — all published by Ryerson Press — were aimed at the high school market, as were *Kaleidoscope* (1972) and *The Speaking Earth* (1972) from Van Nostrand Reinhold and *Stories Plus* (1979) and *New Worlds* (1980) from McGraw-Hill Ryerson.

Other anthologies were directed toward universities and colleges and the general reading public; these included *The Narrative Voice* (1972) from McGraw-Hill Ryerson, *Here & Now: Best Canadian Stories* (1977) from Oberon, and *Making It New* (1982) from Methuen. From 1976 through 1982 he edited — with Joan Harcourt, Clark Blaise, and Leon Rooke — successive editions of Oberon's *New Canadian Stories* and *Best Canadian Stories*. In all of these anthologies Metcalf tried to indicate what he felt represented significant literary achievement. What began as an educational venture was continued in a larger context. He introduced both the new work and the continuing work of generally unknown Canadian writers to the Canadian literary public in the Oberon publications *First Impressions* (1980), *Second Impressions* (1981), and *Third Impressions* (1982).

Since the publication of *The Lady Who Sold Furniture* in 1970, John Metcalf has devoted most of his time to writing, teaching only when it has been financially necessary. He held Canada Council bursaries in 1968, 1969, and 1971. In 1974 he was given a Senior Arts Grant, and again in 1976, 1977, 1980, 1983, and 1984.

Thus are the bare facts fleshed out a little.

Now for the interpretation and evaluation.

Certain generalizations are easy. We can see that John Metcalf suffers the usual paradoxical feelings which afflict trans-Atlantic immigrants, whichever way they are going. Britain has elitist institutions and standards — which are good for art — while North America does not, and art and artistic taste suffer as a result. But Britain's class system is suffocating. Metcalf writes of teaching there that he saw "the children doomed to an easily foreseeable future which was also mine if I didn't remove myself." The system which could preserve standards could also predict one's life.

And his interest in the pastoral — his yearning for the rural life of his boyhood and his return to that kind of life for five years in Delta — might indicate that for John Metcalf the "natural" values are the true ones, and those of society's institutions are questionable. That is roughly the position of the disillusioned Romantic — who at once praises nature and satirizes society. "Gentle as Flowers Make the Stones" can demonstrate both of Metcalf's attitudes. In addition, John has explained that: "I don't write *grotesques* or even caricatures —

153

people are like that everywhere and *more* bizarre.'' It is his job to show what is to be valued and what is to be condemned.

John's interest in Biology, which he himself mocks, is related to his pastoral passions and has given him the background for ''The Years in Exile,'' as well as ''Gentle as Flowers Make the Stones.''

The example of his Latin-teaching headmaster is important, too, because he invoked in John Metcalf that meticulous sense of detail and nuance of meaning which characterizes both his fiction and his criticism.

Equally important is the example of his scholarly brother. John says of his brother that ''if you wish to know anything about Byzantine or medieval Balkan coinage, mints, trade routes, devaluation, etc., he'll tell you. . . a *list* of his publications would fill a book.'' But that same passion for knowledge and detail means that John Metcalf will sometimes do an extraordinary amount of research for a story. For example, I know that he read the entire Book of Mormon as well as related tomes simply as background for his story ''Robert, standing.'' In that story the two Mormon missionaries are essential but not major characters; the major character is a paraplegic writer. Metcalf's research must have gone in other directions, too, or his intuition was working extremely well for that particular story, because a reader who happened to be a paraplegic was so impressed with the accuracy of the story that he assumed that Metcalf was paraplegic as well. Rare praise.

A statement Metcalf has made about his sixth-form English teacher is also important. ''The teacher gave us reading lists around the texts and concentrated on pure textual study. He also made us deliver the speeches in the Shakespeare plays. Same with Milton. Said that if you couldn't deliver the stuff aloud with the correct emphasis and rhetoric, you didn't understand it. Good man. Correct. Five or six essays per term which demanded grotesque amounts of reading. I read about three books a day.''

Because I asked him, Metcalf gave me a statement of his ideas concerning art and literature. It begins with, ''*Ideas have been the ruin of many a good man.*'' The emphasis is his.

He mocks the statement by noting that he is reported to have said this in drunken conversation, but he defends it nonetheless. ''I tend to dislike writers with philosophies. They get in the way of art. I have no 'philosophy' to teach anyone. Only fictional worlds they can experience. What they make of them is up to them.... Mike Taylor [a mutual friend] reckons that I'm deficient because I have no extractable set of ideas. I find that wish for such a set of ideas shocking in him.... All I long for in my writing is an invisible iron control of material, a seemingly effortless flow of rhythm, wit, an exactness of word. All in the service of the story itself.... I also want to combine tragedy (sadness, rather) with comedy. Hugh [Hood] claims that this is bad because the genres should not be mixed but the genres are precisely that — literary modes and models. Life is incredibly funny even at (or particularly at) the most horrendous times.... What happens in a story is always less delightful for me than the story's construction, its grammar, its nuts and bolts — but that's a writer's response.... More and more, I want to be *funny*— and for me that's impossible without an edge of sadness. For example, in ["Girl in] Gingham" (Part 4) where he's thinking about his kitchen and how he'll clean it up, etc., I found the line 'He could hang up strings of onions in the kitchen' very sad and very funny because there's a vision of the 'good life' there, the cook books with coloured pictures, domesticity, etc., contrasted with our knowledge that he'll do no such thing. Also the very rhythm of the sentence has a lugubrious quality. The rhythm...tells you, too, it's a 'delight' he doesn't want or believe in himself.''

Metcalf then says that in re-arranging his books during the reconstruction of his house in Delta, he found himself putting together in one place all the books which he liked the most at that time. The authors gathered together were: Charles Dickens, Evelyn Waugh, Kingsley Amis, Anthony Powell, Roger Longrigg, Richard Yates, P.G. Wodehouse, and Keith Waterhouse. It's an interesting list. Metcalf calls it a ''weird collection.''

Now for more personal anecdotes, wherein the writer (me) presumes upon friendship with his subject and interprets him by what has willy-nilly taken place in their acquaintance.

For example, I like to think of John Metcalf as the tough-minded professional artist. The fellow who intended to be a boxer believes very strongly that a writer should be paid fairly for his work, and he's willing to fight fiercely for that principle. When he was editing *The Narrative Voice* he insisted that the contributors (me among them) be paid something more than twice the pitiful usual rate for their contributions. And we were, although the money eventually came out of John's pocket. That is, he wasn't to start earning royalties on the book until the expenses were paid off. I doubt he made a penny out of it. *The Narrative Voice* was intended — or so he hoped — for use in universities or colleges, but it was generally considered "too difficult" for that level and was used, if at all, for graduate courses.

Then there was the brouhaha in The Writers' Union of Canada. Here you have to remember that John was one of the founding members of The Union, which was organized in an attempt to get writers of books in this country paid at a professional level for their work. (This was — and is — heretical in itself, it being assumed in Canada that writers do something real for their livings and write books on the side as a hobby.)

After the organization had been under way for a couple of years, the idea came up of supporting what was called The Educational Project. In this project various school-teachers around the country were to make up teaching outlines for Canadian Literature in the high schools. Very soon the project was under way and outlines were produced. They dealt with such subjects as "The Immigrant Experience," "Images of Biculturalism, " etc. In short, they used literature as a means of looking at the culture rather than as an end in itself. No trouble in that, you might think, until you realize that such an attitude is an implicit denial of the intrinsic value of art. John was outraged, said so loudly, and resigned from The Union. (He was mollified and came back, but resigned again later on another issue.)

In fact, there are many anecdotes of John's outrage — many of which centre on his powerful pronunciation of the word "bizarre" — and it has to be admitted that John Metcalf in the full flight of denunciation is a marvellous sight. One has only to read *Kicking Against the Pricks* to see his passions for literature and the proper status of art at their most provocative. It is a magnificently bad-tempered book. Names are named and adjectives are applied. But his most devastating technique is to tell the truth precisely, without euphemisms.

But if John Metcalf is willing to attack the failed literature and the ignorance of literature in our culture, he is also eager to proclaim and publish good writing. No one in Canada has done more to insist on the recognition due to excellence. One afternoon in the year after Mavis Gallant published *From the Fifteenth District* I received an anguished telephone call from John. "Do you realize," he said, "that they haven't even *nominated* her for the Governor-General's Award!'' It was John being outraged again; but he was right — it was outrageous to ignore *From the Fifteenth District*.

Nor has anyone except Robert Weaver done more for unrecognized writers. If it were not for John's Oberon publications *First Impressions*, *Second Impressions*, and *Third Impressions*, how could unknown writers move from the little magazines into book publication and national consciousness — such as it is.

When John fights a battle, it is usually for the benefit of all writers, not merely himself. Recently a major publisher contracted for more stories to be put in an anthology than it was thought wise, in the end, to use. Some writers (I was one of them) were sent letters of sad regret. The publisher was sorry, but surely we would understand, etc., etc. All but one of us shrugged our shoulders and accepted meekly the breaking of a legal contract. John Metcalf informed the publisher that he would see the publisher's lawyers in court. The publisher consulted with his lawyers, and an out-of-court settlement was reached. And lo, we *all* got paid! Decision and bout to John Metcalf.

And despite John Metcalf's self-mockery of his life as a teacher and a writer-in-residence, he is a tireless teacher of writing. He is an indefatigable worker at writers' workshops, talking patiently about craft to anyone who wants to know about it, and his essay on punctuation in *Kicking Against the Pricks* is easily the most useful writing on that subject available.

In October 1983 I visited John Metcalf in Ottawa. As usual, we talked far into the night about writing, art, and excellence. I told him I was trying to revise and update an old *Fiddlehead* profile which I had written about him. Was there anything he wanted said?

No, he replied, he couldn't think of anything at the moment. But as we were winding up the evening, he said suddenly: ''A life is not divisible. It's all of a piece.''

And so it is. The John Metcalf who values the status of the artist in society so highly that he believes a serious writer should not take public transport is the same John Metcalf who will denounce the use of art for handy purposes — however sincerely proposed — and who will challenge The Union on a matter of aesthetic principle or a publisher on the matter of payment.

The same John Metcalf who will reject a friend's story (he has been known to suggest burning a piece of failed fiction) will do everything he can to promote the career of an unknown writer who has written good stories.

He is the same John Metcalf who will take on the Canadian literary establishment in *Kicking Against the Pricks* and rail against formal education — but publish innumerable textbooks for the Canadian Literature professors to use in their classes.

He will mock the smugly self-righteous, lament the Christian principles which removed the family farm from his family, and in private act with such Christian generosity that he amazes his friends. He gives away more of his life than any man I know.

In his work he demonstrates what he means by excellence, and in his criticism and letters he serves as the artistic conscience for a large number of Canadian writers. Is it too much to say that he saves some of us from despair and others from temptation? I don't believe so. Besides that, I understand he's a helluva darts player.

Notes

[1]This essay is a revised, updated version of an article published in *The Fiddlehead*, No. 114 (Summer 1977), pp. 57-63.

Barry Cameron
AN APPROXIMATION OF POETRY:
THREE STORIES BY JOHN METCALF

For John Metcalf, the short story is an approximation of poetry in that it offers to the reader through the subtlety and complexity of its linguistic and imagistic patterns a brief but intense insight into life at its most fundamental psychological and emotional level.[1] The words of a Metcalf story are a springboard, points of departure, for the actual story that we, the readers, create with an imaginative response; for, through its conciseness and intensity, a Metcalf story asks us to fill out its narrative or dramatic frame by acts of inference and imagination. In comparison to a play, a Metcalf short story is a self-sufficient scene taken from a drama. In comparison to a novel, a Metcalf short story is a compressed narrative, concentrating on striking details and inviting us to make psychological connections and to draw appropriate conclusions. In other words, the narrative and dramatic dimensions of a Metcalf story, as in poetry, are elliptical. The stories move imagistically and associationally as poems do, and, as in poetry, any descriptions that we receive work less as precise, detailed descriptions of particular objects than as metaphors conveying the attitudes and feelings of the perceiving consciousness. Because of this conception of the short story, Metcalf consistently works with either a first-person point of view, in which case the narrative voice is close to his own, or with a limited, controlled third-person point of view in which the sensibility is first-person perception but which allows Metcalf as writer the possibility of detachment and rhetorical flexibility.

The three stories that I shall examine here were first collected in Metcalf's *The Teeth of My Father* (1975) and later re-issued in his *Selected Stories* (1982).[2] They are concerned in different ways with different aspects of the same dilemma: the plight of the artist in terms of either the relationship between the artist and society or the relationship between the artist's execution of his craft and his own personal life. "Gentle as Flowers Make the Stones," chosen by Metcalf for inclusion in the anthologies *Here & Now: Best Canadian Stories* (1977) and *Making It New: Contemporary Canadian Stories* (1982),[3] is told in a third-person limited point of view. The next two stories in my arrangement, "The Years in Exile" and "The Teeth of My Father," are told in the first person and reveal a further internalization and particularization of Metcalf's treatment of the artist's predicament.

Like other of Metcalf's stories that show the plight of the artist, "Gentle as Flowers Make the Stones" exhibits a prominent satiric strain—ridicule of real estate agencies, hippies, nature-organic freaks, women's liberation, pseudo-poets, pseudo-novelists, *avant-garde* literary magazines, book review editors, *Reader's Digest*, booksellers, the Canadian Authors' Association, academe, and suburbia and the Jewish *nouveau riche*. The satire, however, is not merely invective self-indulgence on the author's part. The attitudes of ridicule are a device of characterization, for we see everything through the eyes of a poet named Jim Haine who lives purely and simply for the art that he practises. Despite the exigencies of his life—his need for money, food, shelter, human companionship, even the necessity to defecate—he must practise his craft. Throughout the story, Haine is composing a poem in his mind, a translation of one of Martial's epigrams that is an elegy for a dead child. The completion of the poem, which is the climax of the story, occurs during a moment of sexual climax with a woman who is presumably emotionally and sexually starved for him. Yet while the entire sexual encounter is taking place, all that is going on in Haine's mind is the birth of the poem that he has been working on all day.

"Gentle as Flowers Make the Stones" suggests that to be an artist is to be utterly cut off from life and all genuine human contact, but it also raises the issue of whether the artist's isolation is self-imposed and what his motives are in choosing to be an artist. The classical, Jonsonian precision of the poem that the poet finally creates is in stark contrast to the chaos and fragmentation of his life. In the poet's obvious joy in creativity lies a strong implication that art is superior to life and that the isolation of the artist is self-willed. The satiric attitudes thus indicate

160

the poet's sense of superiority and his self-distancing from the world. Metcalf intensifies this dialectic between art and life by revealing at strategic points throughout the story that the poet is divorced and making child-support payments. In the context of these expository details, the elegy that the poet is translating becomes a paradoxical lament for his own lost child and for the normal personal life that he has given up to practise his craft — a lament, in other words, for the loss of life itself. The artist has sealed himself away from the world because of the demands of his art.

Jim Haine's compulsion to lie about his occupation emphasizes his sense of vulnerability, his isolation, and his implicit awareness that his profession is unacceptable to society. Any of the tenuously acceptable professions that Haine claims to be his own — "a professor at McGill, a male nurse, a pest-control officer, a journalist" (p. 233) — would be considered more respectable than the profession of poet, and so as poet he withdraws from the world. The initial paragraphs of the story also lead us to an awareness of the nakedness of the artist, stripped of the vestments of normal social existence and persistently attempting to spawn new art despite frustrating odds:

> Fists, teeth clenched, Jim Haine stood naked and shivering staring at the lighted rectangle. He must have slept through the first knocks, the calling. . . .
>
> . . . .
>
> Hour after hour he had watched the two fish cleaning one of the blades of a Sword plant, watched their ritual procession, watched the female dotting the pearly eggs in rows up the length of the leaf, the milt-shedding male following; slow, solemn, seeming to move without motion, like carved galleons or bright painted rocking-horses.
>
> . . . .
>
> He had watched the parents fanning the eggs; watched them stand guard. Nightly, during the hatch, he had watched the parents transport the jelly blobs to new hiding places, watched them spitting the blobs onto the underside of leaves to hang glued and wriggling. He had watched the fry become free-swimming, discover the flat sides of their parents, wriggle and feed there from the mucous secretions. (pp. 229-30)

But as Haine stands listening to the assault upon his door, he sees the parent fish — frenzied by the unnatural noise and vibration — turn and devour their own brood:

161

> He didn't stay to watch the carnage; the flash of the turning fish, the litter floating across the surface of the tank, the tiny commas drifting towards the suction of the filter's mouth. (p. 230)

The painstaking and delicate generative activity of the fish is a metaphor for the poetic process. The parents' devouring of their own brood is a metaphor for how art may, in the face of frustrating odds, occasionally destroy itself.

Even more compelling is the final scene of the story, in which Metcalf, through a startling juxtaposition of the events that are literally taking place and the literal events in the poet's head, dramatizes with a simultaneously pathetic and bitter irony the exact nature of the poet's plight:

> They lay in silence.
> He could feel the sperm getting cold, running down his side, cold on his hip.
> "There's some Kleenex in my purse," she said.
> She wiped his thigh and stomach, and pulling down his shirt, snuggled up against him, kissing his mouth, his chin, his neck. He stroked her shoulders, back, running his hand down to her buttocks and up again. She pulled herself higher until her cheek was against his.
> "Was it good for you, too?" she whispered.
> "Mmm."
> He felt a mounting excitement.
> *All, all, dear ladies, a question of balance.*
> And he'd found it.
> His balancing pole, as it were, commas.
> COMMAS
> No risk of falling now; no staggering run up the incline of a sagging rope.
> *Earth* COMMA *lie lightly on her* COMMA *who* COMMA
> *Living* COMMA *scarcely burdened you.*
> Tears were welling in his half-shut eyes, the lights of the city lancing gold and silver along his wet lashes, the poem perfect.
>
> Gentle as flowers make the stones
> That comfort Liza's tender bones.
> Earth, lie lightly on her, who,
> Living, scarcely burdened you.
>
> Feeling his hot tears on her cheek, she lifted her head to look at him.
> "You're crying," she whispered. "Don't cry."
> She brushed the backs of her fingers against his cheek.

162

"Jim?"
He stirred, shifting himself of some of her weight.
"Jim?"
She nestled against him.
"You know something?" she said. "You're very sweet."
(pp. 248-49)

The total failure here in verbal and emotional communication, the joy of the poet's creative climax and the a-generative birth of his poem in contrast to the nongenerative sexual encounter and joyless sexual climax, and merely the fact that the attempt at human contact is on a sloppy, vulgar level in the back seat of a car — it is not even intercourse — all intensify the ironic pathos of the incident. It seems to me significant that the sexual gratification is not simultaneous and that the fellatio is not a complete act. In terms of the theme of poetic creativity and the odds against which it must take place as well as the sexual and ironic generative dimensions of this scene, the entire episode should also be compared with the generative activity of the fish, the image that initiates the story. Notice, for example, the connection between the description of the fish as "commas" (p. 230) and the poet's discovery that commas are "His balancing pole" (p. 249).

Metcalf's use of a first-person point of view in the final two stories that I shall discuss suggests that his exploration of the problem of the artist's predicament has become more internal and particularized. Although the elderly novelist of "The Years in Exile" is not Metcalf, he might be considered a symbolic surrogate for the author. His aesthetics are strikingly similar to Metcalf's own:

> I have always disliked Wordsworth. Once, I must admit, I thought I disliked him for his bathos, his lugubrious tone. But now I know that it is because he could not do justice to the truth; no philosophical cast of mind can do justice to particularity.
> I am uncomfortable with abstraction, his *or* mine. (pp. 201-02)

> What will the young man say to me this evening? And what can I say to him? It is difficult to talk to these young college men whose minds no longer move in pictures. Had he been here this morning I could, like some Zen sage, have pointed to the Monarchs about the apple leaves and preserved my silence.
> Particular life. Particular life.
> All else is tricks of the trade or inexpressible. (p. 210)

163

The story focuses on the psychic split in the novelist's mind that exists, inherently, since he is a novelist. Because he has fictionalized the past, because he has framed its "insistence" (p. 195) through the internal fictionalizing process of memory, the novelist's visions of his childhood at the age of nine or ten are more real to him than his present moment in Canada as a famous novelist. The fictionalizing operation of memory, as the novelist himself knows, is " 'the most basic form of creativity' " (p. 211). Memory, like fiction, edits, orders, and preserves experience. Memory shapes experience, giving it meaning, and ultimately yields through its mythologizing effects a sense of identity. Home is a psychic state of oneness, of identity, in which one's world is not an external environment but part of one. Consequently, the novelist's memories of his childhood past in England, because he has mythologized the past, are his internal home:

> Many might dismiss such meaningless particulars of memory.
> I know that I am lost in silence hours on end dwelling on another time now more real to me than this chair, more real than the sunshine filtering through the fawn and green of the willow tree. (pp. 195-96)

> Yes, I have thought myself a pilgrim, the books my milestones. But these recent weeks, the images that haunt my nights and days...
> I have seen the holy places though I never knew it. I have travelled on, not knowing all my life that the mecca of my pilgrimage had been reached so young, and that all after was the homeward journey. (p. 197)

Because the novelist's real home lies in his visions of the past, his present moment becomes, as the title of the story implies, a metaphorical condition of exile and expatriation.

The detailed vividness and immediacy of the many recollections throughout "The Years in Exile" both illustrate the novelist's (and Metcalf's) aesthetic about particularity and convey the reality of the novelist's visions. He can smell the honeysuckle; he is able to feel the magistrate's ledger that he as a young boy found in a spoiled mansion named Fortnell House; and he remembers the body of eight-year-old Patricia Hopkins, who gave him at the age of nine a glimpse of "the smooth cleft mound of her vagina," far more clearly "than the bodies of two wives" (p. 211). All of the passages describing his experiences in the past are really metaphors for the novelist's psychic condition of being at home.

164

The past-present, fiction-life dialectic that Metcalf is exploring in this story parallels other dialectics that occur in his work: art and life, reality and fantasy, factual and fictional autobiography, the child and the adult, the individual and society, innocence and experience, order and chaos, the pastoral and the urban, and the natural and the mechanistic. In "The Years in Exile," he specifically identifies the particularity and vividness of the past with nature. The colour of the petunias, the willows, the Monarch butterflies — all objects of the novelist's perception in the present moment — are associated with the reality of the details perceived through memory. The first three paragraphs of the story offer an immediate juxtaposition of the past and the present, the pastoral and the urban, and the natural and the synthetic along with a sense of the novelist's discomfort and alienation in the present moment.

One of the ways in which Metcalf stresses the reality of the novelist's fictionalized dreams of his past is by associating the state of the old man's physical decay with the decay of the eighteenth-century mansion, Fortnell House, which is the focal point of his reveries. The house itself stands for the vitiation of English society, manners, and values. Despite their physical decomposition, however, both the novelist and the house gain vitality through the fictionalizing activity of the novelist. The old man's movement around the lawn throughout the story in order to remain in the sunlight suggests this vitality and his desire or need to persist in the "life" of his reveries, and the story ends with the image being associated specifically with his past. Although the sun has literally "long since passed over the house," the aged novelist remains in the sunlight of his dreams:

> . . .I should go and shave. But I will sit a little longer in the sunshine. Here between the moored houseboats where I can watch the turn of the quicksilver dace. Here by the piles of the bridge where in the refracted sunlight swim the golden-barred and red-finned perch. (p. 212)

The two stories that I have dealt with thus far have examined hypothetically through purely fictional figures the plight of the artist in general. "The Teeth of My Father" deals not only with the general relation between life and art, but also with the particular relation between Metcalf's own life and his own accomplishments as a short story

165

writer. Specifically, it explores the truth of fiction as opposed to the factual truth of life; but it is also a moving elegy for Metcalf's father and a summing-up of Metcalf's rhetorical concerns as a writer.

Early in the story, which incorporates whole stories or parts of others that Metcalf had previously written, the speaking "I" utters a remark that is both an admonition to and a directive for the reader:

> (I have decided to tell the truth. My stories in the River Room were not purely nostalgic; they were calculated to be funny and entertain my friend. My friend was more an acquaintance, a man I admired and wanted to impress. And 'wilful legs' was plagiarized from Dylan Thomas.) (pp. 174-75)

The effect of this remark is multiple. It shatters the art illusion of the narrative up to this point; it suggests the possibility of more than one level of fictional reality in the story (later well-established by the incorporation of other Metcalf stories into the narrative frame); it establishes the fictional structure of the story as an autobiographical one; it draws attention to the fact that the story is indeed fiction and to the writer's performance as fiction writer; and, finally, it invites the reader to realize that whether the following incidents are inventive or factual is irrelevant. The story, because it is fiction, a distillation of experience, has an imaginative truth that is more real, more true emotionally and psychologically, than any factual or historical autobiography. The story appears to be — indeed, professes to be, through the speaking voice of the "I" — "the truth" (p. 174); but it is a truth that is a supreme piece of fiction. "The Teeth of My Father," then, is really about the craft of fiction itself, about the writer's art of shaping or manipulating experience to give it a greater reality.

There are several occasions in the story when Metcalf, as in the admonitory remark that I quoted earlier, deliberately shatters the art illusion to draw attention to the art of the fiction and to the fact that the story is indeed fiction. The narrator's introductions to the incorporated stories serve this function, though an even more obvious instance is the two voices — one in italics and one in ordinary type — of the narrator's comments after he presents the story "Biscuits":

> *It is instructive, ladies and gentlemen, to examine the psychological implications of this sample of juvenilia if we may assume it to be autobiographical either*

166

in fact or impulse.

Yes, you can assume that.

What activity is the child essentially engaged in? In nothing more or less than the act of defining his identity. Through which functions does the child perform this act? Through naming, drawing, and most importantly, writing. And with which parent does this suggest identification?

Exactly so. Exactly so. The father!

Who, who I may remind you, is, in the words of the text, 'far away.' For the perceptive reader, the point requires no further elucidation. (pp. 178-79)

The incorporation of other Metcalf stories into "The Teeth of My Father" has several effects. All the stories have an autobiographical fictional structure, and so we have autobiography within autobiography, fiction within fiction; and despite the reader's factual knowledge that Metcalf did indeed write these other stories, there is the added fiction that the *persona* of "The Teeth of My Father" is the author of the stories. Is "The Teeth of My Father" "*autobiographical either in fact or impulse*" (p. 178)? "*For the perceptive reader, the point requires no further elucidation*" (p. 179).

Many of the incidents here related no doubt are pure invention — the loose box incident, for example. Many are edited or transformed facts — Metcalf's father did not make a new pair of teeth every week. But all are true emotionally and psychologically, more illustrative of the way the father really was from the writer's point of view than any factual truth could be. The story ends with an elegiac lament of an "I" that is if not John Metcalf in fact then John Metcalf in truth:

I did not cry.

On the evening I received news of your death I went to the Esquire Show Bar on Stanley Street in Montreal and listened to King Curtis leading a blues band.

I did not cry.

I was irritated at your funeral by the tear-sodden faces and the predictable rhetoric of the officiating minister. Looking at your coffin, I was not moved. My thoughts were of the borrowed airfare, the yellowed soles of your feet, toenails.

I was not moved to tears.

Yet I did go into your study which still stank of your tobacco and I took your red propelling-pencil and your fountain pen.

Now, ten years later in a life half done, a life distinctly lacking in probity, I use your pen, now twice-repaired, to write my stories, your pencil for corrections.

167

And I am crying now.

Drunken tears but tears for you. For you. For both of us. Standing on the sidewalk in the cold fall evening of another country, my tears are scalding. (pp. 192-93)

Careful examination of John Metcalf's short stories illustrates in truth and fact the subtlety and craftsmanship of his work. Metcalf places severe demands upon his readers. He asks that his stories be read with all the attention and effort that a good poem requires, for his stories are indeed an approximation of poetry.

Notes

[1] This essay is a revised, abridged version of an article published in *Studies in Canadian Literature*, 2 (Winter 1977), 17-35. An earlier version of that article was delivered as a paper to the University of Ottawa Short Story Conference in November 1975.

[2] All quotations in this essay are from Metcalf's *Selected Stories* (Toronto: McClelland and Stewart, 1982).

[3] Comments by Metcalf on "Gentle as Flowers Make the Stones" appear in his essay "Building Castles" published in *Making It New: Contemporary Canadian Stories* (Toronto: Methuen, 1982).

Dennis Duffy
"MORE DEAR, BOTH FOR THEMSELVES AND FOR THY SAKE!": HUGH HOOD'S *THE NEW AGE*

We took a week, my wife and I, in the summer of 1979, and drove slowly along Upper Canada's waterfront from Toronto to Morrisburg, sleeping every night within sight of lake or river.[1] The holiday encompassed a moral geography as well, the map of a vision of Canadian civility that we had chosen as converts. We came to pay homage to what could never for us seem roots, but were instead fruits of a choice we had made. And on that journey ever in the backs of our minds lay the mappings of one writer who, more than any other, had laid out this route for us.

Long ago, in 1962, a sentence from the opening of one of the *Flying a Red Kite* stories, "Three Halves of a House," had taken hold of my imagination: "But a third of the continent leans pushing behind the lakes and the river, the pulse, circulation, artery, and heart, all in one flowing geographical fact, of half the North Americans, the flow we live by all that long way from Minnesota to the Gulf."[2] The idea, the vision of a river like that (I had grown up along the Ohio, itself some punkins when it came to pumping out the flow), caught me. Hood's pregnant sentence sent me to Creighton's *The Empire of the St. Lawrence*; and after that, my imaginative life had a Canadian corner to it. Choosing citizenship in a new country comes about through complex considerations, and my Canadian allegiance stems largely from the facts that my livelihood and my children are here. But in 1967, on the way to Expo, the beginning of Hood's sentence ran through my mind from Kingston to Cornwall; it had opened for me a view of the land's imaginative possibilities and had started me on a new route.

When the cold hand of speculation grabs us by the throat in the early

169

grades of our schooling, we are suddenly told that what we are living is not history but that history lies embalmed in books, slides, and films dealing with the past. We find ourselves adrift on an ocean of facts and impressions. History becomes then a blur of imperial wars and adventurings, controversies, scandals, and catastrophes whose frictions finally culminate in the exhilarating assault by the Old World upon the body of the New. We ourselves shine forth as the thrice-blessed offspring of that union. And one of the first things we learn is the importance of river valley civilizations. Nile, Euphrates, Indus, Yangtse: here, we are told, is where it all began; here lies our historical genesis.

Maps and visual interpretations present us with shapeless blots that appear along both sides of the curved line of the river. As time proceeds, the blobs expand and link up, so that eventually the river pursues its course through canyons of settled space before dissolving within a delta where water becomes indistinguishable from land. When this course runs in time rather than in space, we speak of it as the flowering of a civilization. In "Swinging Deep: Splendeurs et Profondeurs de Québec," a travel piece collected in *The Governor's Bridge is Closed*, Hood describes a journey from the emptiness of the Gulf of Saint Lawrence to the urbanity of Montreal, a spatial/temporal trip along a river that links beginnings ("On the first morning"[3]: the echo of Genesis is deliberate) with the nows. Hood's river journey, his kicking against the current, reveals that the river and the things built along it are no longer discrete entities; they have reached an accommodation. The stream and the settlements intermix as clotted dots within an archipelago.

Yet Hugh Hood, in choosing to write of his own culture, finds himself forced to deal with a civilization characterized by linearity and dispersal rather than by conglobement and increasing density. No matter how closely one follows the Laurentian interpretation of Canadian history, coming to terms with the civilization produced by it entails a splitting of earlier riverain images. For we dwell along only half of the river. The titanic forces of imperial politics tore from nature one of the twin banks of the river valley, so that Upper Canada became a north-shore structure rather than an enterprise advancing along and outward on both sides with the river as its centre. Our side of the river, then, has been forced to look northward, to cast its aspirations not only along the rich alluvial soil and the natural conduit for settlement and trade, but also to the rock and the forest that lie to the north.

That polarity between river and rock has become Canada's version of the desert versus the sown. To be found in every corner of our culture, it seems especially apparent in our literature. Our heroes divide between those reaching maturity only through contesting themselves against all the inimical forces of a natural environment and those attaining their majority through integration into communal social structures. On the one hand lies struggle with, or possible integration into, the world of animals and nature; on the other, the affirmation of historic and familial ties within the settlement. On the one hand lies a vision of Canada as a new and rugged land to be viewed in and for itself alone (The Group of Seven); on the other, a vision of an oceanic flow in which the river rolls on within a continuum that includes the parent country (United Empire Loyalism). "Something godlike about the rivers..."[4] is the narrator's echo in Hood's "Predictions of Ice" of "...I think that the river / Is a strong brown god"[5] in Eliot's "The Dry Salvages." Something Hindu clings to this god, who appears in so many guises in the society he has shaped.

However deeply its artists wished to depict such a society in terms of either primeval scarcity or pastoral plenty, that organism would be rich in contradictions and complexities. On the one hand, John Strachan; on the other, Tom Thomson. Thus Hood's Stoverville is a town established along the great river, with its physical and economic origins springing from the waterfront and yet its highest aspirations keyed to the railway running north to the inland ocean of Lake Superior. On the one hand, the strip settlement of the river; on the other, the reaching out into the *pays d'en haut*, the high country to be subjugated by steel and engineer rather than by canoe and trapper.

Chugging along in the excursion boat through the Thousand Islands, the traveller finds the two shores blended together in the resort archipelago. Yet the line remains, as cottages identical in scale and architecture flaunt differing flags from their boat docks. The Stars and Stripes is set in foundations deriving their strength and significance from processes to the south, while the Maple Leaf begins where the other leaves off, as a base for the thrust northward. Between the shores, resembling a kind of Wagnerian dream transported from the metropolitan area (and opera) to the north, stands Boldt Castle, an instant ruin incorporating its own original bogus ruins on the site. On the one hand, the New York City land speculator's proto-Disneyland; on the other, at Toronto's Casa Loma, the northern mining-stock magnate's attempt to figure forth his romantic fantasy within the limits of a metropolitan area. To us, on the day-tripper's craft, the border-river washed all in its embrace; to the geographer and constitutionalist, the region appears filled with lines and demarcations. And oddly enough, and still at this time, human structures hold their sway over geographical ones. Thus the early inhabitants of Stoverville found in an imperial gunboat an ark to deliver them from the depredations of pirates lurking no farther than across the river. For them existed no between-the-nations summer world of tiny islets dotted with varying pieces of bunting, but a sharp demarcation between a pathway for peaceful trade and the robbers' den along the open main.

To drive along the shore of that river was for us to grasp a host of imaginative constructs that brought home the solidity of the imaginative vision that lies behind the complex narratives of *The New Age* series. Prince Edward County, its seat named for a villainous fighter who had governed Trinidad like a Mongol warlord and then died at Waterloo in the garb of an English country gentleman, bearing a cane rather than a sword, gave us nothing so much as a sense of the settledness, the agrarian continuity that marks *A New Athens*. We left the main highway and stuck to the winding shore, visiting the immense sand dunes that spoke of timeless accretions of small detail, a mark also of the farmhouse residence where we had once stayed. Yes, the County (as its residents know it) was becoming a bedroom community for a booming Belleville; yes, one of the dunes had years ago been sold to a sand-and-gravel firm that had simply carted it all away; yes, the superb cheese factories suffered from the milk quotas a government had imposed in the interests of the multinational food giants — but to the naked eye all seemed a demonstration of the Upper Canadian dream.

Peace, order, and good government could produce a locality which not only nestled into its particular environment but whose churches, schools, and libraries affirmed their ties with the trans-atlantic culture from which these buildings and settlements had sprung. Of course, the ferry from Glenora to Adolphustown bore the name *Quinte Loyalist*, and although the U.E.L. memorials at the original landing place spoke of a project that had undergone considerable modifications and dilution in the course of time, something of the original remained. Driving along that road into Kingston, we stopped and watched a re-creation of an old square-rigged barquetine as it tacked along the river, even as we noted the huge multinational chemical complex — and the hydro-electric plant built to further the ambitions that the complex represented — lying along the road we travelled. The ship had stepped out of the Museum in *A New Athens*, the plants from the concentration of power and technology governing the Toronto of *Reservoir Ravine*.

The reality of Hood's Upper Canada includes the idyllic dreams of the former novel as well as the mammon-ish control systems of the latter. As *Reservoir Ravine* reminds us, underground streams and deep romantic chasms can be found beneath the surface of the driving, entrepreneurial city that long ago turned its back on its own waterfront and has only recently begun to attempt to restore it to the people. The narrator's shocked realization that the reservoir that shaped his early imaginings has been covered over, like the near-death by drowning at the beginning of *The Swing in the Garden*, recalls things gone wrong, recalls powers and principalities that function according to drives more brutal than those of the imagination. Yet for us, as we drove along the river shore, that world seemed less present, however deluded our view.

Perhaps we had joined Mrs. Codrington's view of Stoverville from the river as the yachts passed by in grand review. Hardly possible that, since cruising holidayers lack the spiritual sinews to bear the weight of visionary reconstruction. Yet we soon arrived in Brockville, the other name for Stoverville, and found there a town laid out with no small claims to the realization of a concept of integration, harmony, and human dignity. The shopfronts had been reshaped, but not destroyed, by the demands of modern marketing, while in the centre of town lay a truly public and refreshing space. We stood halfway up the rise from riverbank to where the rise levelled off, gazing at the county offices at the top. In our foreground stood an ornate fountain, while the stone structures that lined the street forced our gaze upward not only to the public buildings but to the Ontario Gothic churches that made up the remainder of the circle in which the county offices sat.

To look at all this from below was a treat; to stroll up to the green that the buildings enclosed and to pass along these foundations one by one, a revelation. We stood within a circle formed by structures expressing man's need for justice, concord, and order here, and expressing his conviction that a system existing elsewhere could translate itself into a model for behaviour here. Looking down from that height, we beheld again the fountain as it played a tinkling parody of the majestic oratorio

173

of the river as it flowed onward in the distance. The circularity of our vantage point, the linearity of our view along the street to the river, the movement and sweep of the flood as it passed in perpetual review combined to form a larger figure composed of various shapes, a single impression of appropriateness. It seemed good to us to be here, on this earth, at this time, at this place, with these sundry folk. Here seemed a locus of potentially conflicting spaces that had resolved themselves into a grander measure. One needn't be a visionary artist to grasp that certain shapes and proportions please, and that this pleasure exerts more than a fleeting hold upon us. We lacked the visionary intensity of Mrs. Codrington; we hadn't the Wordsworthian bridging of space and time that marks Matthew Goderich's moments of exaltation. Yet we were responding to the beat of the imaginative relocation of space that had struck up in us at that moment. We had in some small way replicated the imaginative experience that lies as the key to Hood's fiction.

Small wonder, then, that a few blocks onward we passed a millionaires' row of splendid mansions set above the river front but whose gardens flowed down to the bank itself. The last in the row — I remember it as a pleasant jumble of Queen Anne and Jacobean and Georgian styles, with a great deal of stone trim and decoration — struck me then and there as the Robinsons' house. No writer would wish his work to be interpreted so literally as to have a single house pinpointed as *the* mansion in which part of his story occurs, but certainly the house seemed a seat of the mighty. The entire row lacked the air of imposed magnificence we had always found in Newport, Rhode Island; the houses stood as dwellings accessible from the street and rooted, however haughtily, in the spot they adorned. The Robinson house — for so it shall ever remain in my mind — indicated also the social change that had come about since its foundation. For while its stone fence stretched for a good distance beyond the sides of the dwelling, a newer house stood on each side of the older one. Obviously, bits of the original property had been sold to newcomers, who wisely left standing the fence they had acquired with the titles.

I recalled then that along the public square we had so recently enjoyed stood a one-time custom-house, now converted to another public use. The river trade had long since ceased to necessitate so imposing an establishment, and the buildings, domestic and governmental, showed the losses time had brought. From this, my memory flowed back to a museum display we had come across in Prince Edward

174

County. It had dealt with a post-Confederation boom in barley, when the distilling interests southward had demanded all the barley the region could create in order to see to it that America kept on dreaming. The brief years saw fields converted wholesale to the grain, and shipbuilding and docking proceeding at a frenzied rate (you must understand that "frenzy" in the County is a very relative term). Then one day the U.S. imposed a punitive tariff on barley grown on the other side of the lake, and the entire enterprise folded so quickly that barely a few photographs of it linger in a dusty corner of a county museum.

The mansion, the custom-house, the barley boom — were these the economic indices to Upper Canada, and was the entire region a macrocosm of the Stoverville, Westport and Lake Superior Railway? Were these enterprises and monuments now no more than moments within a dream? And even for us to think that was to plunge backward a month earlier, when George and Sheila Grant had come to dinner, and we had talked of loss, but as always, exuberantly. Fiction, philosophy, friendship, and the objects we had bumped against had melded into a single reality.

We took no literary pilgrimage, we left aside any use of *The New Age* as a guidebook, but what we saw confirmed an imaginative hold that a writer's work had taken upon a place we had come to feel as our own. Months later, a student was to tell me that, during a troubled time in Australia, with her future undecided, it had been a reading of *The Swing in the Garden* that sent her home. When critics take into account Hood's literary achievement, I hope they won't leave that consideration — and our trip — out of the measure.

Notes

[1]This essay is a revised version of a paper delivered to the Hugh Hood Symposium at York University in October 1979.

[2]Hugh Hood, "Three Halves of a House," in his *Flying a Red Kite* (Toronto: Ryerson, 1962), p. 99.

[3]Hugh Hood, "Swinging Deep: Splendeurs et Profondeurs de Québec," in his *The Governor's Bridge is Closed* (Ottawa: Oberon, 1973), p. 77.

[4]Hugh Hood, "Predictions of Ice," in his *Around the Mountain: Scenes from Montreal Life* (Toronto: Peter Martin, 1967), p. 156.

[5]T.S. Eliot, "The Dry Salvages," in *Four Quartets*, in his *Collected Poems 1909-1962* (London: Faber and Faber, 1963), p. 205.

Lawrence Mathews
HOOD AND EVIL

Satan is rightly named the father of lies: absolute evil denies the coherence and familiarity of being absolutely.
— Hugh Hood, *Reservoir Ravine*[1]

In the mainstream fiction of our time, the destiny of man presents its meaning in psychological terms, and a novelist's sense of good and evil is expected to be compatible with contemporary dogma about personality. Again and again, Hugh Hood's work fails to pass this test. A typical complaint is that Hood's vision is flawed by "his unwillingness to deal with evil," that his "affirmation . . . is too easily or simply achieved."[2] These phrases come from a review of *Reservoir Ravine* (1979) — the third volume in Hood's *roman fleuve*, *The New Age/Le nouveau siècle* — but they echo critics' comments about other of his books. Of course the publication of *Black and White Keys* (1982), the fourth volume in the series, has made it impossible for anyone to say that Hood is any longer 'unwilling to deal with evil.'[3] But what I want to argue here is that Hood's treatment of evil in *Black and White Keys* is consistent with his handling of that subject elsewhere in his canon.

In the world of Hood's fiction, the central moral questions have to do with perception. To fall prey to evil is to be convinced by the father of lies — to misperceive the nature of reality, to fail to affirm "the coherence and familiarity of being." The specific forms of personal immorality predicated upon this false conviction — adultery, to take one classic and obvious example — seem not to inspire Hood's imagination. It is the spiritual warfare that interests him, the struggle of light against darkness in the arena of the individual and collective soul.

176

A paradigm of Hood's method is provided by "A Near Miss," a story composed in 1964 and collected in *Dark Glasses* (1976).[4] Denying the expectations of readers schooled in the conventions of nineteenth- and twentieth-century psychological fiction, Hood in this story 'deals with evil' in a way which sheds light on the methods he uses in his longer narratives. Marnie, the narrator and protagonist of "A Near Miss," undergoes an experience which frees her from one of Satan's lies. In presenting her story, Hood includes the material needed for a 'psychological' perspective, but the reader becomes aware of the author's radically different understanding of the action.

At twenty-four, Marnie has a serious problem; she fears and mistrusts men: "I never met a man who didn't make me feel threatened with rape, they're all out for the same thing, men..." (*DG*, p. 47). The one exception is her father: "I trusted my father. He never wanted to rape me, and we almost got to know each other, a near miss" (*DG*, p. 50). She tells her story in a series of flashbacks describing her adolescence in Brockville, university life in Toronto, her courtship and marriage, and finally her father's terminal illness. It is Marnie's father who is largely responsible for her attitude to men, a fact that he recognizes on his deathbed.

But the most noticeable manifestation of maleness in "A Near Miss" is Lieutenant Dunglas, whose portrait hangs in her parents' dining-room. Hood begins the story by focusing our attention upon the heirloom: "Supposed to be an aide of the counter-revolutionary hero for whom this town was named, a young lieutenant with varnished beige cheeks shines in the dark, an ancestral portrait from Mother's side of the family. Tight embroidered collar, red coat, pop eyes, varnish" (*DG*, p. 36). Marnie makes no explicit connection between Dunglas and her father; but somehow the lieutenant becomes for her the symbol of ideal masculinity, even though the portrait suggests qualities — remoteness, repression, the whole panoply of character armour — which Marnie does not consciously associate with her trusted father. When she rejects Ted Harasymchuk, a sexually aggressive artist whom she meets at university, she invokes the image of Dunglas: " 'a decent man, not like you' " (*DG*, p. 43). But when she goes on to assert that " 'I know a real man when I see one,' " Harasymchuk's reply brings her up short: " 'And they're all in the pictures on the wall, aren't they?' " (*DG*, p. 43)

The story seems to develop, then, in conventional Freudian terms. Marnie worships her father's 'decency,' objectified in the Dunglas portrait, but this decency allows no place for her sexuality. How could anyone emulate the serene purity of the lieutenant, embalmed by varnish, body hidden by his uniform? Marnie's fear of men is rooted partly in her fear of her own sexual nature, a fear disguised as disgust at her own body. Hood always chooses his names carefully, and "Dunglas" is based partly on a pun, 'dung-lass,' for what the portrait half-evokes in Marnie is a sense of her own contrasting baseness.

Inevitably Marnie tries to reject this identity in order to make herself into Dunglas' female counterpart. Harasymchuk is the man in her life who comes closest to exposing her bad faith. When he says of her that " 'She thinks her shit doesn't stink,' " Marnie feels "disgusted, and oddly excited" (DG, p. 42). The excitement suggests that her attempt at repression has not been completely successful, but disgust wins the day. In an early scene, Marnie at fifteen shaves her legs, possessed by a "Repugnance to visible body hair" (DG, p. 38) inspired by a Zsa Zsa Gabor TV commercial; as an adult, she ponders the fact that "Sexual folklore is full of disgust and instrumentalism" (DG, p. 47). Marnie is never comfortable with her physical nature. Eventually she marries Paul, an architect accused by Harasymchuk of " 'virginal high thinking' "(DG, p. 49); according to her cousin, Paul " 'looks like the picture on the wall' " (DG, p. 45). She has chosen safety, and she knows it: "Did I marry him for his beautiful blueprints and his Utopian views or because he isn't a sexual threat" (DG, p. 47). She has retained her emotional virginity, 'a near miss' inwardly withholding herself from her husband.

In establishing this sort of situation, an author might be preparing the reader for an epiphany in which Marnie (or, if Marnie is not bright enough, perhaps only the reader) recognizes that she is trapped in the web of Freudian determinism, that — unless she is lucky enough to find a good shrink — her fear of men will continue to warp her life. A more optimistic writer might arrange for her to experience some sort of 'breakthrough' by which she would begin to 'get in touch with her sexuality' (perhaps by means of an affair with someone like Harasymchuk); a process of 'psychological growth' would follow — and her story would resemble Rachel Cameron's in Margaret Laurence's *A Jest of God*.

But Hood does neither of these things. Instead we get a last conversation between Marnie and her father, in which he says he wants " 'to retrieve some of the damage I've done' " (*DG*, p. 51). This damage has to do with Marnie's feelings about men: " 'I want you to believe — you *must* believe — that no proper man will assault you or abuse you. Believe this, and don't be afraid' " (*DG*, p. 51) Marnie replies that she does believe it, forcing the moment to this crisis:

> We looked straight at each other and for once, for once, I got through the screen of another person's looks to the identity beyond. I really felt, as you feel moving water or an electric shock, the living movement of someone else's person. The only time. I knew him, and he gave me the freedom of the kingdom of men. (*DG*, p. 51)

This scene exemplifies precisely what a critic might point to as an "affirmation . . . too easily or simply achieved." Hood wants the reader to believe that the encounter he describes is so powerful for Marnie that her emotional bondage can end immediately. The passage's impact depends partly upon its allusiveness, and most critics would be quick to point out that allusions are a cheap substitute for 'adequate motivation.' Hood could hardly have been unaware of this possibility. In presenting the scene as he does, he is challenging the assumptions upon which such 'psychological criticism' is based. The allusions do not evidence a clumsy attempt on Hood's part to camouflage his supposed ineptitude as a psychologist; instead he is appealing to the standards by which he believes modern psychology should be judged.

The passage brings to mind Robert Browning's poem "By the Fireside," in which the speaker remembers the moment at which he and his wife first declared their mutual love:

> A moment after, and hands unseen
>   Were hanging the night around us fast;
> But we knew that a bar was broken between
>   Life and life: we were mixed at last
> In spite of the mortal screen.
> . . . .
>
> How the world is made for each of us!
>   How all we perceive and know in it
> Tends to some moment's product thus,
>   When a soul declares itself — to wit,
> By its fruit, the thing it does![5]

179

Penetrating the "screen" that ordinarily separates us from others can radically change our perception of the world. The change does not occur as the automatic result of some chain of psychological causes and effects. The soul must declare itself; the person must recognize the moment and respond in the right way. Browning's speaker notes that if his wife had not done so, their love would never have come to fruition: "Had she willed it, still had stood the screen / So slight, so sure, 'twixt my love and her . . . ."[6] Marnie, in getting "through the screen of [her father's] looks to the identity beyond" is performing the act that will change her life, that will give her "the freedom of the kingdom of men" (DG, p. 51).

This last phrase, with its echo of "the kingdom of heaven," suggests the chief literary context that Hood recalls here: the New Testament, specifically the Gospel stories of Jesus' miracles of physical and spiritual healing. Marnie's father (dying in Kingston, town of the king) speaks the truth; Marnie believes him, and is immediately initiated into a new life — a direct analogue of a New Testament conversion story. Northrop Frye's gloss on the term *metanoia* is useful here. Life in Jesus' spiritual kingdom, Frye says,

> is described as beginning in *metanoia*, a word translated "repentance" by the AV, which suggests a moralized inhibition of the "stop doing everything you want to do" variety. What the word primarily means, however, is change of outlook or spiritual metamorphosis, an enlarged vision of the dimensions of human life.[7]

The notion of repentance as "enlarged vision" suggests the other major New Testament reference in the passage, the one identified by Hood's epigraph for *Dark Glasses*: "For now we see through a glass, darkly; but then face to face" (1 Cor. 13.12).[8] Clearly there is a second pun on the lieutenant's name: 'dun-glass,' the dark glass of maleness which has for Marnie obscured the human identity beyond.

The brief concluding section of "A Near Miss" reveals that Marnie has retained the freedom granted to her in the Kingston hospital room. She is making preparations for her father's funeral, in the dining-room over which Dunglas presides. Ironically her father's photograph will now hang beside the portrait; this is the first time that she has related the two. The last sentences of the story measure the distance that Marnie has travelled: "My friends, my gallery, these are not men but pictures. Men you have to touch" (*DG*, p. 52).

This sort of analysis is unlikely to convince a hostile critic that Hood's treatment of his material in "A Near Miss" is artistically successful, or that the understanding of human nature which informs the story is as profound as that offered by modern psychology. The "affirmation" implied by Marnie's story will seem "too easily or simply achieved" to anyone unsympathetic to Hood's psychological and spiritual premises. But "A Near Miss" does provide evidence that Hood is not at all 'unwilling to deal with evil' — though the *way* that he deals with this subject is no doubt unpalatable to many contemporary critics.

II

For some readers, any affirmation implied by a novel about the Holocaust will seem suspect. But in *Black and White Keys* Hood has tried to write such a novel, in full awareness of the odds against him:

> Something had happened for which there was no name and no conception. A great wickedness. Wickedness exceeding the bounds of purely human invention. It had required a mass intoxication far superior to the powers of the unaided human will to bring about this catastrophe. It was not the traceable consequence of three or five or ten or twenty or fifty years of mere misconduct or criminality or cultural antagonism; it had a Scriptural, a prophetic significance. The wrongdoing seemed of a nature coequal with human nature, a permanent destructive possibility.[9]

After this, what affirmation will not seem pathetically false?

In fact, the two sections of *Black and White Keys* dealing with Matt Goderich's wartime adolescence in Toronto provide an analysis of the nature of the false affirmation inspired by popular culture in time of war. The first of these sections ends with a comic account of a professional wrestling match between "World Champion" Lou Thesz and "The Masked Marvel," a ring villain widely believed — if Matt is to be taken literally — to be Hitler in disguise. Good prevails, and the Marvel is unMasked; his true identity is "Freddie 'King Kong' Cox of Cleveland, Ohio" (*BWK*, p. 116). The comic book notion of good and evil shared by Matt and the other wrestling fans — and, by implication, the Canadian people — has been revealed to be empty and banal. Yet

181

this same notion moves the country to dedicate itself to the war effort.

The second section narrated by Matt ends with a more serious unmasking. Here Matt's story parallels Marnie's in certain striking ways. The role corresponding to that of Lieutenant Dunglas is played, improbably enough, by Bing Crosby and Perry Como, *inter alia*. Matt, looking back at his teenage ambition to be a crooner, considers the function of these performers in shaping the collective consciousness of the time: "Those songs were our armour against horror.... Nonsense, banality, sentimentality, spun sugar, insouciance, melody, buoyant rhythm, innocent gaiety, self-indulgence... were skin over ulcers, first protection for wounds, healing, scarring" (*BWK*, pp. 230-31). Like Marnie, Matt has his moment of *metanoia*, though his is ironic. It comes just after V-E Day, as, listening to his Perry Como records, he discovers the famous *Life* photographs of the concentration camps:

> I turned the page. There was another picture, worse than the first, and another worse still on the following two pages. I put the record carefully down on my bed and picked up another, Como's very latest hit. I read the title of the A-side. It said, "Till the End of Time." (*BWK*, p. 233)

The world of Matt's adolescence, in which evil can be represented by The Masked Marvel and warded off by Bing Crosby, whose "filmed image couldn't be brought into any proximity with the facts of war" (*BWK*, p. 211), vanishes instantly. The dark glass of popular culture, apparently designed to shield North American society from the truth about human nature, has been removed. Matt is suddenly face to face with incalculable evil.

Matt's story is 'affirmative,' then, insofar as it enacts a movement from illusion to truth. But the nature of that truth is purely negative. It implicitly defines man as, in Viktor Frankl's terms, "that being who has invented the gas chambers of Auschwitz...." [10] In the other narrative strand of *Black and White Keys*, the story of Andrew Goderich's wartime experience, Hood has tried to dramatize the perception that underlies the second half of Frankl's sentence: "however, he is also that being who has entered those gas chambers upright, with the Lord's Prayer or the *Shema Yisrael* on his lips."[11]

Andrew's story begins where Matt's ends, with an initiation into the truth about the concentration camps. In late 1941 Andrew is recruited by officials of the Canadian government to participate in a rescue mission whose object is to free from Dachau the philosopher Georg Mandel, who, we are given to understand, is a sort of Einstein in his field. The central section of the novel describes the rescue itself, as Andrew and his friend Sam Aaronsohn successfully spirit Mandel away from Dachau, and, by means of an underground railway, get him into Switzerland, although the escape costs Aaronsohn his life, and the enfeebled Mandel dies soon afterward. Following the war Andrew writes a book called *Sin Quantified*, a philosophical treatise on genocide, and is awarded the Nobel Peace Prize for 1950.

Hood runs enormous risks in using this material. Mandel has been the subject of medical experiments which have left him with an artificially-created clubfoot. At the time of his rescue, he has been frozen almost to death in another experiment. He weighs sixty pounds. His body is crisscrossed with scores of cuts. This is not the place for the glib invocation of some triumphantly 'Christian perspective,' nor for ecumenical smarminess. To reduce Mandel to a factor in some theological equation would be to commit a kind of secular blasphemy. But the evil that his story embodies must be confronted, if Hood is not to fail in the task that he has set for himself.

As in ''A Near Miss,'' analogues and allusions help to interpret the action but are ultimately dwarfed by the nature of the characters' own experiences. Andrew muses about the fact that the rescue attempt is to take place on the Sunday after Easter: ''If Mandel were to escape from Dachau, the action would be about as close to an actual descent into the inferno, followed by a miraculous ascent, as life would allow. The world seemed full of analogies to the Christological drama'' (*BWK*, p. 129). But the identification of Mandel and Christ is not insisted upon, even when the literal action makes it difficult to avoid. For example, when Mandel's body temperature rises to the point at which blood begins to flow from his wounds, Hood keeps the reader's attention focused firmly on the physiological facts. Nor is our attention explicitly drawn to the clubfoot as a sign of Satan's power to do harm. For Mandel must be present to the reader as human being, not symbol, if Hood is to have any chance of succeeding. Evil makes itself incarnate in the excruciating details of what has been done to Mandel's body; in contemplating those details, we respond to the horror of evil with the greatest possible intensity.

In the core passage of *Black and White Keys*, Andrew revives the near-

183

ly frozen Mandel by means of his own body heat, "married to a dying man in a fearful parody of a wedding" (*BWK*, p. 154). Then comes a sovereign moment, which is not perhaps one of *metanoia* (since Andrew is already in some sense aware of the "enlarged vision" which that term implies), but is nonetheless the occasion of a spiritual experience on which affirmation can with confidence be based:

> There was some looming entity covering the two men and — this seemed more and more present and given — watching over them . . . . he and his beloved spouse in grace, the great mind, the lord of European thought, were robed in the protection of the Divine Love, in the presence of God. (*BWK*, pp. 155-56)

We are not meant to understand this talk about God as metaphorical. Hood is not using it to describe in some indirect way the triumph of the human will-to-live (exemplified by Mandel's endurance) or the triumph of human altruism (exemplified by Andrew's willingness to risk his life for the philosopher's sake), though he is celebrating these qualities. What Hood is most intent on celebrating is the divine source of value for any human action, celebrating, quite simply, the presence of the God of Jews and Christians, the God who does not despise or abhor the affliction of the afflicted, and does not hide his face from him. The holy marriage of Christian and Jew obliterates the distinction between them, which is — and this has long been a theme in Hood's work — essentially an illusion in any case, perhaps the most diabolical of 'dark glasses' to have warped our civilization's perception of itself.

To speak naturally of divine intervention in the lives of individuals who are not psychotic is of course anathema to the critic who wants 'adequate motivation.' Hood's own remarks on the question are worth quoting here. "I don't think the bulk of extra-conscious motivation is sub- or pre- or unconscious at all," he has said in an interview; "I think it's superconscious in the Latin sense of coming from above, coming . . . from the Holy Ghost — down from above and enlightening and illuminating, not a dark pall cast up from below."[12] If genocide has "a Scriptural, a prophetic significance" (*BWK*, p. 283), so then does any thoughtful response to it that transcends despair about the fate of humanity.

In the face of the apparently complete triumph of evil, Viktor Frankl reports, some men did not lose their perception of the divine, did not

184

believe Satan's lie, but chose to remain open to the vision that Georg Mandel and Andrew Goderich experience. For Hood, embracing this vision is the essential moral act. To deny it is to surrender to "a dark pall cast up from below." To be open to it is to affirm "the coherence and familiarity of being." The dark glass is everywhere in the world of Marnie, of Matt, of Andrew, but Hood's art continually leads his reader to apprehend the Identity behind it.

III

The subject matter demands that the dark glass be particularly dark in the world of *Black and White Keys*. But it is not as though that novel records Hood's belated discovery of the existence of evil. He is merely applying in a different way the principles that have always governed its presentation in his work. The (relative) innocence of vision embodied by the earlier novels in *The New Age/Le nouveau siècle* is far from pre-lapsarian. Even in the worlds of *The Swing in the Garden*, *A New Athens*, and *Reservoir Ravine* (the target of the complaint which I quoted at the beginning of this essay), evil has usurped a place for itself. Comprehensive discussion of this issue is impossible here, but it should be useful to conclude with a brief comment on *Reservoir Ravine*.

In this work, Hood is hardly unwilling to deal with evil. Again and again he allows it to reveal itself in terms of limitation of vision — the perverse human capacity to let ourselves be blinded to what is true and good. For example, materialism is rampant in the Toronto of the Twenties; but in Andrew Goderich's opinion, " 'Money is the most ingenious of all fictions' " (*RR*, p. 227). He and Isabelle choose to make love, not money, the centre of their lives. (Andrew first realizes that he loves her as he watches the worthless money of the Domestic and Foreign Bank of Upper Canada go up in flames.) A second example: one of the speakers in the Hart House debate argues that Canada should act only on the basis of self-interest, but an "unassuming history don" (*RR*, p. 54) — not identified, but revealed in *Black and White Keys* to be Charlie Pope, a civil servant whose career runs suspiciously parallel to Lester Pearson's — appeals successfully to an idea of Canada based on the belief that " 'the Holy Land *is* in Manitoba and in Quebec, and it is the other way around too' " (*RR*, p. 55). Always there is the possibility of responding to what Northrop Frye calls "an enlarged vision of the dimensions of human life." Rejection of such vision leads to Mr. Chastel Baby's suicide, to Mounties riding into the crowd in the Winnipeg General Strike, to the panic after the crash of '29, to anti-Semitism — Hood does not labour these points, but they are made.

A striking minor example of such a point is provided by Matt Goderich's meditation on the word "cunt":

> How can that word, and the flesh it names, come to be the name used for the grossest wish to insult? . . . Herod slaughtered infants in cradles and would have reached into wombs with coat hangers . . . Herod is the abortionist, the king of anti-life. . . . Is it Herod then who makes the cunt the name of insult, a gross murdering stinking dark? (*RR*, pp. 194-95)

Taken in isolation, this passage may appear bizarre: a typological explanation for a contemporary obscenity. But its presence demonstrates Hood's supreme confidence in the method he uses consistently. A psychologist investigating the reasons for the status of "cunt" as an obscenity would be unlikely to find it useful to mention Herod. But for Hood, the reference to Herod furnishes the context needed for right understanding. Hood's reader (who may have his own "unwillingness to deal with evil" as Hood would define it) is forced to consider the issue not as the psychologist would, but as the spectator of a drama depicting spiritual warfare between darkness and light. The method is designed precisely to focus the reader's attention on the question of good — and evil.

Notes

[1] Hugh Hood, *Reservoir Ravine* (Ottawa: Oberon, 1979), p. 207. All further references to this work appear in the text.

[2] Sam Solecki, "Songs of Innocence," rev. of *Before the Flood: Our Exagmination round His Factification for Incamination of Hugh Hood's Work in Progress*, ed. J.R. (Tim) Struthers, and *Reservoir Ravine*, by Hugh Hood, *The Canadian Forum*, Oct. 1979, p. 30.

[3] Solecki, too, acknowledges this; see his "The Gospel of St. Andrew," rev. of *Black and White Keys*, by Hugh Hood, *The Canadian Forum*, Dec.-Jan. 1982-83, p. 38.

[4] Hugh Hood, "A Near Miss," in his *Dark Glasses* (Ottawa: Oberon, 1976), pp. 36-52. All further references to this work appear in the text. The date of composi-

tion of "A Near Miss" is given in J.R. (Tim) Struthers' "A Bibliography of Works by and on Hugh Hood," in *Before the Flood: Our Exagmination round His Factification for Incamination of Hugh Hood's Work in Progress* (Downsview, Ont.: ECW, 1979), p. 243.

[5]Robert Browning, "By the Fire-side," ll. 231-35, 241-45, in his *Poetical Works 1833-1864*, ed. Ian Jack (London: Oxford Univ. Press, 1970), p. 588.

[6]Browning, ll. 196-97, p. 587.

[7]Northrop Frye, *The Great Code: The Bible and Literature* (Toronto: Academic, 1982), p. 130.

[8]Hood has had fun with this image earlier in the story. When, on the eve of their wedding, Paul and Marnie stand beside each other, she notes that "tomorrow night we'll be face to face" (*DG*, p. 47).

[9]Hugh Hood, *Black and White Keys* (Downsview, Ont.: ECW, 1982), p. 283. All further references to this work appear in the text.

[10]Viktor E. Frankl, *Man's Search for Meaning: An Introduction to Logotherapy* (New York: Pocket Books, 1963), p. 213.

[11]Frankl, p. 213.

[12]Hugh Hood, "An Interview with Hugh Hood," by J.R. (Tim) Struthers, in *Before the Flood: Our Exagmination round His Factification for Incamination of Hugh Hood's Work in Progress*, ed. J.R. (Tim) Struthers (Downsview, Ont.: ECW, 1979), p. 76.

Keith Garebian
IN THE END, A BEGINNING:
THE MONTREAL STORY TELLERS

There is no need to be elegiac, to return with honeyed nostalgia to their collective past when they sounded their variable literary passions. There is, to be sure, something ironic about having to commemorate a group who, on occasion, outnumbered their audience — but, then, this is Canada, where the most exquisite tortures of indifference or apathy are devised for many an artist or craftsman of significance. They were strong enough to stay on home-soil and struggle to be heard in spite of the popular trend for writers to take off to Paris or London in order to learn certain modernist modes of art. Nor did they try to be wan, genteel, or European, although in certain cases their sophistication was decidedly inspired by foreign masters.

Unlike Grove, Callaghan, or MacLennan, they were not real pioneers, except in the sense of bringing attention to voice and texture in short fiction. But they were dragon-fighters or, more properly, dinosaur-slayers — the dinosaur being the antiquated conventions that Ray Smith found massively predictable and lumbering in fiction: "If we can reconstruct a novel from a fragment it is a dinosaur, extinct, and no damn use to a writer today."[1] And so, Smith, with the cosmopolitan inspiration of Borges, Barth, Barthelme, Vonnegut, Pynchon, Nabokov, and Brautigan, attempted to slay the dinosaur with "speculative fiction" — "Generally ironic in tone. Aesthetic in approach."[2] He made special claims for fiction's truth even while subverting expectations by glittering, wily, often precious techniques that deconstructed reality into a sum whose parts — like one of the special connotations for the title "Colours"[3] — were versatile variations, particles whose precision, accuracy, and virtuosity could be

188

perceived and appreciated only by alert imagination, intelligence, and a lust for experimental form. In his fiction, Smith approaches the dinosaur with a cluster of weapons — images, moods, words, characters — that trace a line of attack first to the right, then curve to the left, and finally disappear in a puff of smoke. And it is not at all a solemn battle. In fact, it is a game of gestures where even such devices as italics, capital letters, parentheses, and semi-colons have strategic value. And parody rampant is set against sobriety couchant till the field of literature is bespotted by the sometimes overstated colours of aesthetic bravado.

"Symbols in Agony,"[4] a short story that appeared in the signal issue of *Journal of Canadian Fiction* where for the first time all members of the Montreal Story Teller Fiction Performance Group were represented together, gives ample evidence of Smith's penchant for parody. Subtitled "A Canadian Short Story," it is really a rib-tickler with multiple literary targets: genteel, bourgeois sentimental fiction; Westerns (particularly frontier literature); and Canadian naturalism. There is a colourful gallery of caricatures: sensitive Josh who needs a Secret Place for his soul-plumbing sensitivity; his mother Sarah with the unwaveringly "high, firm bosom";[5] Old Doc Miller, one of the town's secret drinkers; Father Dogan, "an out and out drunk, like all Catholics";[6] Indian Joe, Josh's secret soul-mate; and the parade of 'types' that crowd the story for its finale. Some of this comedy is sophomorish, but there is fine subtlety amid the broad burlesque. Understated gesture has a contrapuntal complement in overstated portent: "Joe nodded slightly; Josh returned the gesture. It was a moving demonstration of affection and respect."[7] Passion is empurpled by the pitch and tenor of exaggeration, but the farcical excesses underscore Smith's supple ribbing of conventions: "Claret and port at table did not constitute secret drinking but a mark of gentle society, as shown in numberless English novels."[8]

Parody can date itself quickly and can explode itself by excessive jocularity, but this story lends substance to Dwight Macdonald's view that parody is "an intuitive kind of literary criticism, shorthand for what 'serious' critics must write out at length."[9]

In his more absurdist or fantastical stories, Smith is never as broad in his mode. Indeed, the predominant impression he creates is that of a sly, cryptic, ludic tactician. From his first collection, *Cape Breton is the Thought-Control Centre of Canada* (1969), Smith has baffled many critics by radical experiments with language and form. Part of the critics'

189

problem is their lack of a vocabulary adequate enough to deal with the dichotomy of form and content — a dichotomy which in Smith's case arises from a parodic playfulness that often obscures his serious concerns with subject matter. Although the distinction between form and content has been at the heart of western civilization's literary art, criticism in English has not yet solved the difficulty of vocabulary. Smith, who pointed out the crucial correlation between aesthetics and criticism in a recent and interesting graduate essay on *Moby-Dick*, suggests that "it is necessary, especially when approaching a difficult work, to keep constantly in mind the sense that style and content are one, to emphasize not the separation of analysis, but the unity of synthesis, to emphasize the artist and his procedures and concerns."[10] Part of our approach to a complex work, he adds, "should be to try to get a sense of the author's mind moving in, through, behind, under (whatever) the text as he searches for the efficient form, the embodiment, the realization of the complex of ideas, images, dreams, words, anecdotes and memories in his mind."[11] This valuable suggestion needs to be applied to Smith's own work, which frequently resorts to non-narrative techniques in order to break the smooth surface of a story and to compile disparate elements such as mythology, sociology, ballad, aphorism, anecdote, comic dialogue, statement, and allusion. The artist's balance between form and content must also be held in the reader's mind, and this involves "subtlety, care, patience, and imagination in reading."[12]

Lawrence Garber demonstrates with admirable incisiveness how a story by Smith often calls into question a number of story-telling conventions having to do with narrative continuity, character identities, formal design, and philosophic overview so that we may perceive with sharper clarity the *variables* in literary craft.[13] It is almost as if Smith were a cunning but apolitical Polonius by indirections seeking a direction out. The lack of a firm authorial voice is a deliberate feature, as it often is in post-modernist fiction. Of course, in a fundamental sense, the narrative or non-narrative text is always a ventriloquist's act, for the author has the last resort, the final pull on all the strings, the editorial decision, and is responsible for the virtuoso generation of voices that could never be created *ex nihilo*.

With *Lord Nelson Tavern* (1974), Smith won Kent Thompson's high accolade: "...I think that Ray Smith is the best writer in Canada right now. (Have you read LORD NELSON TAVERN?) He has used the short story as a tool to write a book — which is almost a patented Canadian technique. (See Hood's AROUND THE MOUNTAIN, Laurence's A BIRD IN THE HOUSE, Munro's LIVES OF GIRLS AND WOMEN, Bruce's THE TOWNSHIP OF TIME, and my much inferior Seeg-and-Greta stories .... ''[14] *Lord Nelson Tavern* presents short glimpses — the sort of revelations that Paleologue obtains in the novel itself. Sub-titles, ironic humour, and parody are the crux of Smith's repertoire, and while the cumulative effect is, for some readers, a little trying, the narrative glints with the often enigmatic eccentricities of characters who are caught in their mixture of guilts, perversions, loves, fantasies, and animosities.

Against Smith's compressed technique, Raymond Fraser's booming Maritime vigour and directness seem, with subtle undertows of psychological configuration, like a roaring tide battering the literary shore. Born in Chatham, New Brunswick, in 1941, the same year as the Cape Bretoner Smith, Fraser (the former Associate Editor of *Midnight*, founder of *Intercourse*, executive member of the Flat Earth Society, and self-declared First Lord of the Admiralty of the legitimate Stuart Monarchy[15]) was clearly the group's robust, irrepressible primitive. *The Black Horse Tavern* (1972), his collection of stories, established his gift as an oral taleteller, whose rawness and crudity were redeemed by an unvarnished zest for life and love and honesty. Fraser's narrative ancestors are not only the old salts of every Maritime tavern or watering-hole, but also the more commemorated figures of Mark Twain and Hugh Garner. Today his co-ordinates are probably W.P. Kinsella (in his Silas Ermineskin stories) and Jack Hodgins, who possess, no doubt, greater literary skill and ingenuity, but not necessarily a greater amount of brio. In a classic bawdy tale such as ''Spanish Jack,'' where a randy septuagenarian, under the influence of booze doctored by an aphrodisiac, bites off one of the tits of his wizened wife, salty vulgarity is turned into a pleasurable sensation. In fact, the entire book is blessed by an amiable colloquialism through which Fraser is able to arouse our delight in his wicked sequence of tales that follow hotly one upon another. Fraser's characters thrive on their wits, but their strengths are far from pretentious. The style is straightforward. Sophistication — especially verbal — is used as a target of satire, for Fraser's sympathies are clearly with the failures, bums, and derelicts

191

who populate his stories like a teeming multitude from a purgatorial half-life of stress and misadventure.

Fraser's books (which include *East of Canada: An Atlantic Anthology*, co-edited with Clyde Rose and Jim Stewart) show his attachment to the Maritimes, and his two published novels manifest the raw elements of his achievements as a writer. *The Struggle Outside* (1975) is a satire on revolutionary struggle, set risibly in New Brunswick. Written purportedly in the manner of a combat journal, it is a frequently rollicking political misadventure where violence and cruelty vie against comic clumsiness and naïveté as a small band of the Popular Liberation Party tries a revolution. Full of humorous incident and dialogue, it bounces along to its inevitable dénouement of disillusionment and defeat. In *The Bannonbridge Musicians* (1978), a group of young Maritimers hit the big time in Toronto, and the raunchy anecdotes (which end sadly, in human waste) concentrate on action and dialogue. There is no finesse, but there is certainly tempo. Once again, Fraser's comically grotesque art, always on the verge of pornography, is sharpened and justified by his uncompromising vision of life. Once again, the main characters are what are normally called 'losers,' who are perpetually on the run from tavern to shack to nightclub to highway. The King George Tavern is a principal setting, just as taverns predominate in David Fennario's seedy plays of life in Montreal's scruffy Point St. Charles. Fraser stands as the Fennario of fiction, sharing with the ghetto Montrealer not a raucous absorption in naïve or primitive politics, but an acute ear for the sounds of low-lifers.

Fraser's *The Fighting Fisherman: The Life of Yvon Durelle* (1978) is a highlight in Canadian sports biography, and provides vivid insights into his literary method. Really a collage of newspaper reports, interviews, anecdotes, eye-witness accounts, and the author's candid reactions to his subject, *The Fighting Fisherman* has a vulgar flamboyance that issues from ex-professional boxer Yvon Durelle himself. Having watched Durelle from a distance, once as a boy of eight in Chatham, Fraser formed an opinion or two but still did not have a clear perception of the boxer who became a mythic hero for an entire country, especially for a region noted for rocky fortunes. Although filled to the brim with the effusions of its rough-cut protagonist — all his vulgar humour, gross pranks, demon habits, distresses, and wild caprices — the biography becomes a muted elegy by the end, and achieves a level of

192

genuine pathos for a figure whom Canadian sports legend might have squandered ruthlessly.

Like his main characters, Fraser keeps in motion — retreating to his native region, for a time, then heading for Paris and, most recently, back to Montreal. Aesthetically, he remains apart from the rest of the group, for Fraser's robust, vulgar style appears to grow out of his un-varnished milieus rather than out of literary or intellectual designs. Whereas he gives attention to the primal drives and urges of men and generally allows his characters to speak free of authorial mediation, Blaise, Metcalf, and Hood take calculated pains to deliver their existen-tial truths in forms that are meant to honour sincerity by high craft. ,

Clark Blaise, born in 1940 of a French-Canadian salesman-father, is a *rara avis*, ''the only Canadian writer born in Fargo, North Dakota.''[16] He and his family returned to Winnipeg, his mother's city, whenever his father ran out of work, and Blaise believes that Canada cultivated an unused part of him that America never touched: ''The significant blob of otherness in my life has always been Canada; it sits like a helmet over the United States, but I was the only person who felt its weight.''[17] His parents had moved back to Canada at a time when its differences from the U.S. were ''unforced but extreme.''[18] Canada, to him, was ''a novel that others found dull and difficult, but that I found interesting and accessible from the beginning. You could say that my life was a dissertation on the subject of Canada and the United States, and what it is like, being a part of both.''[19]

This sense of unique bilateralism is conveyed with piquant force in Blaise's first collection of short fiction, *A North American Education* (1973), where, as Robert Lecker observes, the paradoxical impulse is, on one hand, a ''tragic recognition of change,'' and, on the other, a ''recognition that the nature of change can never be precisely ar-ticulated.''[20] The next collection, *Tribal Justice* (1974), is unified by the idea of tribes or groups of people locked into attitudes, loyalties, and feelings. The stories are often vignettes or anecdotes, where climax is metaphysical rather than purely dramatic. In fact, for Blaise ''The most interesting thing about a story is not its climax or dénouement — both dated terms — nor even its style and characterization. It is its begin-ning, its first paragraph, often its first sentence.''[21]

The philosophical tenor of *Tribal Justice* sheds light not only on

Blaise's attitudes towards life, but also on his aesthetics. The narrator of "The March" speaks of his story as "A determinist romance where transcendence lives a microsecond before it dims into nothing new. I am moved by that in art, in life; by the slow revelation of a larger design, the way we live one detail at a time and never know the depth and the extent — the meaning — of what we have made."[22] Blaise's stories, for all their raw texture, can be construed as a slow revelation of a large design — of what it means to be a member of a tribe that is stagnant, inert, or confused. The insights are often as concrete and precise as any by Alice Munro — without her fastidious attention to endings. They are occasionally as richly comic as some by Mordecai Richler — without his emphasis on parody. Although they appear to come at the last minute (just as in John Cheever's rhetorical flourishes) they are not massive or luridly apocalyptic — but simply incremental perceptions of a world where everyone's heart is broken.

Blaise's writing has sharp autobiographical underpinnings, and it yields the sense of a writer seeking to understand his mixed identity in a confused world. Blaise's self participates in four cultures and two continents — partly by his French-Canadian, English-Canadian, and American origins and partly by his marriage to Indian scholar and novelist Bharati Mukherjee. In *Days and Nights in Calcutta* (1977), a documentary record of a visit to India, written in collaboration with his wife, Blaise dramatically sifts the peripheral from the central, forces a swift pace on haphazard events, strives for transitions and epiphanic climaxes, while managing to convince us that his adventures are lived rather than simply verbalized. His open-mindedness produces textures that convey remarkably well the heterogeneous modes and multiple paradoxes of Indian life: right from a Goan orchestra and its singer doing a medley of recent hit tunes in the voices of Streisand, Warwick, Flack, and Fitzgerald, to the garbage heaps and human scavengers of Calcutta; a gray, classic 1937 Citroen with boxes on its sagging canvas roof; Mommy-di carrying a ring of keys around her own house like a mediaeval jailer; and a father-in-law, formerly sympathetic to Hitler, who is now a devout Hindu and prays for three hours daily.

Days and Nights in Calcutta (the title is a variation on Satyajit Ray's film-title *Days and Nights in the Forest*) is reminiscent at times of darkest Naipaulia. It is certainly at times "a circle of hell"[23] — a seething mass of primitive commerce and community, a world where function and duty are decreed in the throes of poverty, squalor, and pain. Husband

194

and wife engage in their separate but intersecting quests, forcing old wounds to the surface, entering into a drama which demands a certain tenderness but, ultimately, a disengagement. Blaise feels his marriage rocked to the core, and his wife laments and deplores the Indian sacrifice of improvisation just for the sake of propriety and obedience. As the Blaises return from India's shadow, their courageous self-exposure becomes not a refinement of sensibility but a provocation of the West's forgotten primitive self.

The primitive self is something that Blaise never avoids. *Lunar Attractions* (1979), his award-winning first novel, is a richly textured book which explores the primal instincts of lust and life in America of the 1950s. An intelligent but vulnerable boy, son of a clairvoyant and a prizefighter, grows up with the dark side of man's nature in central Florida. An only child, he enjoys dual worlds of fevered dream and reality. He identifies with fear, nightmare, and unanswered things; and, at the end, in an explosive climax of orgasmic passion, he seems a strangely mythic figure, like Margaret Atwood's anonymous heroine in *Surfacing*.

Written as a form of psychological fiction, *Lunar Attractions'* many features — light satire, painful comedy, lurid sexual drama — are skilfully interwoven and altered to suggest the different transformations of the protagonist, David Greenwood. The narrative crystallizes at strategic points in shocking images etched in the hero's mind, *tableaux vivants* through which we learn about dark forces that exist beyond our control or our desire for omniscience. It is a chilling, amusing, strangely moving novel about "the most dangerous, most corrupt kind of knowledge,"[24] by a writer for whom the grotesque is a vision of man's battle with the irrational — the demons that would destroy him for his complicated innocence.

Blaise's books are paradigms of cultures and their times. *Lusts* (1983), his second novel, mirrors the 1950s and 1960s in America, as well as the consequences of a dream turning to nightmare and spitting one out at the bottom. Epistolary in form, it tells its story as a mosaic. Rosie Chang, at the University of California in Berkeley, is writing "a frank discussion"[25] of the life and poetic art of the late Rachel Isaacs (Durgin), who suddenly and inexplicably committed suicide in a warm tub only a few feet away from where her husband, Richard, was watching football on television. Rosie solicits correspondence and manuscripts, and receives from Richard Durgin in Rajasthan, India, a story

195

of lusts and redemption. Lusts for sex, power, love, adventure, industrial progress. Redemption for his soul.

On one level, *Lusts* is a story of tragic Rachel, a child of the movie industry, Italian-educated daughter of a German Jewish refugee. Just as the Italian neo-realists (whom she admires) shot their films in silence and then dubbed them in a studio, she writes poetry by first imagining scenes and then adding words to them. The idea that words have meaning apart from things is a kind of liberation. Rachel is wounded by her European Jewishness and by her American citizenship. Europe loses its conscience and does not recognize its brutal violation of her sensitivity. America adopts too casual and too insensitive an attitude to her silent *angst*. As in *Tribal Justice* and *Lunar Attractions*, life refuses to assume a tractable shape. As Richard Durgin admits: "We plan our lives along gentle curves, and I guess that's the safest way of anticipating the unknown. But our lives are really a series of breaks, falls, bubbles, and crashes."[26] Durgin is Blaise's persona — the voice of conscience and the literary creator — who acknowledges that reality is too monstrous for irony, and irony too stern a measure for a simple truth.

Lusts is about Rachel's suicide in the face of a callously intolerant and brutal world. It is also about her husband's penitence, and about the vulnerable 1950s and 1960s. In moving from America to Europe and India, the novel dramatizes Durgin's entry into a new stage of life. In a fundamental sense it is a tale of betrayal. Betrayed by her German father who sells out to Hollywood, betrayed, too, by the men in her lives, Rachel discovers that America also betrays her with Vietnam. The unconscionable comedy of the television programme *Hogan's Heroes* provides the final evidence that she seeks: "proof that the European millions had died in vain, and that her country and her times were incapable of absorbing the lesson."[27] When one of Durgin's tastelessly cruel jokes makes her snap and she commits suicide, there is an allegorical implication. For a long time, America was a shield that she used to keep Europe safe and distant. Her husband has been America for her; and, by propelling her suicide, he (America) kills her. Filled with the ashes of guilt, Durgin, a widower again when his Indian wife succumbs to cancer, does his penance in the East, waiting for redemption.

The ending of *Lusts* is a reminder of Blaise's discovery in *Days and Nights in Calcutta* that "All experience of India is a passage into myths that are still functional, rituals that still signify, art (like the classical dance) that is forever *in creation*."[28] Blaise's total fiction appears to be an

196

entry into myth, a signifying art whose purpose is illumination of the design and texture of life. Blaise is a meditative writer, but the density of his meditation never arrests the flow of his narrative. He addresses himself to existential crises with dramatic flair. Because the retrieval of his buried self is an exploration of thick, multitudinous paradoxes of personal mythology, this existential drama will not wane.

By the very nature of his academic career as English and Writing professor in city after city (in the U.S. and Canada), Blaise appears to be in flight; but his habit of transience is, perhaps, a manifestation of his appetite for new experience — an existential correlative for his lust in fiction to begin anew. In his seminal essay "To Begin, to Begin," he imparts the lesson that "art wishes to begin, even more than end."[29] This conviction may well account for the impressive openings in his fiction ("I cherish openings more than endings"[30]) and for his preoccupation with genesis rather than apocalypse. Blaise's stories, however, do not reveal their machinery nakedly. As John Metcalf attests, they run "on wheels," with Blaise creating the illusion that he is "merely the almost invisible track"[31] on which they run.

John Metcalf, born in 1938 in Carlisle, County Cumberland, in the north of England, is — to use Clark Blaise's term — a "resident alien,"[32] often reviled as a bloody Brit by those super-nationalists who take his cultural criticism as a malicious slur against their identity. But while aesthetically aligned with Kingsley Amis, Keith Waterhouse, and Beryl Bainbridge, and while maintaining proud attachments to Evelyn Waugh and P.G. Wodehouse, Metcalf is no less Canadian for his thoroughly satirical stance against the various individuals, institutions, and systems that demean taste in this land. His short stories, written with the painstaking craft of a master diamond-cutter who studies every surface and edge for his most decisive strike, glint with purity of intention and clarity of revelation. They show a painstaking concern for rhythm, mode of caricature, and texture; every device is a refinement of technique — even the punctuation, whose importance Metcalf deems to be "not exclusive to the wildly avant-garde or to the wiltingly effete but ... common to all writers who are alive to the possible music of prose."[33] Acutely aware that "For many writers of fiction there is a conflict between ear and eye" because "the conventional symbols do not translate fully all the nuances of the voices that speak on the page,"[34] he has tried "for some years now to establish a system of punctuation which is more sensitive to voice than the conventions allow and which, at the same time, is not peculiar to my own individual voice.''[35] This preoccupation is not to be confused with Ray Smith's idiosyncratic deployment of punctuation for parody. Metcalf, who confesses to a bemusement with post-modernism, which he calls ''a sort of literary Rubik's Cube,''[36] approaches fiction as ''a verbal structure''[37] where words are manipulated ''in a delicious order''[38] and where elegance and what Waugh called '' 'an exercise in the use of language' ''[39] count for far more than ideas or philosophy. In Metcalf's fiction, punctuation becomes elegant calligraphy, a score to direct the verbal music to a well-shaped end. ''Italic hereby becomes interior speech — words formulated but not uttered.''[40] A combined use of single and double quotation marks ''helps to establish the consciousness of the character and adds intensity and *drama* to his immobility and concentration''; it also serves for ''irony or the negation of statement.''[41] ''Paragraphing of non-dialogue within dialogue is particularly useful in *orchestrating* dialogue — in building rhythms, in delaying the beat, in establishing pause and silence, and, by absence, in increasing tempo.''[42] Naturally, all this fussing over form puts Metcalf squarely against the crude thematic tradition of Canadian writing, and he admits: ''I haven't got a Garrison Mentality and I'm not at Stage Three or a Victim or on Cloud Nine or whatever the fuck all that twaddle was about. My work suffers from a paucity of Indians and Myth. I have very few readers and the critics are still largely baying at the thematic moon. I just potter about making Ronald Firbank noises.''[43]

Metcalf began his Canadian career with missionary work. He edited anthologies such as *Sixteen by Twelve* (1970) and *The Narrative Voice* (1972) largely because he wanted to remedy an appalling situation in Canadian schools where there was an almost total ignorance of indigenous writers. The Montreal Story Teller Fiction Performance Group was part of this missionary work because it tried to attract a new generation of readers for Canadian literature. As Doug Rollins described in a brief piece on the group, Metcalf and company took ''to toting cartons of their publications to readings.''[44] Metcalf's editorial spadework for Oberon Press's *Best Canadian Stories* and the *Impressions* series also helped to showcase fresh talent and to advance the idea of sophistication in contemporary fiction.

As far as his own work is concerned, Metcalf strives after ''an invisible iron control of material, a seemingly effortless flow of rhythm, wit, an exactness of word.''[45] What happens in a story is always less delightful to him than "the story's construction, its grammar, its nuts and bolts.''[46] Although he perceives life as incredibly funny (even at the most horrendous times), he finds it virtually impossible to deliver this comedy without an edge of sadness. A vivid example occurs in "The Lady Who Sold Furniture,''[47] in the scene where Peter Hendricks, the English teacher, discovers his lover Jeanne's essential dishonesty and amorality as she sells off the furniture in houses she has been hired to manage. Peter's feeling of devastation is first conveyed through shock right in the middle of a busy scene where movers are calling out to Jeanne just as Peter is attempting to confront her with his hurt. The emotional climax modulates into hollow sadness, and Peter's feelings find objective correlatives or contrasts in the still, stale objects around him — the congealed fat and the lace of a fried egg on the stove, a cigarette end floating in the cornflakes bowl, the grating noise of a radio, an empty hall, footsteps booming on the hollow stairs, litter on counter and bare board, and, in the middle of the room, a chair with a broken back.[48]

Another example of emotional colouration is in the careful plotting of "The Estuary,''[49] where David, the protagonist, suffers from "depth fatigue''[50] — apparently a result of an hysteria that even his psychiatrist does not comprehend. After building up David's history of apparently idle chatter and frustrating evasiveness, Metcalf creates a feeling of melancholy trance, heightened by a lyrical beach scene in Wales which culminates in an epiphanic climax. David, strung out by life, spies two large porpoises leaping and frolicking up the estuary. Transported out of his depression and agitation, he empathizes with the creatures whose movements and sounds he construes as a secret semaphore of kinship with him. When he cries out to them, the intensity of his reaction is misinterpreted as irrational and suicidal hysteria by witnesses.

The same quality of dark sadness wells up in the most outrageous comedy of *General Ludd* (1980), Metcalf's second novel. (His first was *Going Down Slow* in 1972, an apprentice-work about a Montreal school-teacher driven to neurosis by the anarchy of school life.) Here Metcalf deploys parody and black comedy to great effect, destroying his social and cultural *bêtes-noires* by ridicule or abuse, and working his way to a new accommodation with reality. As satire, this novel flourishes with a self-conscious moral impulse and battens itself on an ultimately cheerful pessimism that Céline might have envied. A satire on cultural decadence, *General Ludd* casts its protagonist, a poet-in-residence at a Jesuit-run college, as a latter-day Don Quixote tilting apoplectically at the modern world. Decadence here has several manifestations: a gross insensitivity to the spirit of language and, hence, of civilization; the pursuit of technology at the cost of taste; the exploitation of facile sentiment at the price of truth and sincerity; a capitulation to a mass of dunces; the democratization and, hence, the dilution of culture.

Filled with episodic set-pieces (a literary wine and cheese soirée; a nightclub misadventure; turbulent tutorials; a pastoral flight from the ills of city life; a neo-Luddite assault on machines), the novel uses jokes, caricature, and bawdry to startling effect. Sketches of the earnest Indian student, Mr. Bhardwaj, the perversely *schmaltzy* Itzic Zemermann, the culturally barbarous Cosimo O'Gorman, and a motley of academic nitwits, eccentrics, and perverts are droll triumphs. Clearly Metcalf thrives on comedy of humours; and, although the narrative is sometimes slowed by the blandly sincere Kathy, a foil to the hero, it yields distinguished dividends. James Wells, the anarchic protagonist (who in his quasi-madness is appropriately aligned with Ned Ludd, the nineteenth-century opponent of the Industrial Revolution), is a fulsome Jeremiah, full of biblical analogies, but a bit of a fool himself. Obviously a paranoid psychotic near the end, Wells prefers to remain somewhat deluded in his hysterical battle against civilization's real or imagined enemies. Yet although there is much that is impure about his reactionary behaviour, there is also an irreproachable core in his soul. Literature and language matter so deeply to him that he would rather go mad than acquiesce to the Vidigoths intent on vulgarizing and ravaging culture. His soul shares the late W.H. Auden's sentiments: "Time that is intolerant / Of the brave and innocent, / And indifferent in a week / To a beautiful physique, / Worships language and forgives / Everyone by whom it lives."[51]

Although *General Ludd* is at present Metcalf's most ambitious fiction, his truest form is, perhaps, the novella — of which he has given us four specimens: "The Lady Who Sold Furniture," "Private Parts," "Girl in Gingham," and "Polly Ongle."[52] Even at his most banal (as in "Girl in Gingham") Metcalf can take ordinary material and deliver sharp pricks of recognition about fundamental human truths. At his most colourful, Metcalf is a virtuoso of satiric modulation and pitch. "Private Parts" presents an English professor's reminiscence about sexuality and religiosity in his childhood and adolescence. The pastoral opening soon twists into grotesque comic and sexual adventure, as guilt over masturbation and pornographic fantasy is heightened by perverted religious puritanism. By the end, the spent erotic passion of the male protagonist (who is yet another writer) is sublimated by his desire for a new direction in life. Metcalf, as Robert Lecker points out, "does make use of the allegorical mode to broaden the implications of the narrator's tale and to draw our attention to the metaphorical aspects of his experiences."[53]

But Metcalf entreats us not to understand him too quickly: "I would ask you not to approach my stories as things to be understood but rather as things to be lived through and experienced."[54] "Bald and explicit statements" about his stories "are not the equivalents"; the life or reality of his stories is "in pictures, images, turns of phrase, in the echoes and reverberations the stories set up in your head."[55] "Well written stories," Metcalf contends, "are as complex as poems and it's hopeless to approach a story as if it were, say, newspaper prose. A good story needs savouring."[56] Metcalf's elegant textures and often understated wit can be appreciated only through an intelligent consideration of his sentence structure, punctuation, pacing, and dialogue. And his injunctions against paraphrase are not special pleading. He is not moved to vainglorious self-promotion. Indeed, he has frequently expressed dissatisfaction with his own work.

"Polly Ongle," however, should cause him to move from dissatisfaction to jubilation. It manifests both hard craft and delightful play. With flair to spare, it manages a neat balance between satire and black comedy, and its sheer vibrancy and linguistic precision challenge the critic to attempt a close textual examination. Set in Ottawa, the novella centres on forty-six-year-old Paul Denton, a husband and father to three children, who owns an art gallery where he cultivates a fascination for a nubile young woman (nicknamed Polly Ongle for a whimsical reason related to nail polish remover). The opening subject of the work is Paul's engorged but unsatisfied sexual desire. The images of "the hanging plant's soft tendrils," "stiff-hairy stems and open-mouthed flowers," and heavy, green clusters of tomatoes with a "chaste shine" are emblematic punctuation for his concupiscence. The

201

satire of his sexual misery (blamed, comically, on open-plan architecture that eliminates privacy and leads to his wife's anxiety about being caught *in flagrante delicto* by the children) links to his middle-aged character and problems with health. The protracted sexual deprivation becomes increasingly amusing as Paul fantasizes about it. He lives with "a great restlessness and longing as if the frustration of his semi-celibacy" has spread "like a malignancy." It appears that he has had a heart attack, but his unhappiness might be the sole reason for cardiac tautness. Everything feels to be somehow slipping away from him, and he can only daydream of heroic exploits or sexual revolution.

With his house in dire need of renovation, his business a precarious enterprise, his relationship with his punk-rock son fraught with ugly hostility, Paul is evidently on the way to devastation. The early pages of the novella build like a portentous wave before a resounding crash. The satire is freighted with sociological criticism, extremely reminiscent of the arching pessimism in *General Ludd*. Paul sometimes displays the same anger at cultural decadence as Wells does — but, perhaps, not quite so apoplectically.

The emotional power of the rhetoric is shaped by an unusually massive movement consisting of several pages of choler and bile, after which adjectival clauses topple over adverbial phrases like foam in the backwash of passion. In a sudden shift of rhythm and force, the long paragraph of this invective concludes with an exclamatory sentence and two emphatic phrases. Because Metcalf's verbal style is usually lean and wiry, understated rather than amplified, this passage becomes a *tour de force* of theatrical prose, and draws attention to his way with diction and rhythm.

The entire novella seems to be like the Cole Porter song played in a crucial scene, with a fluent passage from major to minor movements — although Metcalf also reverses the pattern. The misty sentimentality at times fits in effectively, because beneath it flows a genuine melancholy generated by Paul's inability to be larger than the miserably deficient life he's forced to lead. There are so many unrequited desires in the story: mundane or domestic, sexual, artistic, and spiritual. Nothing is quite at the right pitch or moment for the protagonist. Paul's fifteen-year-old punker son and his mousey-haired girlfriend and loutish buddies (nicknamed Deet, Wiggs, Munchy, etcetera) are symptoms of an essential malady in the younger generation. But Paul's own generation

202

is not excused for its flaws. His dentist is a comic grotesque; his art gallery is an emporium for Third World junk; and his florid sexual and political fantasies are a pathological condition.

"Polly Ongle" is surely the most theatrical of Metcalf's novellas. Right from The Canadian Grill scene (where Paul wines and dines the girl of his fantasies in an exotic restaurant) and the Iron Guard performance (whose loud, deafening music makes him think of Munch's *The Scream*) to the final tumid monologue (where all his passion erupts before he decides to face front and prepare himself "for the long littleness of life"), the pitch and projection are superbly realized. The story is rich, intense, lyrical, vividly dramatic — and painfully funny. There is a sometimes ineffable sadness sprung out of the gap between desire and fulfilment. The climax is reached outside the restaurant when Paul encounters his wayward son who is drunk and helpless. Suddenly, a dam bursts within the protagonist, and in an idiosyncratic mixture of bitterness, rueful anger, and wrily tender apology, he compulsively unburdens himself in Minto Park, beside a bronze statue of a South American general, champion of Chilean and Peruvian struggle. Whereas the real-life general was a revolutionary hero, Paul is a hero to himself only in fantasy or imagined scenes. Therefore, as the general becomes an extravagant counterpoint to Paul's trivial mundaneness, the protagonist is himself elevated — not by any melodramatic elation of spirit, but by a very convincing and modest adjustment to the nasty shortness of life. It is one thing to dream of "doing sweaty things with Bianca Jagger, of fighting heroically against BOSS to free Nelson Mandela from Robben Island," but there, at his feet, is his vomit- and blood-stained son with whom he must close ranks and march forward — even if only to the beat of a rather tired and awkward drummer.

Metcalf's concern with form and texture is similar to Hugh Hood's preoccupations.[57] Hood, however, offers greater density and complexity, partly because of the paramount importance he attaches to apocalyptic moral imagination. Born in Toronto in 1928, and a resident of Montreal since 1961, Hood is the oldest, the most solidly rooted, and the most spiritually composed of all the Montreal Story Tellers. I remember from my one direct experience of the group at a Montreal comprehensive high school (very much like the one satirized by Metcalf in *Going Down Slow*) that while Blaise and Metcalf performed with perfectly pitched wit and drama, Hood seemed the most self-assured, the most entertained by his own literary gifts. His habit of interrupting a reading to draw attention to a particular felicity of style or thought in his own work seems egotistical to those who do not appreciate his voluptuous optimism about art and the world. As a Catholic, Hood, of course, has a comic vision in the sense that he believes emphatically that the world is saved by Christ's Incarnation, Crucifixion, and Resurrection. Hood's entire body of work is informed by this Christian faith and hope; and, while some critics find that his vision is too free of anguish or the pressures of evil, a more accurate interpretation of his writing would be inclined to see it as a complex of long associative chains bound firmly around a faith in moral redemption.

Hood has spoken frequently about his own method, and has repeatedly invited critics to make allegorical or analogical interpretations of his work without necessarily forsaking the sheen of his realistic textures. In "trying to assimilate the mode of the novel to the mode of fully-developed Christian allegory," he believes that he is "more 'real' than the realists, yet more transcendent than the most vaporous allegorist."[58] His fiction creates relationships with the gospels and biblical parables, and he is one of few novelists today concerned with the holy life or the life of grace. But his allegory is not a primitive species. It is not at all like mediaeval allegory where ideas are always their own images. It never loses its sensory appeal or allows its inner meaning to clash against the literal reality through which the signification is maintained. His imagination is able to bring together various meanings at a single moment of action — like Dante's synchronous method — by conducting correspondences of the natural to the supernatural.[59] He starts with the commonest of things — streets, buildings, geography, ordinary people — and significant emblems emerge.

From his very first book of short stories — an early sign that his signature was, indeed, genuine — Hood's emblems fortify ideas and structures. The title story in *Flying a Red Kite* (1962) turns the human spirit, after several travails, into a sacramental. Most of the other stories in the book coalesce around two complementary themes: various gifts of the spirit, and the alarming "doubleness"[60] — or dichotomies of guarded assurance and tormenting suspicion — in life. The most successful stories show his attention to texture. In fact, *Flying a Red Kite* is such a virtuoso performance that it is hard to believe it is a beginner's collection. The emblems are organizing principles rather than sheer symbolic elements, and the apocalyptic endings obtain a special force.

Hood's short stories in themselves should surely earn him a significant reputation for all time. Seemingly incapable of writing a boring paragraph, Hood successfully mediates between the secular and the sacral, keeping his characters intensely human while probing their souls with deft sensitivity. In *Dark Glasses* (1976), he examines characters who fight spiritual battles against fear, guilt, deception, and other imperfections. Taking as his guiding text a quotation from St. Paul ("For now we see through a glass, darkly; but then face to face..." — 1 Cor. 13.12), Hood focusses his twelve stories on the themes of vision and the imperfection of human knowledge. The stories derive most of their force from qualities of light and disguise, and are arranged so that they begin with problems of penetrating existential paradoxes and end with an allegory of man's fate.

In *None Genuine Without This Signature* (1980), Hood turns to the signatures of our times (in sports, commerce, media, human relationships, music, etcetera). The language dances differently from story to story, acquiring additional grace from the signature of Hood's calm, spiritual self. The most striking experimental pieces are probably "Gone Three Days," "The Good Listener," and "Doubles," but the signature theme culminates in "The Woodcutter's Third Son" and "None Genuine Without This Signature, or, Peaches in the Bathtub." These two stories powerfully convey Hood's didactic craft, with the first one casting a spell of language and wit, while the second is offered to us as a mental movie.

Despite the not inconsiderable successes of these and other short story collections such as *Around the Mountain: Scenes from Montreal Life* (1967) and *The Fruit Man, The Meat Man & The Manager* (1971), of four early novels, and of the volume of essays *The Governor's Bridge is Closed* (1973), Hood's career commenced its steepest ascent with an epical series. The opening came with *The Swing in the Garden* in 1975, the first volume in a projected twelve-volume *roman fleuve* collectively entitled *The New Age/Le nouveau siècle*. The bilingual title is instructive of Hood's ambition to unite the whole country in fiction. Although *The Swing in the Garden* oppressed some readers because of its density of apparently trivial sociological detail and its seeming formlessness, it has since come to be regarded as "an innovative high point in Canadian fiction''[61] and as a repository of references for the entire series. In telling the story of young Matt Goderich (whose name alludes specifically to the biblical Matthew, author of the first gospel, and *Godes rice*, the kingdom of God), Hood is also telling the story of the country's coming of age in the years prior to the outbreak of World War II.

Influenced as much by Coleridge and Wordsworth as he is by Proust, Joyce, and Anthony Powell,[62] Hood achieves such encyclopaedic and original dimensions in his long fiction that these works invariably present a problem of labelling for critics. Thus, is *The Swing in the Garden* the ''documentary fantasy''[63] that Hood would have us believe it is? Or is it simply a Canadian version of Proust? Or is it a new form — a moral apocalyptic fiction with historical authenticity as its surface and spiritual optimism as its buoyant principle?

Actually the novel has to be placed in its proper context. It is but part of a series that is millennial in that the final volume (and Hood has already planned the general shape of the entire series) will be completed by 2000. Hood suggests that *The New Age* should be read like the Bible, Blake's *The Four Zoas*, or Joyce's *Finnegans Wake*.[64] This suggestion helps us to treat *The Swing in the Garden* not so much as a conventional novel but as a piece of fiction that assimilates realism, satire, and romance. The book's pastoralism (it is a quieter novel than any of its successors) yields not the innocence of prelapsarian Adam but an innocence put to the test. Like the biblical Adam, however, Matt Goderich finds the world and its history opening before him once he is expelled from the Edenic womb of his infant environment. There is a swing out of the garden of innocence into the fallen world. Whereas the biblical Adam was a creator in his inventory of the world, Matt is a creator in his cross-references, ramifications, and annotations. Strong intellectual illuminations charge Matt's consciousness, so that we grasp the special complexities of Canadian society as it grows up with Matt Goderich.

A New Athens (1977) is Hood's Book of Revelation. As Lawrence Mathews argues, it ''is ordered by means of a clear biblical structure'' that ''does not violate the conventions of realism.''[65] Matt here is a pilgrim who begins, like Wordsworth, with an excursion and, as his mind composes relationships among a multiplicity of experiences, connects the human and the divine through apocalyptic emblems that have an aesthetic intelligibility. An art historian with a degree in Art 'n' Ark (Art and Architecture), Matt uses ''The Janus-headed impulse of the historian, the looking before and after''[66] to lead us from the new

Athens (an Ontario town) to a New Jerusalem. As John Mills has argued, the anagogic method used so strongly in *White Figure, White Ground* (1964), Hood's first novel, now acquires a polished sophistication.[67] Matt combines the secular and the sacral without the slightest bit of damage to the narrative. Beginning on the road of Old Adam, he finds his world eventually absorbed into a visionary painting by his mother-in-law, Mrs. Codrington, which depicts the heavenly city on top of an enormous height irradiated by the glory of the Divine.

This apocalyptic vision of redemption — with Athens leading to Jerusalem — is extended in *Reservoir Ravine* (1979) where the New Jerusalem crystallizes in the image of a beautiful bride coming down from God in Heaven, all dressed for her husband. *Reservoir Ravine* is, perhaps, the only instance of a long fiction in which marriage occupies a central anagogical position. Marriage and generation are made the source of the deepest interlocking relationships and themes. Out of the context of the marriage of Matt's parents arise the issues of contracts, incarnations, and witnesses to time — the very material of human experience. The narrative form is peculiar, related in the third person and focussing on the years from 1921 to 1930, except for Chapter 11 which is set several decades later and in which Matt, now forty-nine years old, gives a first-person account of his gestation and all the factors that have made him the sort of person he is.[68] Chapter 11 has at least one reference to some event or character from each of the previous ten chapters, and it thereby is a compendium of past influences on his present consciousness. Serving as a witness to his parents' covenant of love, Matt is a Raphael figure who stirs "the waters"[69] of history and finds healing benediction for the productions of time that eternity loves.

The central characters of *Reservoir Ravine* are Matt's parents, Isabelle and Andrew, who first meet each other in the mid-1920s, "arguably the most exciting and transformative years of the century."[70] After an account of Isabelle's childhood and the pleasures and exceptional intellectual achievements of her youth, Hood leads to the parents' courtship, romance (that passes through fire and then ice before moving over water) and a wordless marriage proposal. Following the nuptials and honeymoon, the novel traces the rising fortunes of Andrew, a brilliant socialist philosopher who is preoccupied with the idea of justice. The final two chapters are Matt's, as he plays his Raphael role — comforting his old, blind mother, and serving as important witness to his parents' love and the *Zeitgeist* of Canada prior to the 1970s. The novel's only 'digression' is Hal Forbes's eye-witness retrospective, in Chapter 6, of the Winnipeg General Strike. Hal, a former suitor of Isabelle's, provides testimony about the incredible unrest in a country that Hood sees as having the potential to be another Holy Land once its two linguistic races have learned to love each other. Hal's memories suggest that Canada has to right itself and clear its conscience.

At the end of the book, the world of Matt's parents has changed. Germany is on the brink of a sinister new order (here Samuel Aaronsohn, an academic colleague of Andrew's, is a European witness to omens of world catastrophe) and philosophy is losing its way. This mood deepens in the next novel, *Black and White Keys* (1982), which is Hood's most explicit engagement with the problem of evil — at least in a historical context, as opposed to the purely fictive context of *You Cant Get There From Here*. A novel in two major tones, divided into five unequal chapters that alternate points of view, *Black and White Keys* tells two concomitant stories during World War II — Andrew Goderich's startling secret mission to rescue a renowned Jewish philosopher from the Dachau concentration camp; and Matt's experiences in the Toronto of the same era. Andrew's eerie, suspenseful adventures, most of which occur in shadow and darkness, are the black keys of the novel, whereas young Matt's intimations of the emotional tone of Canada in the early and mid-1940s are the white keys. However, the design is not quite that simple, because Andrew's story, while circumscribed by sorrowfully violent and sinful events, ascends to a plane of joyful and even glorious redemptive significance, whereas Matt's nostalgic reveries (about popular music, Hollywood movies, and other emblems of moral style) end portentously with signs of the Holocaust and cosmic destruction. The entire novel has a unity of idea, and becomes a symphonic analogy in which life, even in its most horribly iniquitous phases, unfolds as a Christological comedy of grace and salvation.

While there is no inherent philosophical anomaly about Andrew Goderich's wartime role (a leftwing Catholic, he has unusual moral courage and resigns from his tenured university position on a matter of principle), there is some question about its psychological credibility. Some readers may have to suspend disbelief in order to accept his unusual wartime heroism. There is also a problem with Andrew's winning of the Nobel Peace Prize in 1950, for here Hood too obviously

208

violates historical fact in order to serve his own moral fiction.

Despite these questions the book is suspenseful and subtle. The religious analogies are created intriguingly. Like his patron saint, Andrew is a missionary and a fisher of men. He spends much of his time crossing water — first the Atlantic, then lakes and seas in Europe — and his attempted resurrection of the great Jewish philosopher condemned to die at Dachau begins on Good Friday. The Dachau adventure becomes Andrew's metaphorical descent into Hell. At the same time, however, it yields a moment that innocently parodies the sacrament of marriage, as Andrew tries to revive the gravely ill philosopher by bodily warmth in a hayloft. A different form of parody[71] occurs when Matt's own story exhibits correspondences with the events and insights in his father's life. Hood's writing proves to be poignantly poetic even in times of great tension.

The question, of course, is how far Hood will stretch *The New Age* aesthetically. He has already made meditation a respectable element of Canadian fiction — Blaise has too, but in a more dramatic, less discursive manner — and he has sharpened our sense of the allegorical scope of modern literature. Even if the series were to fail at the end — and I bet that it will not — it will certainly be immortalized for having shown the country its own forms and features, and for having manifested our potential for moral greatness.

And so on to the millennium, whose vague shape makes it impossible to decide the fate of the disbanded group of Montreal Story Tellers, none of whom, ironically, was born in Montreal. The group played a brief but important role in stimulating parts of the Canadian clerisy to appreciate the quick quiddity of fiction — ah, the short story in oral reading could be as compelling as a poem — but, more importantly, it alerted readers to the subtler elements of form. While Ray Fraser, closest to the roots of mass culture, showed that popular literature could produce its own excellence without genuflecting to academic standards from on high, he was *l'homme moyen sensuel* among the élites — an important popularist who drew attention to the secret self of a non-élitist population and who found representations of its communal dreams. Free, as usual, from any sense of commitment to élitist literature, he takes off on foreign tours, and plans God knows what hilarious outrages to puritanical decency.

209

As for the others, Ray Smith, who had for a time appeared to muffle his creative voice, entertains his students at Dawson College in Montreal with a different mode of his lessons in fiction, and is preparing new stories for publication. His contribution — small in quantity, large in quality — lingers. Before Jack Hodgins brought the world of Gabriel García Márquez to Vancouver Island, before John Mills won acknowledgement for adjusting our literature to the tones of Céline and Burgess, before Leon Rooke delighted us with his bizarre superrealism, Ray Smith was practising an interior emigration of postmodernism — sending it from Canadian city to town, preparing the way for his successors. John Metcalf, an English expatriate, labours in Ottawa, scoring prose as if it were music for live performance, plotting further elegant and witty assaults on a Canadian literary establishment that still refuses to abandon its sanctimonious reverence for home-grown literary sod-busters. Clark Blaise, like the sea in its chains, rolls onto the shores of Canada and, after spending some of his compelling force, slips away for American shores where his ethnic mixture and his wife's Indian background will not meet with inhospitality. There he commands respectful attention on the book pages of *The New York Times* and wins fellowships to pursue his literary career. Only Hugh Hood remains wholly and unperturbedly himself. Equally at home in Montreal (where he teaches and resides) or in Toronto (his birthplace and publishing home), he is an all-Canadian voluptuary of the finest things in writing. I predict he will not be the Canadian Proust, Tolstoy, or Balzac — as some critics like to believe he is — but will be, at the end, an utter original who already has influenced a younger generation of writers by showing that there is a vital way by which to make our literature morally, intellectually, and aesthetically ambitious and luxuriant. He and Clark Blaise show brilliantly that it is possible to compose the most thoughtful fiction without necessarily reducing poetic texture or literary mode. And despite living and writing in Montreal, long a beleaguered centre of a dwindling English population, they and the others in their group showed that Canadian literature did not need an anxiety-neurosis by which to consolidate its mythology. They accepted that in their end as a serendipitous group there could be only a beginning of new hopes for fiction in Canada.

Notes

[1]Ray Smith, "Dinosaur," in *The Narrative Voice: Short Stories and Reflections by Canadian Authors*, ed. John Metcalf (Toronto: McGraw-Hill Ryerson, 1972), p. 202.

[2]Smith, "Dinosaur," p. 206.

[3]Ray Smith, "Colours," in his *Cape Breton is the Thought-Control Centre of Canada* (Toronto: House of Anansi, 1969), pp. 1-17; rpt. in *Sixteen by Twelve: Short Stories by Canadian Writers*, ed. John Metcalf (Toronto: Ryerson, 1970), pp. 205-18.

[4]Ray Smith, "Symbols in Agony: A Canadian Short Story," *Journal of Canadian Fiction*, 1, No. 2 (Spring 1972), 18-24.

[5]Smith, "Symbols in Agony: A Canadian Short Story," p. 19.

[6]Smith, "Symbols in Agony: A Canadian Short Story," p. 21.

[7]Smith, "Symbols in Agony: A Canadian Short Story," p. 18.

[8]Smith, "Symbols in Agony: A Canadian Short Story," p. 22.

[9]Dwight Macdonald, Preface, in *Parodies: An Anthology from Chaucer to Beerbohm — and After*, ed. Dwight Macdonald (New York: Random House, 1960), p. xiii.

[10]Ray Smith, "Golden Gleamings: A Study of Non-narrative Material in *Moby-Dick*," unpublished graduate essay, Concordia University, 1983, p. 2.

[11]Smith, "Golden Gleamings: A Study of Non-narrative Material in *Moby-Dick*," pp. 8-9.

[12]Smith, "Golden Gleamings: A Study of Non-narrative Material in *Moby-Dick*," p. 13.

[13]Lawrence Garber, "Ray Smith's *Cape Breton is the Thought-Control Centre of Canada*: The Diagnostics of the Absurd," in *The Montreal Story Tellers: Memoirs, Photographs, Critical Essays*, ed. J.R. (Tim) Struthers.

[14]Kent Thompson, Letter to J.R. (Tim) Struthers, 27 Aug. 1975.

[15]"Raymond Fraser," in *The Writers' Union of Canada: A Directory of Members*, ed. Ted Whittaker (Toronto: The Writers' Union of Canada, 1981), p. 81.

[16]Clark Blaise, "Memories of Unhousement: A Memoir," *Salmagundi*, No. 56 (Spring 1982), p. 4.

[17]Blaise, "Memories of Unhousement: A Memoir," p. 13.

[18]Blaise, "Memories of Unhousement: A Memoir," p. 13.

[19]Blaise, "Memories of Unhousement: A Memoir," p. 15.

[20]Robert Lecker, *On the Line: Readings in the Short Fiction of Clark Blaise, John Metcalf, and Hugh Hood* (Downsview, Ont.: ECW, 1982), p. 24.

[21]Clark Blaise, "To Begin, to Begin," in *The Narrative Voice: Short Stories and Reflections by Canadian Authors*, ed. John Metcalf (Toronto: McGraw-Hill Ryerson, 1972), p. 22.

[22]Clark Blaise, "The March," in his *Tribal Justice* (Toronto: Doubleday, 1974), p. 121.

[23]Clark Blaise, in *Days and Nights in Calcutta*, by Clark Blaise and Bharati Mukherjee (Garden City, N.Y.: Doubleday, 1977), p. 297.

[24]Clark Blaise, *Lunar Attractions* (Toronto: Doubleday, 1979), p. 155.

[25]Clark Blaise, *Lusts* (Toronto: Doubleday, 1983), [p. 1.]

[26]Blaise, *Lusts*, p. 145.

[27]Blaise, *Lusts*, p. 245.

[28]Blaise, in *Days and Nights in Calcutta*, p. 151.

211

[29]Blaise, "To Begin, to Begin," p. 24.

[30]Blaise, "To Begin, to Begin," p. 24.

[31]John Metcalf, "Telling Tales," in his *Kicking Against the Pricks* (Downsview, Ont.: ECW, 1982), p. 71; rpt. (revised) in *The Montreal Story Tellers: Memoirs, Photographs, Critical Essays*, ed. J.R. (Tim) Struthers.

[32]This phrase echoes the title of *Resident Alien*, a proposed collection of memoirs and stories by Blaise.

[33]John Metcalf, "Punctuation as Score," in his *Kicking Against the Pricks* (Downsview, Ont.: ECW, 1982), p. 95.

[34]Metcalf, "Punctuation as Score," p. 95.

[35]Metcalf, "Punctuation as Score," p. 97.

[36]John Metcalf, "Communiqué," in his *Kicking Against the Pricks* (Downsview, Ont.: ECW, 1982), p. 5.

[37]Metcalf, "Communiqué," p. 6.

[38]Metcalf, "Communiqué," p. 7.

[39]Metcalf, "Communiqué," p. 6.

[40]Metcalf, "Punctuation as Score," pp. 99-100.

[41]Metcalf, "Punctuation as Score," p. 100.

[42]Metcalf, "Punctuation as Score," p. 108.

[43]Metcalf, "Communiqué," p. 8.

[44]Douglas Rollins, "The Montreal Storytellers," *Journal of Canadian Fiction*, 1, No. 2 (Spring 1972), 6.

[45]John Metcalf, as quoted in Kent Thompson, "John Metcalf: A Profile," *The Fiddlehead*, No. 114 (Summer 1977), p. 61; rpt. (revised) in *The Montreal Story Tellers: Memoirs, Photographs, Critical Essays*, ed. J.R. (Tim) Struthers.

[46]Metcalf, as quoted in Thompson, "John Metcalf: A Profile," p. 61.

[47]John Metcalf, "The Lady Who Sold Furniture," in his *Selected Stories* (Toronto: McClelland and Stewart, 1982), pp. 9-100.

[48]Metcalf, "The Lady Who Sold Furniture," pp. 93-94.

[49]John Metcalf, "The Estuary," in his *Selected Stories* (Toronto: McClelland and Stewart, 1982), pp. 136-50.

[50]Metcalf, "The Estuary," p. 136.

[51]W.H. Auden, "In Memory of W.B. Yeats," as quoted in John Metcalf, *General Ludd* (Downsview, Ont.: ECW, 1980), p. 237.

[52]"The Lady Who Sold Furniture" was published in *The Lady Who Sold Furniture* (Toronto: Clarke, Irwin, 1970) and in *Selected Stories* (Toronto: McClelland and Stewart, 1982). "Private Parts" and "Girl in Gingham" appeared together under the title *Girl in Gingham* (Ottawa: Oberon, 1978), then under the title *Private Parts: A Memoir* (Scarborough, Ont.: New American Library, 1980). "Polly Ongle" was written in 1983.

[53]Lecker, *On the Line: Readings in the Short Fiction of Clark Blaise, John Metcalf, and Hugh Hood*, p. 89.

[54]John Metcalf, "Author's Commentary," in *Sixteen by Twelve: Short Stories by Canadian Writers*, ed. John Metcalf (Toronto: Ryerson, 1970), p. 202.

[55]Metcalf, "Author's Commentary," p. 203.

[56]John Metcalf, "Building Castles," in *Making It New: Contemporary Canadian Stories*, ed. John Metcalf (Toronto: Methuen, 1982), p. 177.

[57]In writing the section of this essay on Hugh Hood, I wish to thank ECW Press for allowing me to use phrases or sentences from the discussion of Hood that I prepared for *Canadian Writers and Their Works*, ed. Robert Lecker, Jack David, and Ellen Quigley, Fiction Series, VII (Toronto: ECW, 1985); and I wish to acknowledge the echoes from my book *Hugh Hood* (Boston: Twayne, 1983).

[58]Hugh Hood, in "Hugh Hood and John Mills in Epistolary Conversation," *The Fiddlehead*, No. 116 (Winter 1978), p. 145.

[59]See Barry Cameron, " 'Incarnational Art': Typology and Analogy in Hugh Hood's Fiction," rev. of *Before the Flood: Our Exagmination round His Factification for Incamination of Hugh Hood's Work in Progress*, ed. J.R. (Tim) Struthers, *The Fiddlehead*, No. 133 (July 1982), pp. 89-91.

[60]Hugh Hood, "Nobody's Going Anywhere!", in his *Flying a Red Kite* (Toronto: Ryerson, 1962), p. 159.

[61]Robert Lecker, "A Spirit of Communion: *The Swing in the Garden*," in *Before the Flood: Our Exagmination round His Factification for Incamination of Hugh Hood's Work in Progress*, ed. J.R. (Tim) Struthers (Downsview, Ont.: ECW, 1979), p. 187. This book is a richly authoritative collection of critical pieces on Hood's work.

[62]See the marvellously informative interview with J.R. (Tim) Struthers in *Before the Flood: Our Exagmination round His Factification for Incamination of Hugh Hood's Work in Progress*, ed. J.R. (Tim) Struthers (Downsview, Ont.: ECW, 1979), pp. 21-93.

[63]Hugh Hood, in "An Interview with Hugh Hood," by Robert Fulford, *The Tamarack Review*, No. 66 (June 1975), p. 77.

[64]Hugh Hood, in "At Home with the Hoods," by Keith Garebian, *The Montreal Star*, 19 Nov. 1977, Sec. D, p. D-1.

[65]Lawrence Mathews, "The Secular and the Sacral: Notes on *A New Athens* and Three Stories by Hugh Hood," in *Before the Flood: Our Exagmination round His Factification for Incamination of Hugh Hood's Work in Progress*, ed. J.R. (Tim) Struthers (Downsview, Ont.: ECW, 1979), p. 223.

[66]Hugh Hood, *A New Athens* (Ottawa: Oberon, 1977), pp. 58-59.

[67]John Mills, "Hugh Hood and the Anagogical Method," in *Before the Flood: Our Exagmination round His Factification for Incamination of Hugh Hood's Work in Progress*, ed. J.R. (Tim) Struthers (Downsview, Ont.: ECW, 1979), pp. 110-11.

[68]On the last page of Chapter 12 (which is also the end of the novel) Hood actually changes from the third person to the first person, presumably as a narrative strategy to indicate that the child Matthew is about to be born.

[69]Hugh Hood, *Reservoir Ravine* (Ottawa: Oberon, 1979), p. 222.

[70]Hood, *Reservoir Ravine*, p. 12.

[71]By 'parody' I mean, of course, a deliberate imitation of a form; and I mean it in a positive way — as an analogue of some other experience.

J.R. (Tim) Struthers
A CHECKLIST OF WORKS
BY THE MONTREAL STORY TELLERS

CLARK BLAISE

FICTION

"Thibidault et fils." M.F.A. Thesis Iowa 1964.

New Canadian Writing, 1968: Stories by David Lewis Stein, Clark Blaise and Dave Godfrey. Toronto: Clarke, Irwin, 1968.

A North American Education: A Book of Short Fiction. Garden City, N.Y.: Doubleday, 1973.
—————————. Toronto: Doubleday, 1973.
—————————. Don Mills, Ont.: PaperJacks, 1974.
—————————. New Press Canadian Classics. Toronto: General, 1984.

Tribal Justice. Garden City, N.Y.: Doubleday, 1974.
—————————. Toronto: Doubleday, 1974.
—————————. Don Mills, Ont.: PaperJacks, 1975.
—————————. New Press Canadian Classics. Toronto: General, 1984.

Lunar Attractions. Garden City, N.Y.: Doubleday, 1979.
—————————. Toronto: Doubleday, 1979.
—————————. Toronto: McClelland and Stewart–Bantam, 1980.
—————————. London: Melbourne, 1981.
—————————. New York: Bantam, 1983.

Lusts. Garden City, N.Y.: Doubleday, 1983.
—————————. Markham, Ont.: Penguin, 1984.

NON-FICTION

Blaise, Clark, and Bharati Mukherjee. *Days and Nights in Calcutta.* Garden City, N.Y.: Doubleday, 1977.

WORKS EDITED

Blaise, Clark, and John Metcalf, eds. *Here & Now: Best Canadian Stories.* Ottawa: Oberon, 1977.

Metcalf, John, and Clark Blaise, eds. *78: Best Canadian Stories.* Ottawa: Oberon, 1978.

Blaise, Clark, and John Metcalf, eds. *79: Best Canadian Stories.* Ottawa: Oberon, 1979.

Blaise, Clark, and John Metcalf, eds. *80: Best Canadian Stories.* Ottawa: Oberon, 1980.

RAYMOND FRASER

FICTION

The Black Horse Tavern. Montreal: Ingluvin, 1972.

The Struggle Outside: A Funny Serious Novel. Toronto: McGraw-Hill Ryerson, 1975.

The Bannonbridge Musicians. St. John's, Nfld.: Breakwater, 1978.

POETRY

Poems for the Miramichi. Montreal: Poverty, 1966.

Waiting for God's Angel. Montreal: Poverty, 1967.

I've laughed and sung through the whole night long seen the summer sunrise in the morning. Montreal: Delta, 1969.

The More I Live. Montreal: Wandering Albatross, 1971.

Stop the Highway.... An Anthology of 4 Montreal Poets: Ray Fraser, Clifford Gaston, Bob Higgins & Bryan McCarthy. Montreal: The Greater

Montreal Anti-Poverty Coordinating Committee, 1972.

NON-FICTION

The Fighting Fisherman: The Life of Yvon Durelle. Toronto: Doubleday, 1981.

WORKS EDITED

Fraser, Raymond, and John Brebner, eds. *Tom-Tom.* St. Thomas Univ., Chatham, N.B.: Moncton, n.d.

Fraser, Raymond, et al, eds. *Intercourse: Contemporary Canadian Writing,* Nos. 1-12/13 (1966-70).

Fraser, Raymond, Clyde Rose, and Jim Stewart, eds. *East of Canada: An Atlantic Anthology.* Portugal Cove, Nfld.: Breakwater, 1976.

HUGH HOOD

FICTION

Flying a Red Kite. Toronto: Ryerson, 1962.
_____. Ryerson Paperbacks. Toronto: Ryerson, 1967.

White Figure, White Ground. New York: E.P. Dutton, 1964.
_____. Toronto: Ryerson, 1964.
_____. Pocket Book Edition. Richmond Hill, Ont.: Simon & Schuster, 1973.
_____. New Press Canadian Classics. Toronto: General, 1984.

Around the Mountain: Scenes from Montreal Life. Toronto: Peter Martin, 1967.

The Camera Always Lies. New York: Harcourt, Brace & World, 1967.
_____. New Canadian Library, No. 160. Toronto: McClelland and Stewart, 1982.

A Game of Touch. Don Mills, Ont.: Longman, 1970.
    Re-issued with a new dust jacket by ECW Press in 1980.

The Fruit Man, The Meat Man & The Manager. Ottawa: Oberon, 1971.

You Cant Get There From Here. Ottawa: Oberon, 1972.

_____. New Press Canadian Classics. Toronto: General, 1984.

The Swing in the Garden. Pt. I of *The New Age/Le nouveau siècle.* Ottawa: Oberon, 1975.

_____. Downsview, Ont.: ECW, 1980.

_____. The New Age: Volume One. New Press Canadian Classics. Toronto: General, 1984.

Dark Glasses. Ottawa: Oberon, 1976.

A New Athens. Pt. II of *The New Age/Le nouveau siècle.* Ottawa: Oberon, 1977.

_____. Downsview, Ont.: ECW, 1981.

_____. The New Age: Volume Two. New Press Canadian Classics. Toronto: General, 1984.

Selected Stories. Ottawa: Oberon, 1978.

Reservoir Ravine. Pt. III of *The New Age/Le nouveau siècle.* Ottawa: Oberon, 1979.

None Genuine Without This Signature. Downsview, Ont.: ECW, 1980.

Black and White Keys. Pt. IV of *The New Age/Le nouveau siècle.* Downsview, Ont.: ECW, 1982.

The Scenic Art. Pt. V of *The New Age/Le nouveau siècle.* Toronto: Stoddart, 1984.

NON-FICTION AND CRITICISM

"The Architecture of Experience (Studies in the Relation of Cosmology to Poetry in the Seventeenth and Early Eighteenth Centuries)." M.A. Thesis Toronto 1952.

"Theories of Imagination in English Thinkers 1650-1790." Diss. Toronto 1955.

Strength Down Centre: the Jean Béliveau Story. Scarborough, Ont.: Prentice-Hall, 1970.

Puissance au centre: Jean Béliveau. Trans. Louis Rémillard. Scarborough, Ont.: Prentice-Hall, 1970.

—————————. Montréal: L'Homme, 1972.

The Governor's Bridge is Closed. Ottawa: Oberon, 1973.

Scoring: The Art of Hockey. Illus. Seymour Segal. Ottawa: Oberon, 1979.

Trusting the Tale. Downsview, Ont.: ECW, 1983.

WORKS EDITED

Hood, Hugh, and Peter O'Brien, eds. *Fatal Recurrences: New Fiction in English from Montréal.* Montreal: Véhicule, 1984.

JOHN METCALF

FICTION

New Canadian Writing, 1969: Stories by John Metcalf, D.O. Spettigue and C.J. Newman. Toronto: Clarke, Irwin, 1969.

The Lady Who Sold Furniture. Toronto: Clarke, Irwin, 1970.

Going Down Slow. Toronto: McClelland and Stewart, 1972.

—————————. Don Mills, Ont.: PaperJacks, 1975.

The Teeth of My Father. Ottawa: Oberon, 1975.

Metcalf, John, and John Newlove. *Dreams Surround Us: Fiction and Poetry by John Metcalf and John Newlove.* Delta, Ont.: Bastard, 1977.
    "Of this edition of 150 copies 130 are numbered and signed. The remaining 20 copies are for private distribution by the authors."

Girl in Gingham. Ottawa: Oberon, 1978.

Private Parts: A Memoir. Scarborough, Ont.: New American Library, 1980.

General Ludd. Downsview, Ont.: ECW, 1980.

—————————. Toronto: General, 1981.

Selected Stories. New Canadian Library, No. 168. Toronto: McClelland

and Stewart, 1982.

NON-FICTION

Kicking Against the Pricks. Downsview, Ont.: ECW, 1982.

WORKS EDITED AND TEXTBOOKS

Metcalf, John, ed. *The Razor's Edge.* By W. Somerset Maugham. Canadian Educational Edition. Don Mills, Ont.: Bellhaven House, 1967.

Metcalf, John, ed. *The Daughter of Time.* By Josephine Tey. Canadian Educational Edition. Scarborough, Ont.: Bellhaven House, 1968.

Metcalf, John, ed. *Flight of the Phoenix.* By Elleston Trevor. Canadian Educational Edition. Scarborough, Ont.: Bellhaven House, 1968.

Metcalf, John, and Gordon Callaghan. *Rhyme and Reason.* Toronto: Ryerson, 1968.

Rittenhouse, Charles, John Metcalf, and Juliette Dowling. *Wordcraft 2.* Toronto: J. M. Dent, 1968.

Rittenhouse, Charles, John Metcalf, and Juliette Dowling. *Wordcraft 3.* Toronto: J.M. Dent, 1968.

Rittenhouse, Charles, John Metcalf, and Juliette Dowling. *Wordcraft 1.* Toronto: J.M. Dent, 1969.

Metcalf, John, and Gordon Callaghan, eds. *Salutation.* Toronto: Ryerson, 1970.

Metcalf, John, ed. *Sixteen by Twelve: Short Stories by Canadian Writers.* Toronto: Ryerson, 1970.

Rittenhouse, Charles, and John Metcalf. *Wordcraft: Senior.* Toronto: J.M. Dent, 1970.

Metcalf, John, ed. *Kaleidoscope: Canadian Stories.* Photographs by John de Visser. Toronto: Van Nostrand Reinhold, 1972.

Metcalf, John, ed. *The Narrative Voice: Short Stories and Reflections by Canadian Authors.* Toronto: McGraw-Hill Ryerson, 1972.

Metcalf, John, ed. *The Speaking Earth: Canadian Poetry.* Toronto: Van

Nostrand Reinhold, 1973.

Harcourt, Joan, and John Metcalf, eds. *76: New Canadian Stories.* Ottawa: Oberon, 1976.

Blaise, Clark, and John Metcalf, eds. *Here & Now: Best Canadian Stories.* Ottawa: Oberon, 1977.

Harcourt, Joan, and John Metcalf, eds. *77: Best Canadian Stories.* Ottawa: Oberon, 1977.

Rittenhouse, Charles, and John Metcalf. *Wordcraft: Junior.* Toronto: J.M. Dent, 1977.

Metcalf, John, and Clark Blaise, eds. *78: Best Canadian Stories.* Ottawa: Oberon, 1978.

Blaise, Clark, and John Metcalf, eds. *79: Best Canadian Stories.* Ottawa: Oberon, 1979.

Metcalf, John, ed. *Stories Plus: Canadian Stories with Authors' Commentaries.* Toronto: McGraw-Hill Ryerson, 1979.

Blaise, Clark, and John Metcalf, eds. *80: Best Canadian Stories.* Ottawa: Oberon, 1980.

Metcalf, John, ed. *First Impressions.* Ottawa: Oberon, 1980.

Metcalf, John, ed. *New Worlds: A Canadian Collection of Stories with Notes.* Toronto: McGraw-Hill Ryerson, 1980.

Metcalf, John, ed. *Second Impressions.* Ottawa: Oberon, 1981.

Metcalf, John, and Leon Rooke, eds. *81: Best Canadian Stories.* Ottawa: Oberon, 1981.

Metcalf, John, ed. *Making It New: Contemporary Canadian Stories.* Toronto: Methuen, 1982.

Metcalf, John, ed. *Third Impressions.* Ottawa: Oberon, 1982.

Metcalf, John, and Leon Rooke, eds. *82: Best Canadian Stories.* Ottawa: Oberon, 1982.

Metcalf, John, and Leon Rooke, eds. *The New Press Anthology: Best Canadian Fiction # 1.* New Press Canadian Classics. Toronto: General, 1984.

RAY SMITH

FICTION

Cape Breton is the Thought-Control Centre of Canada. Toronto: House of Anansi, 1969.

Lord Nelson Tavern. Toronto: McClelland and Stewart, 1974.
_____. New Canadian Library, No. 158. Toronto: McClelland and Stewart, 1981.

ACKNOWLEDGEMENTS

Though written at the invitation of the editor of this volume, the memoirs by Hugh Hood, John Metcalf, and Clark Blaise first appeared, in earlier versions, in the following publications: Hugh Hood's *Trusting the Tale* (Downsview, Ont.: ECW, 1983), John Metcalf's *Kicking Against the Pricks* (Downsview, Ont.: ECW, 1982), and *Canadian Literature*, No. 100 (Spring 1984).

Barry Cameron's "Points of Reference: Approaching Clark Blaise" is excerpted from his monograph on Blaise published in *Canadian Writers and Their Works*, ed. Robert Lecker, Jack David, and Ellen Quigley, Fiction Series, VII (Toronto: ECW, 1985).

Kent Thompson's "John Metcalf: A Profile" is a revised, updated version of an article published in *The Fiddlehead*, No. 114 (Summer 1977).

Barry Cameron's "An Approximation of Poetry: Three Stories by John Metcalf" is a revised, abridged version of an article published in *Studies in Canadian Literature*, 2 (Winter 1977).

Dennis Duffy's "'More dear, both for themselves and for thy sake!': Hugh Hood's *The New Age*" is a revised version of a paper delivered to the Hugh Hood Symposium at York University in October 1979.

Some phrases or sentences in the Hugh Hood section of Keith Garebian's "In the End, a Beginning: The Montreal Story Tellers" are adapted from his monograph on Hood published in *Canadian Writers and Their Works*, ed. Robert Lecker, Jack David, and Ellen Quigley, Fiction Series, VII (Toronto: ECW, 1985); and certain passages in the same section contain echoes from the author's book *Hugh Hood* (Boston: Twayne, 1983).

Much of the Hugh Hood section of J.R. (Tim) Struthers' "A Checklist of Works by The Montreal Story Tellers" is derived from his "Hugh Hood: An Annotated Bibliography," in *The Annotated Bibliography of Canada's Major Authors*, ed. Robert Lecker and Jack David, V (Downsview, Ont.: ECW, 1984).

The editor also wishes to acknowledge, with gratitude, the support of King's College (an affiliate of The University of Western Ontario), in particular a research grant which assisted in the completion of the manuscript of this book.

Note on the Editor

J.R. (Tim) Struthers is a leading critic on Canadian short fiction. Born in London, Ontario, he holds a Ph.D. in English from The University of Western Ontario and was awarded a Social Sciences and Humanities Research Council post-doctoral fellowship for 1982-83 and 1983-84. His highly regarded first book, *Before the Flood*, a collection of articles on Hugh Hood by various hands, was published by ECW Press in 1979 and reprinted in 1984 — followed by his extensive scholarly study "Hugh Hood: An Annotated Bibliography" in Vol. V of ECW Press's *The Annotated Bibliography of Canada's Major Authors*. Several of his articles have been anthologized, including the award-winning essay "Alice Munro and the American South."

On July 1, 1985, J.R. (Tim) Struthers joined the Department of English at the University of Guelph.

Véhicule Press, P.O.B. 125, Place du Parc Station,
Montreal, Quebec, Canada H2W 2M9

Printed in Canada

Typeset in Bembo by Zibra, Inc., Montréal, Québec
Printed by Les Éditions Marquis Ltée, Montmagny, Québec

THE MONTREAL STORY TELLERS